Encore! Hana Hou!

THE HAWAI'I MOVIE AND TELEVISION BOOK

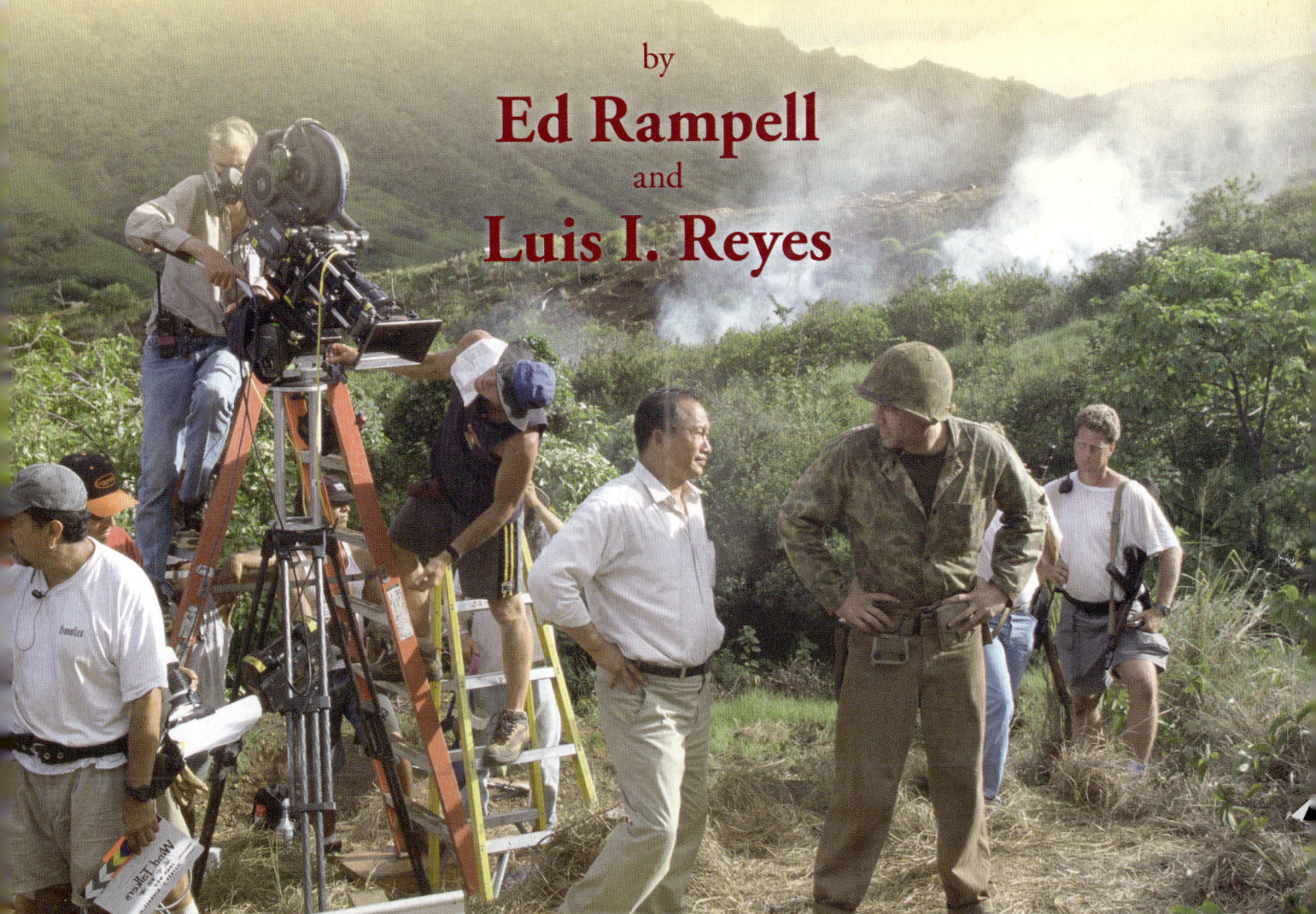

by
Ed Rampell
and
Luis I. Reyes

Other books by the authors

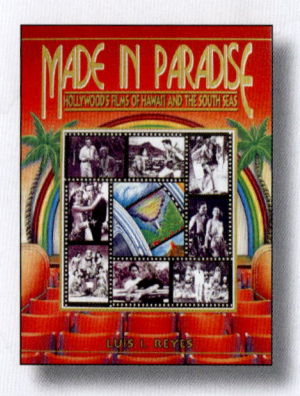

**Made in Paradise:
Hollywood Films of Hawai'i
and the South Seas**

by Luis I. Reyes and Ed Rampell

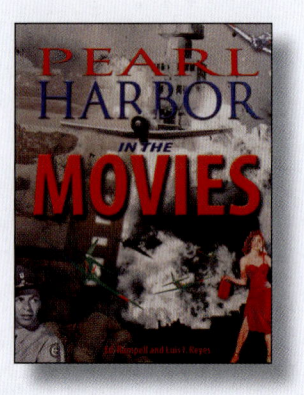

Pearl Harbor in the Movies

by Ed Rampell and Luis I. Reyes

ED RAMPELL

**Progressive Hollywood,
A People's Film History of the United States**

LUIS I. REYES

Hispanics in Hollywood

(Co-author Peter Rubie)

Director Curtis Bernhardt, Charles Buchinski (later known as Charles Bronson), Henry Slate, Rita Hayworth, Aldo Ray, and Rudy Bond chat between scenes for Columbia's 3D Technicolor production, *Miss Sadie Thompson*. This scene was filmed at the historic Hanalei Pier in Hanalei, Kaua'i. LUIS REYES ARCHIVES

Encore! Hana Hou!

THE HAWAI'I
MOVIE
AND TELEVISION BOOK

CELEBRATING 100 YEARS OF FILM PRODUCTION THROUGHOUT THE HAWAIIAN ISLANDS

by
Ed Rampell
and
Luis I. Reyes

Mutual Publishing

This book is gratefully and lovingly dedicated to my parents, Arlene Rampell and the late lamented Richard Rampell, who among many other things taught me to love the movies. Since they took me to see my first film, *South Pacific*, they have encouraged my two great passions—motion pictures and the Pacific Islands.

—Ed Rampell

This book is dedicated to my daughter, Arlinda Marie Makamae Reyes and my son Lui Keonimana Reyes as well as my Hawaiian 'Ohana Betty Kaleohano, Jolynn Kaohi Chew and Pat Hurley Cafferty.

—Luis I. Reyes

Copyright © 2013 by Mutual Publishing

All rights reserved. No part of this book may be reproduced in any form or by any electronic or mechanical means, including information storage and retrieval devices or systems, without prior written permission from the publisher, except that brief passages may be quoted for reviews.

ISBN: 978-1939487-02-5
Library of Congress Control Number: 2013947752

Cover design by Jane Gillespie
Interior design by Courtney Tomasu

Photos from Dreamstime.com: pg. x (palm tree silhouette) © Raja Rc, pg. 3 (film projector background) © Lenart, pg. 18 © Sippakorn Yamkasikorn, pg. 20 © Bortn66, pg. 36 (award background) © Hugolacasse, pg. 36 (pencil) © Anatoly Maslennikov, pg. 36 (notepad) © Gines Valera Marin, pg. 182 (spotlight) © Dmytro Denysov, pg. 183 (tablet) © Marincas_andrei, pg. 186 (television) © Nikmerkulov, pg. 186 (tablet) © Aleksandr Bryliaev, pg. 187 (television) © Thosstock, pg. 192-193 (film strip) © Oana Stoica

First Printing, November 2013
Second Printing, April 2015

Mutual Publishing, LLC
1215 Center Street, Suite 210
Honolulu, Hawai'i 96816
Ph: 808-732-1709 / Fax: 808-734-4094
email: info@mutualpublishing.com
www.mutualpublishing.com

Printed in China

Photographic Credits:
Paramount Pictures, Warner Bros., Time Warner, Turner Entertainment Company, RKO Pictures, MGM, United Artists, Lucas Films, Walt Disney Pictures, NBC-Universal, Republic Pictures, Twentieth Century Fox, CBS Productions, ABC, Angela Tillson and a Whale of a Time Productions, Tim Ryan and the Luis Reyes Archives. Because of corporate mergers, buyouts and transfers of rights over a period of 100 years, films and television programs copyrights are reserved and are listed by their original release dates and copyright holders.

Half title page: Director John Woo (left) and star Nicolas Cage on the set of Metro-Goldwyn-Mayer Pictures' epic drama *Windtalkers*. MGM
This page: Robert Young and Sally Eilers find romance among the palms near the Royal Hawaiian Hotel while shooting a scene for *The Black Camel*. LUIS REYES ARCHIVES
Opposite page: The principal cast of *Hawaiian Eye* on a set at the Hilton Hawaiian Village. LUIS REYES ARCHIVES

Table of Contents

Film & Television Titles	vii
Prefaces	viii
Acknowledgments	x
Introduction	1
Chapter One South Seas Cinema	2
Chapter Two Crime Fighters in Paradise	10
Chapter Three Made in Paradise	30
Chapter Four Locations! Locations! Locations!	153
Chapter Five Development of the Modern Hawai'i Film Idustry	180
Bibliography	194
Index	195
About the Authors	198

Note: Whenever possible the authors have referred to original books and archived film and television publicity, newspapers, periodicals, and publications material as primary source material to compile information for this book, and due to the nature of modern research utilized the World Wide Web which has innumerable Film, Television, Cable, Hawai'i- and South Seas-related and dedicated web sites from which information was drawn from and cross referenced. Interviews were conducted with individuals who are knowledgeable with the subject matter covered in the book.

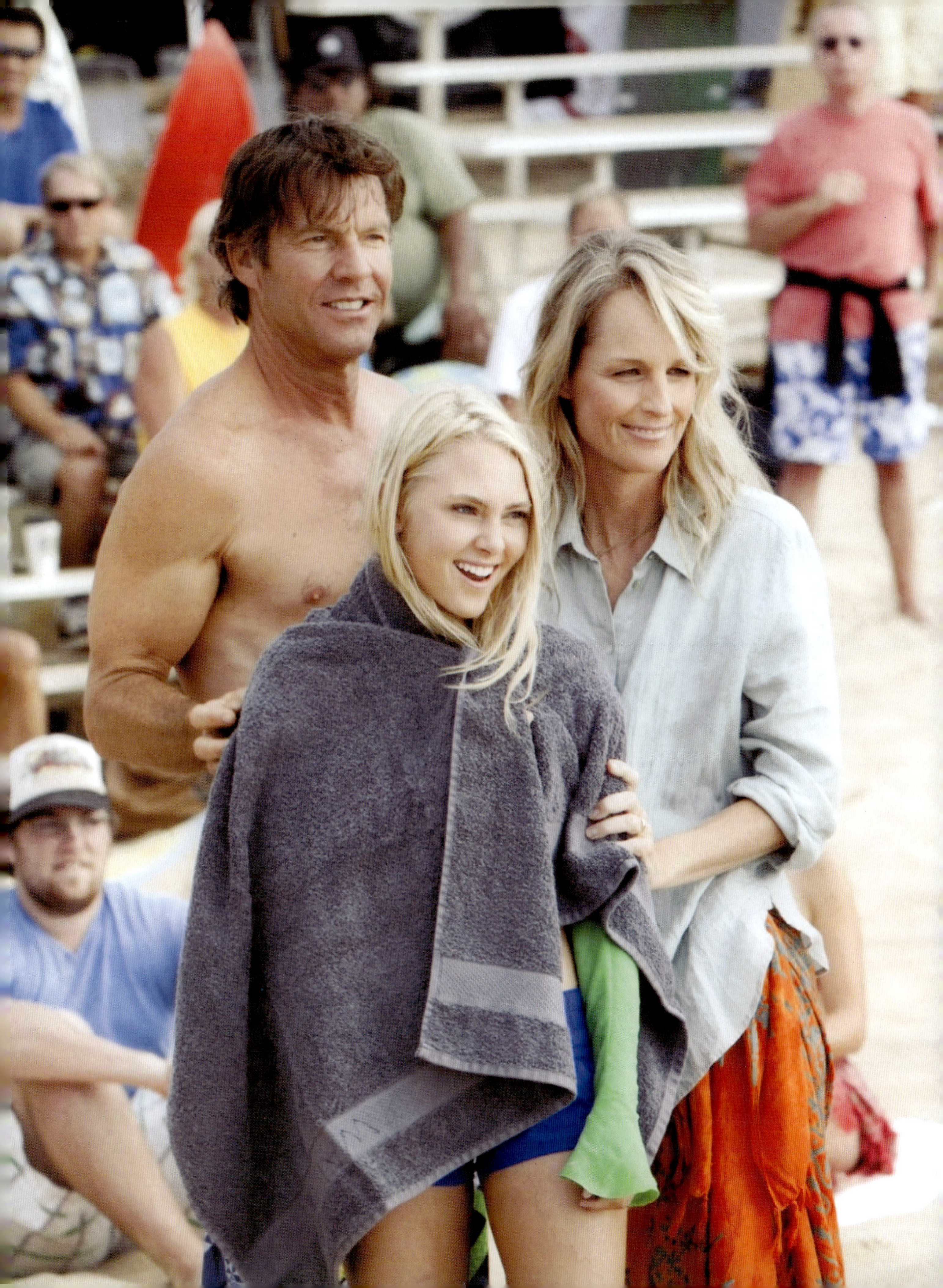

Film & Television Titles

Title	Page
50 First Dates	104
Along Came Polly	104
Avatar	116
Battleship	144
Baywatch Hawaii	86
Beyond Paradise	75
Big Bounce, The	103
Big Jim McLain	16
Bird of Paradise (1932)	34
Bird of Paradise (1951)	37
Black Camel, The	14
Blue Crush	98
Blue Hawaii	49
Blue Lagoon: The Awakening	148
Charlie's Angels: Full Throttle	100
Descendants, The	131
Die Another Day	97
Dog the Bounty Hunter	25
Donovan's Reef	51
Dragonfly	97
Fantasy Island	81
Final Fantasy: The Spirits Within	90
Flight 29 Down	108
Flirting with Forty	115
Forgetting Sarah Marshall	113
From Here to Eternity	39
George of the Jungle	72
Godzilla (1998)	77
Godzilla (2013)	150
Happy Birthday, Tūtū Ruth	188
Hawaii	53
Hawaii Five-0 (reboot)	24, 124
Hawaii Five-O (original)	20, 56
Hawaiian: The Legend of Eddie Aikau	151
Hawaiian Eye	18, 48
Hawaiian Love	33
Hawaiian Room, The	191
Heatstroke	116
Hereafter	121
Homealani	190
Honoka'a Boy	121
Hop	141
Hunger Games, The: Catching Fire	149
In God's Hands	74
Indiana Jones and the Kingdom of the Crystal Skull	114
Janet Jackson: All For You, Live in Concert From Hawaii	100
Johnny Tsunami	85
Journey 2: The Mysterious Island	145
Jurassic Park	64
Jurassic Park III	91
Just Go With It	142
Kai Wahine	191
Keao	189
Kekohi	189
King Kong	61
Krippendorf's Tribe	78
Lani Loa	79
Last Resort	147
Legend of Chang Apana, The	15
Lilo & Stitch	92
Lost	106
Lost World, The: Jurassic Park II	71
Magnum P.I.	23, 62
Maunalua	188
Meet the Deedles	78
Mighty Joe Young	73
Mister Roberts	43
Moke Action	137
Moloka'i: The Story of Father Damien	82
North Shore	108
Off the Map	146
Outbreak	68
Pa'ahana	191
Papa Mau: The Way Finder	129
Paniolo O Hawai'i —Cowboys of the Far West	87
Pearl Harbor	88
Perfect Getaway, A	118
Picture Bride	67
Pirates of the Caribbean: At World's End	110
Pirates of the Caribbean: On Stranger Tides	138
Planet of the Apes	90
Predators	123
Princess Ka'iulani	119
Punch-Drunk Love	99
Queenie: The Spirit of a Dancer	189
Race the Sun	69
Raiders of the Lost Ark	63
Release Our Water	190
Rise of the Planet of the Apes	130
River, The	143
Rundown, The	101
Shark God, The	32
Six Days Seven Nights	75
Snakes on a Plane	109
Soul Surfer	139
South Pacific	45
Special Delivery	115
Sweepstakes, The	190
Tears of the Sun	102
Tempest, The	122
Time Machine, The	94
To End All Wars	91
Too Rich: The Secret Life of Doris Duke	83
Tora! Tora! Tora!	59
Tropic Thunder	111
Tyrannosaurus Azteca	115
Very Brady Sequel, A	70
Waikiki Wedding	35
Waterworld	66
Wind on Water	80
Windtalkers	94
You May Not Kiss the Bride	141
You, Me and Dupree	109

MOVIE CREDITS KEY:

The films are listed as follows:
 Title
 Year, Releasing Company
 Director
 Screenplay
 Producers
 Cast: Actor (Character)

In the case of broadcast television or cable:
 Title
 Year, Network or Cable Company
 Teleplay

Preface

Before its opening, the Hawai'i-set movie *The Descendants* was screened at the Directors Guild of America's (DGA) state-of-the-art theater complex in Hollywood. Afterwards, *The Descendants*' director/co-writer, Alexander Payne, commented on his casting of lead actor George Clooney: "Clooney is one of the American stars I admire most. He has a real screen presence, like an old time Hollywood star…"

Payne was interviewed on the DGA stage, and afterwards I approached him. He remembered meeting me at the 2004 memorial service for the Czech director Jiří Weiss, a movie mentor to both of us. When I told Payne about our previous movie/TV history book *Made In Paradise, Hollywood's Films of Hawaii and the South Seas*, he suggested creating a sequel featuring the Hawai'i movies made since the original book came out in 1995. This way, Payne said, "You can write about *The Descendants*." The result of his recommendation, dear reader, is what you are reading now.

—Ed Rampell

Preface

As an islander by way of Puerto Rico and Manhattan, I have always been fascinated by the images of our fiftieth state and its multiethnic population. Hawai'i's enormous impact on America popular culture, from its annexation in 1898 through today, is evident in music, movies, television, clothing styles, literature and the popular lexicon. When I was a baby boomer growing up in the decade following Hawai'i's statehood in 1959, it seemed that between Don Ho, Elvis, Olympic and surfing legend Duke Kahanamoku, Hula Hoops, Hawaiian Punch, Dole's pineapple juice and United Airlines' Menehune characters, Hawaii was in some way, shape or form ever present in my consciousness.

The big screens of my Upper West Side Manhattan neighborhood movie houses, The RKO Nemo on 110th street and The Loew's Olympia on 107th street, became my portals to the world. I spent many an afternoon living out fantasy island adventures with the screen's beautiful people. Hawai'i's breathtaking scenery in its Technicolor grandeur first came to my view in Elvis Presley's *Blue Hawaii* and John Wayne's *Donovan's Reef*. A few years later, on the small television screen, *Hawaii Five-0* brought the islands home every week in color. My high school graduation night was spent at then New York's world-famous Hawaii Kai Restaurant and Nightclub, whose bamboo façade and Tiki torches promised an unforgettable evening of exotic drinks, hula dancers, and Hawaiian music.

I was so immersed in the Hawai'i movie culture that I felt quite at home when I finally could visit Hawai'i after attending University of the Pacific in California. I understood and recognized that most of the movie images of Hawai'i, its people, and culture (like those of any other place) were stereotypical and false. However, the movies of my youth came to life as I visited the filming locations, which were even more beautiful and stunning in person than on the big screen. The cameras were not rolling, and the movie stars were no longer there, but the real star was—Hawai'i. Up until that time, there was very little information on Hawaii filming locations or its film history except in a few travel brochures and Bob Schmitt's pioneering book, *Hawai'i in the Movies*. These experiences eventually led me to write *Made in Paradise* (1995) with co-author Ed Rampell and now this present volume, a sequel and update.

—Luis I. Reyes

Acknowledgments

The writing of this book would not have been possible without the support and *aloha* of Alma. *Aloha wau iā 'oe.*

Special thanks to my unforgettable professors at Hunter College's Cinema Department: **Chairman Joel Zucker, Ken Roberts, Dick Tomkins, Jerome Coopersmith, Emilie De Brigard** and the late **Jiří Weiss**; and my friend and Hunter College classmate, **Brian Camp.**

And finally, my very deepest *mahalo nui loa* to the **peoples of Polynesia, Micronesia and Melanesia,** who welcomed this errant "Native" New Yorker to their Islands.

—Ed Rampell

Eric Caidin, Hollywood Book and Poster
Mike Hawks, Larry Edmunds Book Store
Anne Archer of The Margaret Herrick Library of the Academy of Motion Pictures Arts and Sciences
Stephanie and **Randy Spangler**
The South Seas Cinema Society
DeSoto Brown of the Bishop Museum
Michelle Yu, HPD
Georja Skinner, chief officer, Hawai'i Creative Industries Division
Matt Locey
Doug Mossman
Ernie Malik
Harry Donenfeld, Maui Film Commissioner
Benita Brazier
Diana Su, Royal Hawaiian Hotel
Stephanie Reid, Princeville Resort
Brandi Peralta, Kualoa Ranch
Frank Lonardo, Turtle Bay Resort
Henry Fordham, IATSE Local 665

And special thanks to:
Angela Tillson and **A Whale of a Time Productions**
Tim Ryan
Brenda Ching, Hawai'i SAG/AFTRA
Art Umezu, Kaua'i Film Commissioner
Jake Anderson and the **Hawai'i International Film Festival**
Patrick Dugan and **Tyler Kruse** of the Anthology Group
Walea Constantinau, Honolulu Film Office
John Mason, Big Island Film Commissioner
Donne Dawson, Hawai'i State Film Commissioner
Jane Gillespie and **Courtney Tomasu**

—Luis I. Reyes

Introduction

The Hawai'i Movie and Television Book documents, with production information and critical commentary, the Hollywood films and television shows made in Hawai'i since 1995 to the present while spotlighting significant film achievements of the past. It also covers television and the iconic fictional island crime fighters. In addition, the book includes an Island film location guide to sites accessible to the general public and a history of the present-day Hawai'i film industry.

Hawai'i played a role in the formative years of Hollywood. It shares a legacy that began a hundred years ago with the consolidating of the U.S. film industry on the West Coast at the beginning of the twentieth century spanning the first feature films made in 1913 through its territorial status, World War II, statehood and now into the current twenty-first century.

Since 1995, more than fifty major Hollywood theatrical feature films were made in the Hawaiian Islands, many of them blockbuster productions, with at least an additional twenty-five broadcast network and cable episodic TV shows. Much of the recent surge in film activity is due in large part to Hawai'i's economic initiatives to attract filmmakers and to the development of a local and experienced professional workforce and support services.

The cameras are still rolling with a new generation of stars. George Clooney, Ben Stiller, Adam Sandler, and Drew Barrymore are leaving their footprints in the sands of Hawai'i's palm-lined beaches where such film icons as Burt Lancaster, John Wayne, Rita Hayworth, Henry Fonda, and Elvis once stood.

Hollywood filmmakers who have brought their own unique vision of Hawai'i and its backgrounds to the screen range from the legendary pioneering film directors Cecil B. DeMille and John Ford to the modern day Steven Spielberg, Clint Eastwood and most recently Alexander Payne.

Films made in Hawai'i fall into several categories, South Seas Cinema (*Bird of Paradise* and *Six Days Seven Nights*), World War II-era settings (*From Here To Eternity* and *Pearl Harbor*), Hawai'i as itself (*50 First Dates* and *The Descendants*), and Hawai'i as elsewhere (*Jurassic Park* and *George of The Jungle*). Film crime dramas in paradise have been relatively few, appearing exclusively in the television arena (*Hawaii Five-0*, *Magnum P.I.*) and now the new version of the weekly network television series *Hawaii Five-0* reboot.

Due to the profound changes in the entertainment industry caused by the computer and the internet, people are watching more movies and TV on more technological digital devices than ever before. More people are seeing Hawai'i as either content or backdrop in the movies and on television than ever before.

Like the movies we love so much and return to again and again, *The Hawai'i Movie and Television Book* reminds the reader of the cinematic images that have become indelibly linked the world over between Hollywood and Hawai'i.

Enjoy the show, Be There, Aloha!

Kono Kalakaua (Grace Park), Danny Williams (Scott Caan), Steve McGarrett (Alex O'Loughlin), and Catherine Rollins (Michelle Borth) holding hands and floating on surfboards while at the scattering of ashes for a scene in *Hawaii Five-0*. CBS PRODUCTIONS

CHAPTER 1

South Seas Cinema
Birth of a Film Genre

Opposite page, top left photo: A young Joel McCrea on location in Kāneʻohe for *Bird of Paradise.* LUIS REYES ARCHIVES
Opposite page, bottom: Poster art for *Aloma of the South Seas.* LUIS REYES ARCHIVES
This page, top left: The original *The Blue Lagoon* (1949) starring Jean Simmons and Donald Houston. LUIS REYES ARCHIVES
This page, top right: Marlon Brando as Fletcher Christian and Tarita as Maimiti in 1962 remake of *Mutiny On The Bounty.* LUIS REYES ARCHIVES/MGM
This page, bottom: The stars of *Son of Fury,* Tyrone Power and Gene Tierney. LUIS REYES ARCHIVES

What is South Seas Cinema?

South Seas Cinema is the film genre set in and/or shot in the islands of Polynesia, Melanesia, and Micronesia. Sometimes the story is specific to the location and involves island life. South Seas Cinema is as distinct a film genre as the Western, Musical, and Film Noir are, and like them has unique identifying characteristics. While the South Seas genre quickly became a pop culture staple and has undergone changes over its existence, certain constants have remained.

One of its main characteristics is a tropical isle setting similar to the "Wild West" being the locale for the Western or a seedy urban landscape

Dolores Del Rio performs a Hollywood version of a "native" dance in the first motion picture adaptation of *Bird of Paradise*. Del Rio is one of many Hispanic actors and actresses who played Polynesians. Del Rio dances topless (beneath her leis) and reveals her navel in this pre-code 1932 feature—South Seas cinema without sensuality is like pancakes without the syrup.

for Film Noir. A second and perhaps even a more key factor is the theme of paradise or utopia, which sets South Seas Cinema apart from other genres and is its hallmark. Islands are depicted as remote oases beyond civilization and its discontents where life is easy and the fruits of the sea and land are free and abundant. In these Elysian enclaves, noble savages inhabit leisure societies devoted to pleasurable pursuits and free from civilization's nightmares of industry and work. Liberated from the anxiety and stress of the daily struggle, scantily clad men and women freely pursue lovemaking and other joyous pursuits unencumbered by Western notions of shame and guilt.

LUIS REYES ARCHIVES

Sources and Origins

As Trevor Graham's 2005 Australian documentary *Hula Girls, Imagining Paradise* points out, the fantasy of a heaven on Earth, of what Captain Bougainville called the "Nouvelle Cytherea" (the "new isle of love"), is derived from ancient Greek and Biblical allusions, as well as Western literary and illustrative conventions predating motion pictures. The genre reflects the influences of Rousseau's philosophy, explorer logs, novels by Herman Melville, Pierre Loti, and Robert Louis Stevenson, the canvases of Paul Gauguin, and the vogue of photographic reproductions in late nineteenth century postcards.

In the case of Hawai'i, influences originated with the early drawing of ship artists John Webber and Louis Choris of nature life and the exoticness of the women. Authors of South Pacific literature also wrote about Hawai'i in the same rhapsodic romantic vein: Melville, Stevenson, Jack London, Somerset Maugham, Charles Nordhoff, and James Norman Hall, Rupert Brooke, and Mark Twain. Some of their literary works went on to become the grist for Hollywood's movie mill.

On February 5, 1897, motion pictures were screened at the Honolulu Opera House. A year later, an Edison camera crew en route from Asia to New Jersey stopped for one day in O'ahu and shot the first Pacific Islands moving pictures: *Honolulu Street Scene, Wharf Scene, Honolulu,* and *Kanakas Diving for Coins*. (Kanaka can be translated to mean "Pacific Islander.")

In its formative years, South Seas Cinema manifested in newsreels, ethno-films, travelogues, and documentaries. By 1912 and 1913, French filmmaker Gaston Méliès was making fiction films in New Zealand, Tahiti, and Java while Hollywood's first features, including Universal's *The Shark God* and *Hawaiian Love*, were filmed in and around Honolulu.

The first thirty-year period of the genre saw some noteworthy pictures such as D.W. Griffith's 1920 *The Idol Dancer* and *The Love Flower*, silent films starring Richard Barthelmess, with footage cameraman Billy Bitzer shot in the Bahamas doubling for Oceania. *Hidden Pearls* starring the first Asian film star, Japanese-born Sessue Hayakawa, was filmed by Paramount Pic-

Betty Compson stars in the Paramount movie *The White Flower* (1923). Compson also plays the title role in *The Bonded Woman* (1922), in which she follows an alcoholic first mate from Honolulu to Samoa to clear his name. Apparently, both Compson films were lensed at the same time in Hawai'i.

LUIS REYES ARCHIVES

4   South Seas Cinema

tures on the Big Island in 1918. In 1923, popular silent film star Betty Compson filmed two features on Oʻahu for Paramount, *The White Flower* and *The Bonded Woman*. In 1926, the legendary detective Charlie Chan appeared in the serial *House Without a Key* while Roaring Twenties' "It Girl," Clara Bow, starred in Victor Fleming's 1927 *Hula* with a brief appearance by Olympic swimming champion and surfer Duke Kahanamoku.

Along with studio-shot features, a parallel trend began in which nonfiction and fiction films were being filmed at actual island locations. The cinema is uniquely qualified to show armchair travelers faraway lands and tribes with the more "exotic" the better. Filmmakers traveled far and wide to bring home moving images of distant places and peoples. (One of the unintended legacies of the genre's patrimony is that through realistic rendering, contemporary islanders can see a photographic record of their ancestors.)

Clara Bow is the "It Girl" in Paramount's *Hula*.

The Golden Age: Return to Nature

By 1929, not only had talkies taken over filmdom, but a new period in South Seas Cinema ushered in building on the conventions and formulae of the initial period. The stock market crash, the Great Depression and the spread of global fascism marked and shaped this subsequent era of the genre. It featured the "Sarong Girl" Dorothy Lamour's rise to stardom; numerous Oscars®, including the only Best Picture Academy Award for a South Pacific-set movie (1935's *Mutiny on the Bounty*, remade in 1962 with Marlon Brando and Tarita, shot on location in Tahiti); and a succession of classics with more than a dozen outstanding works released at a rate of more than one a year.

The uninhibited, sexually free Hula Girl, or Sarong Girl, is a South Seas Cinema staple. The template had already been set by the motion picture's precursors, such as Joseph Banks, a botanist aboard Captain Cook's ship, who wrote in 1769 of "a very pretty girl with a fire in her eyes" who bewitched him. From Dorothy Lamour to Maria Montez to France Nuyen to Tarita—Caucasian, Hispanic, Asian, and indigenous actresses have incarnated the enchanting, sexy Sarong Girl. Despite Hollywood's puritanical Production Code, partial nudity—real or suggested—has endured as a genre staple.

Another feature of the genre is the remoteness of the locale. The islands are a return to nature and the Golden Age, far from the maddening crowd. The genre's recurring dream of paradise lured viewers to its idyllic isles—"your special island" where, as Bloody Mary sings in *South Pacific*, "the sky meets the sea."

Bizarre native rituals were another sta-

Marlon Brando as Fletcher Christian and Tarita as Maimiti in 1962 remake of *Mutiny On The Bounty*.

South Seas Cinema 5

Although she didn't have a drop of Polynesian blood, Dorothy Lamour epitomized America's fantasy of the sultry, sensuous, scantily clad "sarong girl." Not only did she look great in a sarong, but she could sing, too! Lamour starred in a series of jungle movies, including this remake of *Aloma of the South Seas* (1941), as well as a series of "Road" films with Bob Hope and Bing Crosby. *Aloma* ends, literally, with a bang, as a volcano explodes; natural disasters are a staple of Pacific "flicks."

Far right photo: Juanita Hall as Bloody Mary sings Rodgers & Hammerstein's delightful "Happy Talk" in an effort to entice Lt. Cable (John Kerr) to marry her daughter Liat (France Nuyen), with a vision of a happy-go-lucky life in paradise in *South Pacific* (1958). The then-seventeen-year-old Vietnamese-French actress France Nuyen delightfully pantomimes the words to the "Happy Talk" song.

Yvonne DeCarlo performs a "native" dance. Al Kikume stands third from the right in this scene from *Hurricane Smith*.

ple including gathering and preparing for luau feasts serving exotic foods. There was also tattooing, as in *Moana*, and cannibalism, like in the 1958 Melville-inspired *Enchanted Island*. Human sacrifice of not-so vestal virgins occurred in the various versions of *Bird of Paradise* and *King Kong*.

Hawai'i's Unique Role in South Seas Cinema

From its inception, Hawai'i has played a central role in this genre as moving pictures came to Hawai'i early. As early as 1913, fiction films—including *The Shark God* and *Hawaiian Love*—had been filmed on O'ahu. Almost half of all South Seas genre movies have been set and/or made in Hawai'i, which made movies and TV produced in the islands inseparable from the genre. Movies with Hawai'i content share many of the genre's conventions.

By 1913, features were being made in what was then the Territory of Hawai'i, which was even warmer and sunnier than California. Proximity, political bonds and weather contributed to Hawai'i becoming a tropical movie back lot for Hollywood.

Hawaiian music was introduced at the 1915 International Exposition in San Francisco. Sol Ho'opi'i's lap steel guitar and falsetto singers, as well as Hawaiian dancers, were introduced on the world stage along with the ukulele. Broadway's Tin Pan Alley began adapting pseudo-Hawaiian tunes into their shows at the time when sheet music and recording devices like records, record players, and the radio were coming into prominence.

As soon as sound and talkies were developed, Hawaiian music began to be used as part of background music scores, especially in films with South Seas settings. Even World War II movies set in the Pacific Theater always had the obligatory scene of an American Naval

South Seas Cinema

or Army radioman tuning in to Hawaiian music that would become synonymous with Honolulu and the American homeland. When Imperial Japanese aircraft were en route to attack Pearl Harbor, the pilots could tell they had reached Hawai'i from the Hawaiian music picked up on their radio transmitters emanating from Honolulu radio stations.

Enhanced by the widespread appeal of Hawaiian music, the growing popularity of the South Seas genre made Hawai'i a far more accessible locale for Hollywood filmmakers, even if the stories were supposedly set elsewhere in the South Pacific, as with the O'ahu-filmed 1932 *Bird of Paradise* and the 1950 Kaua'i-filmed *Pagan Love Song* with Esther Williams. The islands were still what celebrated American author Mark Twain had called "the prettiest fleet of islands ever to anchor in the Pacific," ideal eye candy for tropical exteriors with stunning and lavish scenery. Hawai'i was the tip of the Polynesian triangle, and authenticity took a backseat to budgetary concerns and storytelling. Pacific Island locations became increasingly interchangeable.

Five-year-old Larry Ramos and his 'ukulele are the center of attention in this scene from the MGM musical *Pagan Love Song*. Rita Moreno is also captured in this scene.

Anti-Utopian Subversion

The Golden Age of South Seas Cinema came to a crashing halt with the December 7, 1941 surprise attack on Pearl Harbor by Japan. The paradise image of the isles was destroyed (at least temporarily). Audiences could not willingly believe in the false fairyland Shangri-La of the islands when newsreels depicted the USS *Arizona* smoldering and sinking. For the most part, motion picture paradises were subverted.

In the Pacific Theatre's features and documentaries, South Sea production morphed and became part of the war effort with agitprop ranging from training shorts, such as 1943's offensively titled *Jap Zero* featuring Ronald Reagan, to features like *Air Force* starring John Garfield, which fictionalized the Dec. 7 debacle and its aftermath. During the war, the movies boosted the morale of military personnel and home-front audiences. Noted directors, such as John Ford (1942's *Battle of Midway* and 1943's *December 7th*) and Frank Capra *(Why We Fight)*, focused their lenses on the island-hopping campaign in the Pacific, as John Wayne, Clark Gable, Tyrone Power, Robert Montgomery, and Jimmy Stewart among many other stars fought to make the world safe for democracy on and off the screen.

Immediately after World War II, traditional South Seas Cinema fell into a period of dormancy. The grim reality of the bloody battlefields of island-hopping Pacific campaigns were at odds with Hollywood's lush tropical escapist fantasies. There were no friendly natives to greet you, just enemy gunfire. Beautiful Dorothy Lamour in her sarong was nowhere to be found on battlefield islands. There was also less island unfamiliarity as hundreds of thousands of American soldiers, sailors, and Marines got their first glimpse of Hawai'i on their way to combat.

A new postwar sub-genre of South Seas Cinema emerged—the war film based on plays, novels, and stories written by World War II veterans such as James Jones, Herman Wouk, and James Michener. This military sub-genre has used Hawai'i well as a primary filming location for more than half a century, e.g. *From Here To Eternity* (1953) and *Pearl Harbor* (2001).

As the war years got further away, the movies largely returned to type with their tropical

South Seas Cinema

Burt Lancaster and Deborah Kerr in *From Here to Eternity* at Hālona Cove, southeast Oʻahu, in one of the most famous scenes in cinema history.

Far left: *From Here to Eternity* (1979) six hour television mini-series based on the novel and film, starred William Devane as Sgt. Milton Warden and Natalie Wood as Karen Holmes, filmed on Oʻahu. The contemporary mini-series format allowed for the full and frank dramatization of the 858-page novel for the first time. The film version only used a portion of the novel.

Led by the kahuna (Maurice Schwartz, who had a background in Yiddish theater), Kalua (Debra Paget) performs one of South Sea cinema's "bizarre native rituals": firewalking. In face, villagers of Apooiti, Raiatea, in French Polynesia are renowned for walking on red-hot stones, which are used for cooking in the imu (earthen oven). It is a Polynesian form of saying grace. Firewalking is still practiced in Fiji.

Oscar®-winning actor Tom Hanks stars in *Castaway* (2004) directed by Bob Zemeckis in Fiji. Hanks also starred in *Joe Versus the Volcano* (1990) which was filmed in Hawaiʻi.

Four young Hawaiʻi sugar plantation workers played by Robert Andre, Warren Fabro, Russell Omori, and Shaun Shimoda are accused of rape in *Blood and Orchids*. Hawaiʻi's real-life Massie case was the island equivalent of the infamous Scottsboro Boys case, another racist miscarriage of justice.

tropes of paradise and postwar clichéd archaic images. Hollywood rehashed the conventions and imagery of the genre's first five decades. In the next half century and beyond, a sporadic South Seas Cinema resurgence followed with *Bird of Paradise* (1951), *Mutiny on the Bounty* (1962), *The Blue Lagoon* (1980) and *Castaway* (2004) among many other films. Filmmakers deployed new high-tech wizardry, including Technicolor, Cinerama, 3D, Computer Generated Imagery, IMAX, and more, for its most popular stars to cavort amongst the palms and beyond the reefs.

The cinematic subversion of Utopianism did persist via crime dramas. TV's crime-fighting trend included the 1959-1963 *Hawaiian Eye*, starring Robert Conrad, Troy Donahue, Poncie Ponce, and Connie Stevens as the singer Cricket Blake. This was followed by the long-running 1968-1980 original *Hawaii Five-O* with Jack Lord, James MacArthur, Kam Fong, and Zulu as the anti-crime elite unit that answers directly to Hawaiʻi's governor (Richard Denning). From 1980-1988, *Magnum P.I.* continued the tradition with Tom Selleck as a private eye. The real-life Massie Affair, about a purported 1931 rape by local youths of a Navy officer's wife, was fictionalized in the 1985 miniseries *Blood and Orchids* with Kris Kristofferson, Jose Ferrer, Jane Alexander, and Sean Young. Other television Hawaiʻi law-breaking series included 1988-1992's *Jake and the Fatman* with William Conrad and Joe Penny; 1992's *Raven* with Jeffrey Meek and Lee Majors; and 1994's *One West Waikiki* with Cheryl Ladd. In 2010, CBS reincarnated *Hawaii Five-0*, starring Alex O'Loughlin and Scott Caan in the Steve McGarrett and Danno roles.

In the last decade, the genre has morphed itself into contemporary Ha-

South Seas Cinema

wai'i-content films such as *Soul Surfer, The Descendants,* and *Forgetting Sarah Marshall* as well as the long-running network television series *Lost*. As with any film genre, South Seas Cinema is adaptable to reflect the values and concerns of society.

Soul Surfer (2011) is based on a contemporary faith-based true story of a teenage surfer from Hawai'i who loses her arm during a shark attack off Kaua'i. This narrative has its origins in the man against nature myths and legends present in Polynesian culture in which man (in this case woman) is pitted against the evils spirits "Gods" incarnate represented by the shark. The film shows the heroine triumphing over those spirits and regaining her true self in the process. *Soul Surfer* also directly links to one of the first feature films made in Hawai'i called *The Shark God* in 1913.

The Descendants (2011) follows a missionary descendant family in modern Hawai'i, keepers of the land that has been passed down through the generations. Moral infidelity upsets their utopia and sets off a chain of events that the protagonist must overcome to come to terms with himself and as a family steward of the land.

Forgetting Sarah Marshall (2008), a romantic comedy, has the Caucasian protagonist coming to a Polynesian paradise (even though man-made, a resort hotel in Hawai'i) to forget his past love. There he finds happiness with a local girl (though in fact she isn't, but has all the trapping of one). Complications result from an encounter with his old flame, who, unbeknownst to him, is also vacationing at the same resort with another man.

Lost (2004-2010) is a modern science-fiction adventure version of survival on a deserted island, a staple of South Seas Cinema. In this case, surviving nature and loneliness is not the problem; rather the challenge is in surviving the group. A commercial jetliner crash lands on a strange island. With no hope of immediate rescue, the survivors must learn to live with one another or perish. All of the resulting backstories on the individual castaways and their motivations are channeled through an omnipotent force.

Filmed entirely in Hawai'i, though not set there, the Emmy® award-winning *Lost* became the most critically acclaimed, highly rated, and honored dramatic television series ever made in Hawai'i. Combining traditional elements of the genre with science fiction, *Lost* demonstrates that South Seas Cinema will be with us in some form or another as long as people wish to escape civilization and dream of a perfect society symbolized by a tropical island or perhaps a tropical planet in a galaxy paradise far… far… away from earth as we know it.

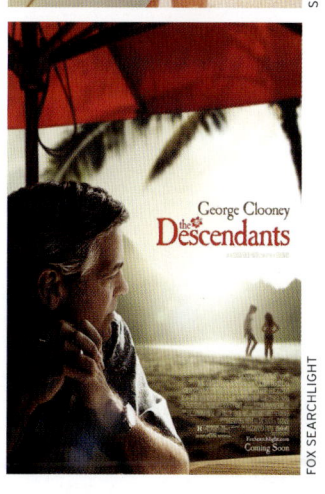

The cast of *Hawaii Five-0* reboot. *Left to right* : Grace Park, Daniel Dae Kim, Alex O'Loughlin and Scott Caan.

South Seas Cinema

This page, left: Jack Lord as Det. Steve McGarrett, head of *Hawaii Five-0* CBS/LEONARD FREEMAN PRODUCTIONS;
top right: Cast of *Hawaii Five-0* Reboot *(left to right)* Daniel Dae Kim, Scott Caan, Grace Park and Alex O'Loughlin CBS PRODUCTIONS;
bottom right: Robert Conrad as Tom Lopaka on the first Hawai'i set TV series *Hawaiian Eye* WARNER BROS TV
Opposite page, left: John Wayne as two fisted Big Jim McLain WARNER BROS.; *center*: Tom Selleck as Magnum P.I. UNIVERSAL TV;
right: Warner Oland as Charlie Chan LUIS REYES ARCHIVES/TWENTIETH CENTURY FOX

CHAPTER 2

Crime Fighters in Paradise

Murder in Paradise or the Snake In Eden

The idea of crime in Paradise dates back to the biblical reference of Adam and Eve at creation in the Garden Of Eden. There, Paradise was lost due to their disobeying of the Lord God through Satan in the form of a serpent or snake. Throughout folklore, literature and popular culture, the snake has been demonized and the reptile vilified. Hawai'i was often referred to as a "Paradise" by early European explorers and missionaries. The idea of crime in such an idyllic place takes on Judeo-Christian overtones. *Hawaii Five-O* creator Leonard Freeman once stated that the show's theme was "The Snake in Eden." The angel man defeating the snake men can easily be McGarrett.

To add fact to fiction, snakes are not native to the Hawaiian Islands, and Hawai'i actually has one of the lowest violent crime rates in the United States.

From the 60s' signature suited *Hawaii Five-O* team to the new young designer sportswear style *Hawaii Five-O* reboot, fighting crime and keeping paradise pure and safe from the bad guys is the mission of the good guys and gals, also known as Crime Fighters in Paradise.

Charlie Chan

"Perhaps listening to a Chinaman is no disgrace"

—Charlie Chan to Captain Flannery
in *Behind That Curtain*, later retitled *Charlie Chan's Chance*.

Charlie Chan, the aphorism-spouting fictional literary Chinese detective, (except for Duke Kahanamoku) was perhaps Hawai'i's best-known figure and a movie icon during the first half of the twentieth century. Chan derives from the literary tradition of Sherlock Holmes that has survived through popular fiction to film and television into many incarnations, most notably Nick and Nora Charles of *The Thin Man* series, Agatha Christie's Hercule Poirot, and Ellery Queen.

The Chan plots are constructed so similarly that their conventions became ritualistic for the reader or the moviegoer. Always there is the obvious suspect. Then Chan commandeers, spotting clues, spouting aphorisms, keeping everyone in the dark until the last moment. Gathering all the suspects and possibilities together, he exposes the true culprit, usually the last person anyone would expect.

Earl Derr Biggers created the character of Charlie Chan in 1925 and acknowledged that the career of Honolulu policeman Chang Apana inspired him. While vacationing in the islands in 1919, Biggers read about Chang in a Honolulu newspaper.

Charlie Chan appeared in six Biggers novels published from 1925 to 1932, in 48 theatrical feature films from 1926 through 1981 and in the magazine *The Saturday Evening Post*. The popularity of the Chan detective stories led to more novels, and *The Saturday Evening Post* paid $25,000 for the third one, *Behind That Curtain* (1929). Chan's theatrical feature film run began in 1926 with *The House without a Key,* set in Hawai'i at the present site of the Halekulani. Chan captured the American public's imagination despite starting out as only a supporting character in the first novel.

Pathé Studios produced *The House without a Key* in 1926 with Japanese actor George Kuwa as Chan. A year later, Universal followed with *The Chinese Parrot* with another Japanese actor, Sojin, as Chan. The Fox Film Corporation acquired the rights to the Chan novels. While Earl Derr Biggers was alive, he allowed only for the contracted studios to adapt his novels into films. All six novels were adapted, but the studios could not create new Charlie Chan stories. In 1933, after Diggers passed away, his widow sold the rights to the Charlie Chan character to Fox Studios. To meet the growing popularity and demand for more Charlie Chan movies, the studio assigned screenwriters to develop new stories for production. In 1929, the Fox series began with *Behind That Curtain* in which Korean actor E.L. Park played Chan in a small supporting role.

Chan finally got into his leading role in *Charlie Chan Carries On,* which was produced by Sol Wurtzel, and actor Warner Oland portrayed Chan. The Swedish-born actor had played

Warner Oland as Honolulu's own crime solver Charlie Chan.

Crime Fighters in Paradise

Asian characters both on stage and in previous films, usually as a villain, typical for the screen portrayals of Asians at the time. Though many actors were considered, Oland won the role and starred in sixteen Chan films produced at Fox studios from 1931 until his death in 1938. Sidney Toler took over the Chan role and starred in eleven films for Twentieth Century Fox. He then brought the screen rights himself and arranged a new series for Monogram Pictures in 1944. In that series, Toler starred in eleven Chan films, and then Roland Winters starred as Chan in six films after Toler's death. From 1957 to 1958, a thirty-nine-episode television series, *The New Adventures of Charlie Chan*, was produced in England for syndication, starring J. Carrol Naish in the title role. In 1973, Ross Martin starred as Chan in a made-for-TV film, *The Return of Charlie Chan*. In 1981, English actor Peter Ustinov played Chan in the color theatrical feature film, *Charlie Chan and the Curse of the Dragon Queen*.

Though Charlie Chan worked as a detective in the Honolulu Police Department, very few of his onscreen cases took place in Hawai'i. Instead, Honolulu usually served as a point of departure for the globetrotting Chan. He was usually solving mysteries in places around the world, such as Egypt, Shanghai, San Francisco, Paris, Monte Carlo, Germany, and London. Chan traveled to over two dozen cities and five continents and was even mentioned as having worked a case in Australia. Only three films, *The House without a Key*, *Charlie Chan's Greatest Case*, and *The Black Camel*, actually take place in Hawai'i. Of the three films, only *The Black Camel* was filmed on location in Hawai'i. Other films where at least some of the storyline takes place in Honolulu include 1931's *Charlie Chan Carries On*, 1936's *Charlie Chan's Secret*, 1936's *Charlie Chan at the Racetrack*, 1938's *Charlie Chan in Honolulu*, 1939's *Charlie Chan in Reno*, and 1940's *Charlie Chan's Murder Cruise*. Charlie Chan and his large family lived in a house on Punchbowl Hill in Honolulu.

Asian-American groups have been sensitive to the portrayal of the fictional Charlie Chan for many years. Chan had been played mainly by Caucasian actors and was based on stereotypical Caucasian perceptions of Asians. With his shuffling walk, soul patch, and oriental Confucious philosophy, Chan is considered an offensive Asian stereotype even though he was a positive, intelligent, law abiding character who usually bested his Caucasian counterparts. Together with his Americanized number one son and family (all played by ethnic Asians) Chan portrayed Chinese-American assimilation into a rigid segregated American society of the time in a somewhat idealized and simplistic Hollywood manner. It is time for a new interpretation of Charlie Chan with an Asian-American actor as Chan, much like the recent *Sherlock Holmes* series of films with Robert Downey Jr.

Victor Sen as Number one son and Sidney Toler as Charlie Chan.

Crime Fighters in Paradise   13

The Black Camel
1931 Fox Film Corp.

DIRECTED BY	**Hamilton MacFadden**
SCREENPLAY BY	**Barry Conners and Philip Klein, adapted by Hugh Strange from an original story by Earl Derr Biggers**
PRODUCED BY	**Hamilton MacFadden**
CAST	**Warner Oland (Charlie Chan), Sally Eilers (Julie O'Neill), Bela Lugosi (Tarneverro alias Arthur Mayo), Victor Varconi (Robert Fyfe), Robert Young (Jimmy Bradshaw), Otto Yamaoka (Kashimo)**

The Black Camel is the only Charlie Chan movie that was filmed almost entirely on location in Hawai'i. More surprisingly, for an early talkie film, it was an expensive production for its time period (Depression Era), which brought an entire cast, crew, and equipment to Hawai'i via Matson liner for a month of filming. Fox Film Corporation experimented with and developed a sound-on-film process. It eased the process of shooting sound films on location in such productions as *In Old Arizona* (1929) and *The Big Trail* (1930), as opposed to other studios such as Warner Bros. that developed a sound-on-disc process. To control production costs and technical sound recording problems, many film companies shot mostly on specially made sound stages in Hollywood studios. Despite the myth that early talkies were static, *The Black Camel* has fluid camera movements and made full use of the scenic Hawai'i locations in its composition of shots. The film captured the size and scope of The Royal Hawaiian Hotel (which had opened just a few years prior in 1927), most noticeably in the scenes between Oland and Lugosi in the hotel lobby, outside gardens, and lanai. Driving scenes show background process shots of Punchbowl hill and the now dilapidated Natatorium swim stadium in Waikīkī.

The title of the book and movie *The Black Camel* is attributed to an old Eastern saying: "Death is the black camel that kneels unbidden at every gate." In the film, a Hollywood screen heartthrob, Denny Mayo, turns up murdered while filming a movie on location in Hawai'i. Suspicion turns to a psychic advisor with a spiritual nature. But when Charlie Chan of the Honolulu Police Department uncovers a link to the unsolved murder, he soon discovers that fame can be murder.

Original 1931 poster art for *The Black Camel* and modern DVD release cover artwork prominently features Warner Oland as Charlie Chan and Bela Lugosi as Tarneverro. *The Black Camel* is the only surviving film of the first three early Chan films with Oland and is the only one that was filmed mostly on location in Hawai'i.

Real-life Honolulu detective Chang Apana poses for a picture with his screen counterpart, actor Warner Oland as Charlie Chan, during location shooting of *The Black Camel* at the Royal Hawaiian Hotel in Honolulu. Apana was the inspiration for author Earl Derr Biggers Honolulu Chinese detective Charlie Chan.

Crime Fighters in Paradise

Hawaiʻi, Honolulu, and the famed Waikīkī Beach in the 1920s and 1930s were known as the playground of the rich and famous. Well-heeled tourists arrived in Hawaiʻi by the luxury Matson ocean liner at Front Street near the Aloha Tower, after a five-day sea journey from San Francisco. Once on shore, the tourists rode on an automobile or a streetcar line that passed rice and taro fields to reach Waikīkī. Air passenger service to Hawaiʻi from the mainland was not available until Pan American Airlines inaugurated The China Clipper in 1936, which made the 2,400 mile trip in twenty-one hours.

While filming in Honolulu, Chang Apana, the inspiration for Charlie Chan, visited the filming set location at the Royal Hawaiian Hotel and posed for a publicity photo with actor Warner Oland as Charlie Chan at Kailua Beach in May 1931.

A Hungarian-born actor who became exclusively identified with the horror film genre, Bela Lugosi played the mystic Tarneverro, in his first role following his star-making success as the title role of Count Dracula in Universal's *Dracula* (1931). Dwight Frye, who plays a servant, played Renfield in *Dracula* and also Fritz in *Frankenstein*. Studio-contract player Robert Young made his film debut as the Island's public relations man. Young had a long career in films and later television, where he became best known due to two long-running series, *Father Knows Best* (1954-1960) and *Marcus Welby M. D.* (1969-1976).

Songs featured in the film include "Uheuhene" and "Na Lei o Hawaiʻi," words and music by Charles E. King; "I Have a Thought in My Heart for You," words and music by Sol Hoopii, Jr; and "Aloha ʻOe," words and music by Queen Liliʻuokalani. Out of all the direct film adaptations of Biggers' Charlie Chan novels, *The Black Camel* is the only film that still survives.

The Legend of Chang Apana
2009

DIRECTED BY **Michael Wurth**
PRODUCED BY **John Noland, Cary-Hiroyuki Tagawa, Lisa Dowd**
CAST **Cary-Hiroyuki Tagawa (Chang Apana)**

A five-minute short film executive produced by John Noland to serve as a pilot for a possible television, cable or web series. This film is based on the story of real-life Hawaiʻi detective Chang Apana, who inspired Earl Derr Biggers to create the character of Charlie Chan. The locally produced independent short has exteriors at Honolulu's Chinatown and against a studio green screen. Jon Brekke serves as the executive producer, and Colin Fong the stunt coordinator on the project. Veteran screen actor Cary-Hiroyuki Tagawa *(Mortal Kombat, Pearl Harbor, Memoirs of a Geisha)* plays Chang Apana, the HPD detective noted for using a horse whip, instead of a gun.

Now, Charlie Chan holds an honorable place as the first of Hawaiʻi's iconic fictional crime fighters, but many followed in his wake on the big and little screen.

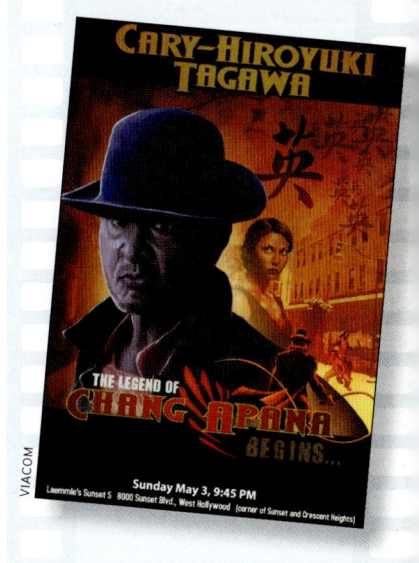

Crime Fighters in Paradise

Big Jim McLain
1952 Warner Bros.

DIRECTED BY **Edward Ludwig**
SCREENPLAY BY **James Edward Grant, Richard English, Eric Taylor**
PRODUCED BY **Wayne-Fellows Productions**
CAST **John Wayne (Jim McLain), Nancy Olsen (Nancy Vallon), James Arness (Mel Baxter), Alan Napier (Sturak), Madame Soo Young (Mrs. Namaka), Honolulu Chief Of Police Dan Liu (Dan Liu, Honolulu Chief of Police), Red McQueen (Phil Briggs)**

John Wayne, an American film icon, was one of the most popular box office film stars of his time in a career that spanned almost 50 years from 1929 until his death in 1979. Wayne embodied American ideals and manifest destiny, both on-screen and off. Though best known for his Western film cowboy roles, Wayne was strongly associated with Hawai'i and the Pacific due to his tough two-fisted portrayals as a man of action in movies in which he often depicted a seaman, American naval officer, Marine or soldier.

In *Big Jim McLain,* possibly one of his worst films, he plays a House Un-American Activities Committee investigator. In this role, he comes to the then-territory of Hawai'i to uncover Communist subversives there. *Big Jim McLain* was one of the first modern motion pictures filmed in post-war Hawai'i. A company of seventeen Hollywood actors and actresses and fifty-one technicians were flown to and from the Islands for six weeks of intensive filming. A score of Hawai'i residents in featured and bit parts augmented the Hollywood cast headed by Wayne, which included his co-stars Nancy Olson, James Arness, and Alan Napier. From beach boy to banker, Honoluluans and their neighbor Islanders volunteered to act. Some of the most prominent and influential citizens of Honolulu accepted feature parts to add to the picture's ring of authenticity and acquitted themselves well. With the permission of the city Police Commission, Honolulu's Island-born police chief Dan Liu portrayed himself and shared considerable key footage with Wayne.

A routine lackluster movie, *Big Jim McLain* strangely lacks action, with a convoluted messy plot. It was so incomprehensible to overseas audiences that for the foreign release, the movie was titled *Marijuana*, which was ironic, given the conservative political nature of John Wayne. Filmed on location in black and white, the film remains a visual record of the then-contemporary territorial Hawai'i. Produced in 1951 during the Joe McCarthy anti-Communist witch hunt in America, the movie made money at the box-office due to the stars' popularity and drawing power. The movie made so much money that it enabled Wayne to set up his own production company under a non-exclusive deal with Warner Bros studio chief, Jack Warner. Wayne-Fellows Productions quickly became Batjac

The foreign poster art for *Big Jim McLain,* whose plot was so incomprehensible to foreign audiences that the film was retitled *Marijuana*.

Crime Fighters in Paradise

Productions and produced a number of Wayne films.

Locations for *Big Jim McLain* included the Honolulu police station, Kukui Street, Waikīkī, the Royal Hawaiian Hotel, the Edgewater (which served as company headquarters), and the Outrigger Canoe Club, all of which opened their doors and turned over their grounds to the Wayne-Fellows Production company. Scenes were also shot at Kalaupapa Settlement for Hansen's Disease victims on Molokaʻi, which required permission from the territorial government. A scene in the film has Wayne and Arness making a pilgrimage to Pearl Harbor, the site of the USS *Arizona*.

Wayne loved Hawaiʻi and vacationed there frequently on the yacht, Araner, that belonged to his mentor, director John Ford. As a college student, Wayne made his first trip to Hawaiʻi in 1927 by stowing away in a Matson Liner. When discovered, he was put in handcuffs and chained for the rest of the voyage back to San Francisco, where he was released due to the intervention of an influential friend. He married his third wife Pilar and honeymooned on the Big Island during the production of *The Sea Chase* in 1954. Duke, who was quite a swimmer, held center stage with Hawaiʻi's own Olympic champion Duke Kahanamoku in the film *Wake of The Red Witch*. The former also visited his friend—the *other* Duke—who was then Acting Sheriff of Honolulu during the production of *Big Jim McLain*.

The Duke greets the Duke—John "Duke" Wayne visits his friend Duke Kahanamoku who was honorary Sheriff of Honolulu while filming *Big Jim McLain* on location in Honolulu.

Wayne made four films on location in Hawaiʻi: *Big Jim McLain, The Sea Chase, In Harm's Way,* and *Donovan's Reef.* His other South Seas-themed films include *Seven Sinners, The Fighting Seabees, They Were Expendable, Flying Leathernecks, Sands of Iwo Jima, Wake of The Red Witch, Operation Pacific,* and *The High and The Mighty.* He also starred in a 1937 Universal chapter serial called *Adventure's End,* which was set in the South Seas, starring as pearl diver Duke Slade.

John Wayne at Honolulu Airport filming scenes for his production of *Big Jim McLain* in 1951.

Crime Fighters in Paradise

Hawaiian Eye
1959-1963 ABC Television Series, produced by Warner Bros.

CAST **Robert Conrad (Tom Lopaka), Anthony Eisley (Tracy Steele), Grant Williams (Greg Mackenzie), Connie Stevens (Cricket Blake), Poncie Ponce (Kazuo Kim), Mel Prestidge (Lt. Danny Quon), Troy Donahue (Philip Barton), Doug Mossman (Moke)**

"The Soft Island Breeze brings you strange melodies
And they tell of exotic mysteries under the tropical spell of
Hawaiian Eye! Hawaiian Eye! Hawaiian Eye!"

–Theme music composed by Mack David and Jerry Livingston

Famous opening tiki logo credit sequence for the popular TV series *Hawaiian Eye*.

Doug Mossman as night security guard Moke on *Hawaiian Eye*. Mossman also served as technical advisor on all things Hawaiian for the series. In a career that spans more than fifty years, Mossman has guest starred on most of the Hawai'i-based television series. Mossman also became a regular on *Hawaii Five-O* and for one season, a member of *Five-O* as Detective Frank Kamana. The actor recently guest starred on an episode of the new *Hawaii Five-0* Reboot. He also produced and created a short-lived NBC series *The Westwind*.

Hawaiian Eye is a Honolulu-based private detective agency owned and operated by Tom Lopaka (Robert Conrad) and Tracy Steele (Eisley). Lopaka, born and raised in the Islands, and Steele, who hails from Chicago, work in a poolside office at the luxurious Hawaiian Village Hotel, which is now the Hilton Hawaiian Village. Assisted by Cricket Blake (Stevens), a beautiful singer/photographer who performs at the hotel Shell Bar, they strive to eliminate the sources of trouble that invade their tropical paradise. Maui-born Poncie Ponce, who was discovered during a Los Angeles nightclub engagement by a Warner Bros. producer, played Kazuo Kim, a 'ukulele-playing taxi driver and featured regular.

Born in the Islands and of Hawaiian-Scotch ancestry, Douglas Kinilau Mossman played Moke, the night security guard at the agency. A graduate of Kamehameha Schools and the University of Hawai'i, Mossman also served as a technical advisor on the series, making sure everything was Island authentic. During the initial planning of the series, one of his first assignments was to sit in a screening room, view as many Warner Bros. movies as possible and extract any footage that could be used in the series that gave the idea of the tropics.

Warner Bros. produced 134 one-hour episodes of this filmed series for the ABC Television network in

Crime Fighters in Paradise

Robert Conrad starred as Tom Lopaka on the first Hawai'i-set TV series *Hawaiian Eye*. Conrad went on to even greater fame as James West in the popular TV series *Wild Wild West* and later returned to the Pacific as Major Pappy Boyington in the World War II series *The Black Sheep Squadron*.

black and white. The show made its debut on October 7, 1959, just a few months after Hawai'i received statehood, so there was much interest in the new Island state. During its debut season, a tagline for the series was, "If you haven't visited the newest state yet, *Hawaiian Eye* television series is the next best thing to it." The opening title sequence of the show included such Hawaiian landmarks as the Blow Hole, Diamond Head, Lanikai, Aloha Tower, and 'Iolani Palace.

Mack David and Jerry Livingston wrote the popular series' theme music and song, which ran over the Tiki-themed opening title sequence credits.

The first four episodes' exteriors were shot in Hawai'i. Otherwise, the use of stock footage and imaginative set design created the illusion of being in Hawai'i. Most of the episodes were shot largely in and around Los Angeles at the Warner Bros. studio and backlot in Burbank. In 1962, the cast and crew filmed four additional episodes on location in Hawai'i.

This detective series with a Hawai'i background was originally based on the successful *77 Sunset Strip* TV series formula. This formula also included the Miami-set series *Surfside 6* and the New Orleans locale of *Bourbon St Beat,* wherein characters and storylines could be transferred from one Warner Bros TV series to the other.

In the late fifties, an actress asked Robert Conrad to help her with an audition for Warner Bros. producer William T. Orr. Conrad did and soon wound up with a contract and later a starring role as Tom Lopaka in *Hawaiian Eye.* That was the first role to be cast for the show and was the first major television role for actor Robert Conrad.

Crime Fighters in Paradise   19

Hawaii Five-O
1968-1980 CBS

CREATED BY **Leonard Freeman**

CAST **Jack Lord (Steve McGarrett), James MacArthur (Danny Williams), Kam Fong (Chin Ho Kelly), Zulu (Kono Kalakua), Richard Denning (The Governor), Khigh Dhiegh (Wo Fat)**

"Book 'em, Danno!"
—McGarrett to Danny Williams

On September 20, 1968, *Hawaii Five-O* debuted as a two-hour pilot movie-of-the-week on the CBS Television Network, and six days later the hour-long series premiered. Beginning with its inspired, ahead-of-its-time, pre-music video title visualization, and theme music by Morton Stevens, who would have guessed that a fictional elite Hawai'i police unit would leave such an indelible impression on the worldwide television landscape?

Hawaii Five-O was a crime series set in the lush surroundings of Hawai'i. *Five-O* (for Fiftieth State) comprises an elite four-people Hawai'i state police unit headed by former U.S. Naval Commander Steve McGarrett (Lord) who reports only to the governor (Denning). The unit tackled high-felony crimes, espionage, and drug trafficking. "The Five-O special investigating unit handling cases too big or too far reaching for any other local agency," according to the CBS program's production notes.

The other members of the team included fresh-faced, college-educated Danny "Danno" Williams, played by James MacArthur, Chin Ho Kelly, played by Kam Fong, who in real life was a veteran Honolulu policeman, and Kono, played by Zulu, a Native Hawaiian entertainer.

In her authoritative *Booking Hawaii Five-O* (McFarland 1997, North Carolina, London), author Karen Rhodes states "episodes of *Hawaii Five-0* are tales of investi-

The classic pre-music video opening wave title credit sequence for *Hawaii Five-O* was assembled and edited by Reza Badiyi.

Jack Lord as Steve McGarrett with the signature Hawaiian landmarks of Waikīkī and Diamond Head in the background.

20 Crime Fighters in Paradise

gation, pursuit, and arrest. The investigation phase is characterized by what we will call the Process, the way the team gathers the clues and correlates them into a coherent theory to solve the problem. Each team member contributes according to his own abilities and expertise. The main stage upon which the Process plays is McGarrett's office, which rather than being a private reserve for the head man, serves as the nerve center for the entire team."

Writer and producer Leonard Freeman originated the idea for the popular show after his mother-in-law, who lived in Honolulu, suggested he develop "something about Hawai'i so that he and his wife could visit more often." During a meeting with then-Governor John A. Burns, Freeman learned that Burns was planning to start a special police task force to deal with unusual crimes in the Islands and was going to call the force *Five-O*. According to production manager Bernie Oseransky, "Lenny went back and wrote a script for a television series called *The Man* which became *Hawaii Five-O* based on that unit." His series idea developed into a straightforward police drama that took place in the 50th State (hence the Five-O) nine years after its entry into the Union. Freeman originally chose Actor Richard Boone, who resided in the Islands for years, for the role of McGarrett. However, Boone turned it down, and Jack Lord became a last-minute casting choice.

Jack Lord as Steve McGarrett radios his team in front of *Hawaii Five-0's* 'Iolani Palace Headquarters.

Jack Lord was a working actor, whom stardom and fame seemed to have eluded, though he possessed all the leading-man qualities. He had appeared in several major films (such as the 1962 James Bond thriller *Dr. No*) and a prior short-lived television rodeo series *Stoney Burke*. Lord was almost forty-seven years old when he seized the opportunity of a lifetime with the role of McGarrett, which became as much his creation as Freeman's over the series' long run. The suit, the hairstyle, the catch phrases, and the square-jawed no-nonsense intensity made up McGarrett's identity. Lord directed *Five-O* episodes over the years and was nominated for a Directors Guild of America Award for the critically acclaimed episode *Why Won't Linda Die?*

Native Hawaiian entertainer Zulu (Gilbert Francis Lani Damian Kauhi) as Kono Kalākaua on *Hawaii Five-0*.

As the first television series filmed entirely on location in Hawai'i, *Hawaii Five-O* brought color images of Hawai'i into homes around the world for years beyond its twelve-year run (you can still find reruns aired on the tube). The long-running series was the first series using locations primarily on O'ahu and in and around Honolulu. *Hawaii Five-O* conveyed a representative image of Hawai'i, its beauty, its racial and ethnic mixtures, and culture. Some have said that Hawai'i served as the real star of the series, and many viewers have tuned in to see Island locales and locals. The program also got credit for promoting Hawai'i as a tourist destination. "It was considered the ultimate travelogue for Hawai'i," David Poltrack, executive vice president of research at CBS, told the *New York Times* when Lord died in 1998. "The ascent

Crime Fighters in Paradise   21

of Hawai'i as a major tourist destination coincided with the strong years of the program. It really hit a chord."

Its twelve-year run provided benefits of over $100 million to Hawai'i via the tourism it attracted. The series created a spending effect of almost $180 million on Hawai'i's economy, paid an estimated $16 million in sales taxes, created 7,992 jobs a year and, more than any other single production, developed Hawai'i as a film center in the Pacific.

To a great extent, *Hawaii Five-O* came to define and represent Hawai'i to the world. However, what kind of image did *Five-O* project? *Hawaii Five-O* came to television when America needed reassurance in law and order and in its traditional values and heroes. It was the era of the Vietnam War, the Civil Rights and the Women's Liberation Movement, student protest, hippies, and acid rock music. Martin Luther King Jr. and Robert Kennedy have been assassinated, Richard Nixon became president, and the first manned Apollo space mission was successfully launched.

Under the guise of a police drama, *Hawaii Five-O,* over the span of its twelve seasons, dealt with contemporary issues, some of which still resonate today. These include environmental concerns, overdevelopment, cultural identity, illegal drugs, political assassination, gun violence, prison reform, police brutality, homosexuality, illegal aliens, problems of returning war veterans, biological germ warfare, and the exploitation and abuse of women.

The *Five-O* series began production in an old military warehouse near Pearl City. CBS

Jack Lord as Steve McGarrett finally has his longtime nemesis Red Chinese agent Wo Fat (Khigh Diegh) behind bars and holds the key after twelve seasons on the air.

Jack Lord, director Alvin Ganzer and guest stars Ricardo Montalban and Carolyn Barret rehearse a scene before rolling the cameras on the first episode of *Hawaii Five-0* filmed at the Henry J. Kaiser Estate.

22 Crime Fighters in Paradise

would produce twenty-four episodes a season at a cost of $210,000 per episode. It would take eight days to film an episode that would comprise twelve-to-sixteen-hour work days. Each time a company move was made, the camera, cables, microphones, sound equipment, etc., were piled into seventeen trucks and, with two generators, were moved to the next location. This effort was a good deal more cumbersome than using a sound stage or the back-lot of a Hollywood studio, but resulted in a far-more realistic and interesting effect.

Filming was comprised of 70 percent exterior shots to take advantage of the exotic beauty of the Islands. Leonard Freeman and Jack Lord soon became partners: Freeman watching the shop in Hollywood, developing scripts, hiring guest stars and directors, and Lord running the show in Hawai'i. The exposed film dailies were air freighted overnight to Hollywood for processing, editing, and post-production work until completion of the episode.

At its height, *Hawaii Five-O* was airing in 80 countries, and 300 million viewers watched it weekly. Its primetime network run spanned twelve seasons, from September 1968 until April 1980. Until 1993, when the original *Law and Order* series surpassed it, *Hawaii Five-O* was the longest-running police drama on American television. Today, it continues to enjoy enormous popularity through syndication, online Internet viewing, the release of remastered DVDs of the series' twelve seasons and, of course, the series' reboot on CBS.

Magnum P.I.
1980-1988 CBS

CREATED BY **Glen Larson, Don Bellisario**

CAST **Tom Selleck (Thomas Magnum), John Hillerman (Jonathan Q. Higgins), Roger E. Mosley (T.C.), Larry Manetti (Rick Wright)**

The ruggedly handsome six-foot-four Tom Selleck progressed from a comparatively unknown actor to an internationally famous star of television and motion pictures with his role as the Hawai'i-based detective, Thomas Magnum on the TV series *Magnum P.I.*

A retired Navy officer who served in Vietnam, Thomas Sullivan Magnum lands an idyllic life, keeping tabs on security at a lush beachfront mansion on O'ahu's southeast coast near Waimānalo, while running an adventurous private-eye business. His companion is the estate's knowledgeable but stuffy British major domo, Jonathan Q. Higgins (Hillerman), who disapproves intensely of Magnum's freewheeling ways and attempts to thwart Magnum's capers at every turn.

In the first two-hour special episode of *Magnum* on December 11, 1980, the fun-loving detective boldly takes on Navy higher-ups to track down the coldblooded murderers of his best friend. Magnum becomes a target in the process and calls for help from resourceful fellow members of his special combat team in Vietnam, now residing in Hawai'i, helicop-

Tom Selleck found international stardom in his role as Hawai'i's *Magnum P.I.* and is playing a top cop presently on the hit CBS television New York set series *Blue Bloods*.

Crime Fighters in Paradise   23

The principal cast of *Magnum P.I.*: Roger E. Mosely as T. C. Calvin, Larry Manetti as Rick Wright, Tom Selleck as Thomas Sullivan Magnum and John Hillerman as Jonathan Q. Higgins.

Legendary Hawai'i Film veteran and Oscar® winner Frank Sinatra *(From Here To Eternity, Devil At Four O'clock, None But The Brave)* with Tom Selleck. "Old Blue Eyes" was a fan of *Magnum P.I.* and accepted a guest starring role and donned a Hawaiian shirt in a specially written episode.

ter pilot T.C. Calvin (Mosley) and Rick Wright (Manetti), the manager of the upscale Waikīkī-based King Kamehameha Club. Thus began the eight-year, 162-episode run of *Magnum*, the one-hour detective series filmed entirely in Hawai'i.

During the series' eight-year run, Tom Selleck won an Emmy® Award in 1984 for Best Actor in a Drama series and four nominations, one Golden Globe® award and seven Globe® nominations. John Hillerman won an Emmy® Award in 1987 as Best Actor for his portrayal of Higgins.

The CBS Network asked Glen Larson, producer of hit series, such as *McCloud, Switch, Battlestar Gallactica, The Fall Guy* and *Knight Rider,* for a script. He gave them *Magnum*, the story of a James Bond-style private eye, ex-CIA agent who lived on the private estate of an author named Robin Masters. Magnum lived in the guesthouse all by himself except for his killer Doberman and a roomful of gadgets. Larson didn't want to proceed with the project and turned the script over to Donald Bellisario, who had his own private-eye pilot script, H. H. Flynn. He combined his script with Larson's to create *Magnum P.I.*

Hawaii Five-0 was going off the air after twelve seasons, and CBS persuaded Bellisario to set *Magnum* in Hawai'i to make use of the production facilities built there. The pilot made in the spring of 1980 received an order to go to series before it even aired. The initial episode shown on December 11, 1980, ranked number 14 for the year and had an overall rating of 21.0. *Magnum P.I.* aired in syndication all over the world well before the end of its primetime life and continues to be popular. Charles Floyd Johnson served as the supervising producer in Hawai'i, and Mike Post and Pete Carpenter composed the theme music. Tom Selleck also served as the executive producer during the last two seasons of the series. Bellisario went on to produce the South Seas-set *Tales of the Gold Monkey* (1982-1983), the long-running television series *JAG* (1995-2005) and *NCIS* (2003-). *Magnum P.I.* contributed $100 million directly into Hawai'i's economy during its initial series run.

Crime Fighters in Paradise

Dog the Bounty Hunter
2004-2012 A&E Cable Network

PRODUCED BY **Simeon Hutner, Adriana Pacheco, Sylvia Waliga, Lorca Sheppard, Jen Lerman, Kimberly Tomes**

CAST **Duane "Dog" Chapman, Leland Chapman, Tim Chapman, Beth Smith, Justin Bihag**

This long-running reality series details the job of bounty hunter Duane "Dog" Chapman at his Da Kine Bail Bonds facilities in Honolulu, Hawai'i, and Denver, Colorado. Dog catches fugitives with the help of his business partner and wife, Beth Smith Chapman, sons Leland and Duane Lee, daughter "Baby" Lyssa Chapman, nephew Justin Bilhag, and associate Tim Chapman.

Dog brings in the bad guys and encourages others to turn their lives around. He has made more than 6,000 captures in his twenty-seven-year career and over the course of 244 half-hour episodes. Dog knows firsthand the position of the criminals he seeks as he himself served a prison sentence for armed robbery and first-degree murder and landed a five-year sentence in Huntsville Prison, Texas, in the late 1970s after a drug deal gone awry.

Dog the Bounty Hunter follows the title character and his company in their search for fugitives, drug dealers, and arsonists. The show also profiles Dog's journey as a father and husband, and family dynamics that are both personal and work-related come into play.

To Dog, finding a clown for his son's birthday party or picking up the right flowers for his wife on their anniversary are just as important (if not more important) than bringing a criminal to justice. The unscripted *Dog the Bounty Hunter* was videotaped all over the Hawaiian Islands and took cable television viewers into areas of Honolulu and Hawai'i off the beaten tourist path.

The series had a loyal viewership for eight seasons on the Arts and Entertainment Cable Television Network and worldwide through syndication. Dog the Bounty Hunter was so well known that he made a guest appearance playing himself in an episode of the third season of the *Hawaii Five-0* Reboot.

DA KINE BAIL BONDS is located at 1381 Queen Emma Street in Downtown Honolulu. Phone: (808) 921-2245.

Duane "Dog" Chapman got his name from a gang member. Dog is "God" spelled backwards.

Crime Fighters in Paradise

Hawaii Five-O
2010-( ) CBS Television

PRODUCED BY   **Peter Lenkov, Roberto Orci, Alex Kurtzman**

Based on the series *Hawai'i-Five-O*, Created by Leonard Freeman

CAST   **Alex O'Loughlin (Steve McGarrett), Scott Caan (Danny Williams), Daniel Dae Kim (Chin Ho Kelly), Grace Park (Kono Kalākaua), Masi Oka (Dr. Mark Bergman), Mark Dacascos (Wo Fat)**

Steve McGarrett (O'Loughlin), a former Navy Seal who grew up in Hawai'i, is tormented by revelations disclosed during the search for his father's murderer. Gov. Pat Jameson (Jean Smart) asks McGarrett to head an elite law-enforcement team to combat crime in the Islands with free reign, and this select squad will report directly to the governor. McGarrett is reluctant at first, but seizes on this opportunity as it will allow him to investigate his father's murder. Danny Williams (Scott Caan) is a transplanted streetwise New Jersey policeman who is going through a divorce and raising a young child. Detective Chin Ho Kelly (Daniel Dae Kim) was an HPD Officer who was trained by Steve's father before being wrongfully accused of corruption and relegated to a federal security patrol. McGarrett believes his side of the story and recruits Chin, who is made a police officer again and a member of Five-0. Chin Ho's cousin and an HPD rookie, Kono Kalākaua (Grace Park), a Hawaiian character, serves as the sole female member of the team during most of the series. The *Hawaii Five-0* team is headquartered at Ali'iōlani Hale, the Hawai'i State Judiciary Building on King Street—unlike in the original series when McGarrett was headquartered at 'Iolani Palace (which was eyebrow raising for some real-life Hawaiians offscreen).

The opening title sequence uses the original theme music reworked and contains a close zoom shot of buff Alex O'Loughlin on a balcony of the Ilikai Hotel, the

Principle cast of *Hawaii Five-0* Reboot: Daniel Dae Kim, Scott Caan, Alex O'Loughlin and Grace Park.

Daniel Dae Kim stars as Chin Ho Kelly, an HPD Officer mentored by Steve McGarrett's father, who joins the *Hawaii Five-0* team.

26   Crime Fighters in Paradise

same one that square-jawed Jack Lord stood on in the original opening credits. Perched upon their lanais, looking down on the mere mortals, both of these intrepid crime fighters suggest Cassius' remarks in Act I, Scene 2 of Shakespeare's *Julius Caesar*: "Why, man, he doth bestride the narrow world Like a Colossus, and we petty men Walk under his huge legs and peep about…"

The new series has a strong interplay between McGarrett and Williams. They often humorously banter and bicker like an old married couple who, despite their differences, really love each other, whereas the interaction between Jack Lord and James MacArthur was far more formal and restrained. The current incarnations of the characters are polar opposites—Danno is a cautious mainlander who openly dislikes Hawai'i and stays there only because of his daughter, while the local-to-da-max tattooed McGarrett is a daredevil. Despite their cultural differences, the Jersey and the local boy learn to work together, with their droll relationship taking its inspiration from various buddy cop movies.

In Season Three, Emmy® Award-winning actress Christine Lahti joined the cast as Doris McGarrett, Steve's mother. She had been presumed dead, which explained the mystery of Shelbourne in season 2. Dennis Chun portrays Sergeant Duke Lukela, a member of HPD and an earnest cop, and is, in a bit of clever casting, the son of actor Kam Fong, the original Chin Ho Kelly. During the second season, actor Edward Asner returned in a guest role as world-class smuggler August March, who was introduced thirty-eight years ago in a 1975 episode of the original *Hawaii Five-O*, *Wooden Model of a Rat*. In the new version, no mention is made of his previous *Five-O* encounter, except for Asner saying that he remembered a young policeman, John McGarrett—Steve's dad—taking him to prison. Isolated footage of Asner from the original series was used in several flashback sequences.

Cast of *Hawaii Five-0* Reboot, *left to right:* Daniel Dae Kim as Chin Ho Kelly, Scott Caan as Danny "Danno" Williams, Grace Park as Kono Kalākaua, and Alex O'Loughlin as Steve McGarrett.

McGarrett (Alex O'Loughlin) catches up with his arch-nemesis, Wo Fat (Mark Dacascos).

Crime Fighters in Paradise

Jack Lord as Steve McGarrett of *Hawaii Five-0* stands in front of the Honolulu Police Department Headquarters with his signature black four-door Ford Mercury automobile.

HONOLULU POLICE DEPARTMENT (HPD)

The city of Honolulu is located on the island of Oʻahu and serves as the capital city of the state of Hawaiʻi. The jurisdiction of the Honolulu Police Department (HPD), established in 1932, encompasses the entire island of Oʻahu, which has the largest population in the state and is divided into eight patrol districts. *Hawaii Five-0* is a fictional state police force; Hawaiʻi actually has no state police. Each of the four counties in the state is responsible for its own police force.

The HPD began cooperating with motion-picture companies in 1951 when the Police Commission gave permission to police chief Dan Liu to play himself in a featured role in John Wayne's film *Big Jim McLain* and to allow on-site filming. Several former Honolulu police officers went on to Hollywood fame playing policemen, including Mel Prestidge who played HPD's Lt. Quon on *Hawaiian Eye,* Ted Nobriga who co-starred as Keolo, an Aliʻi Nui in the 1966 big-screen epic *Hawaiʻi* and Kam Fong who played Chin Ho Kelly on *Hawaii Five-O*. The idea for the original *Hawaii Five-O* series came from a meeting between Leonard Freeman and then-Hawaiʻi Gov. John A. Burns, also a former policeman, who said that he wanted to start a state police unit, but was never able to. When *Hawaii Five-O* went into production, the HPD, then under Police Chief Francis Keala, tacitly approved the show. Many off-duty police officers worked on the series as extras and in bit parts in scenes involving uniformed HPD officers. The Chief also allowed filming at police headquarters. HPD provided support in traffic and crowd control and security while the show was filming on location. So credible

Warner Oland as Charlie Chan discusses a route map with his HPD Officers in a scene from *Charlie Chan At The Racetrack* (1936) Hawaiian character actor Al Kikume (in white hat) looks over Chan's shoulder.

Crime Fighters in Paradise

was McGarrett and his team that several foreign police agencies believed the Hawaii Five-O unit actually existed and formally inquired to HPD and the Hawai'i state government for assistance. Former Honolulu police officer Mike Cho serves as a technical adviser for the new *Hawaii Five-0* series. Though the new *Hawaii Five-0* features the HPD, the department has not officially sanctioned its participation in the series. Thus, the TV series does not follow official HPD policy and procedures. The insignia on the badges and cars seen on the series are designed especially for the series and are not official HPD badge insignia. The exterior of the HPD headquarters in the series is actually the former *Honolulu Advertiser* building at 605 Kapi'olani Blvd., Honolulu.

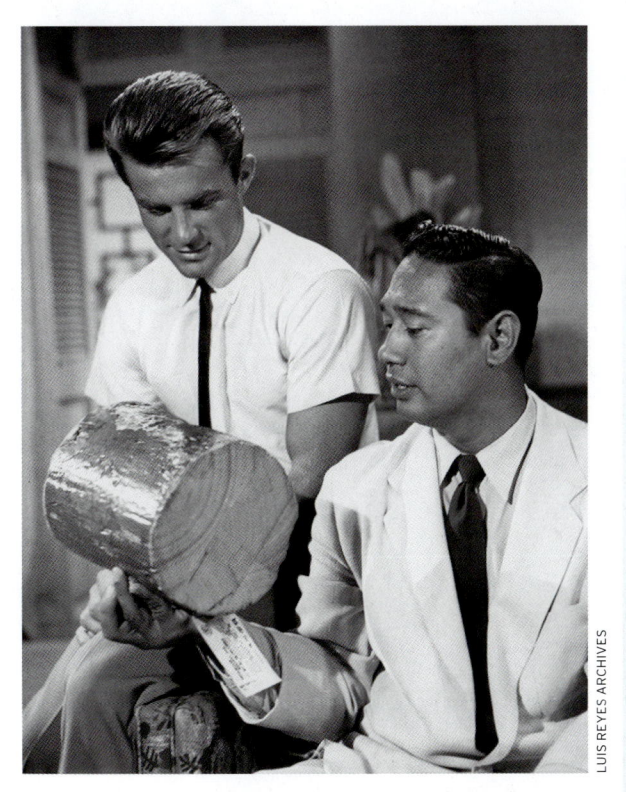

HONOLULU POLICE DEPARTMENT LAW ENFORCEMENT MUSEUM

801 South Beretania St., Honolulu, HI 96813; Monday-Friday 8:00 AM- 4:30 PM; Phone: (808) 529-3351. honolulupd.org

Far left: The exterior of the old *Honolulu Advertiser* newspaper building on Kapi'olani Blvd. and South St. was used to portray HPD headquarters in an episode of the new *Hawaii Five-0* Reboot when a bomb threat causes evacuation of the building just moments before the blast.

Robert Conrad as Tom Lopaka examines a piece of evidence with Mel Prestidge as HPD Lt. Quon on the popular Hawai'i-set TV series *Hawaiian Eye*.

Display and exhibit cases at the HPD Law Enforcement Museum in downtown Honolulu.

John Wayne at the Honolulu Police Station.

Jake and The Fatman, a CBS series filmed from 1987 to 1992, featured William Conrad as tough Hawai'i-born, former HPD officer turned district attorney Jason Lochivar "Fatman." His special investigator, Jake Styles, was played by Joe Penny. The first season of the crime drama took place in Los Angeles. In the second season the show moved to Hawai'i and halfway through the fourth season, it moved back to L.A.

Crime Fighters in Paradise   29

CHAPTER 3

Made in Paradise

Top left photo: Jack Lemmon receives a congratulatory kiss from Eva Marie Saint on the occasion of his Best Supporting Actor Oscar® win for *Mister Roberts*. LUIS REYES ARCHIVES; *top right:* Donna Reed and Frank Sinatra proudly hold their Oscars® for Best Supporting Actress and Best Supporting Actor respectively for their roles in *From Here to Eternity*. LUIS REYES ARCHIVES; *Left column, top photo:* Nicolas Cage and Adam Beach in *Windtalkers* MGM; Left column, center: *Dog The Bounty Hunter* A&E NETWORKS; *Left column, bottom photo:* Rita Hayworth and Jose Ferrer in *Miss Sadie Thompson* filmed on Kaua'i. LUIS REYES ARCHIVES; *Above photo:* Writer Director Alexander Payne and Novelist Kaui Hart Hemmings at *The Descendants* screening at The Hawai'i International Film Festival. COURTESY RAE HUO/HIFF

This book is being published in a landmark year for Hawai'i's motion picture patrimony: The 100th anniversary of the production of the very first made-in-Hawai'i feature films. While a Thomas Edison camera crew had shot actuality footage in the Republic of Hawai'i 15 years earlier, the first fiction films with actors, costumes, a plot telling a story, and presumably some sort of rudimentary script were shot on location in O'ahu in 1913. Although they were black and white and silent, the "flickers" *Hawaiian Love* and *The Shark God* spoke loudly in terms of establishing the motion picture pattern for the many movies to be shot and/or set in Hawai'i in the coming years.

This chapter looks at the feature films and television shows shot and/or set in Hawai'i since 1995 and significant film and television show achievements of the past. From Bing Crosby's 1937 *Waikiki Wedding* to Alexander Payne's 2011 *The Descendants*, many of these films which were filmed in part or entirely in Hawai'i, were presented with or nominated for Academy Awards by the Motion Picture Academy of Arts and Sciences.

Among this select handful recognized by their motion picture industry peers for excellence, Hawai'i films and talents include a disproportionately high number of Oscar® winners and nominees, ranging from contemporary movie stars such as George Clooney, Robert Downey Jr., and Ben Affleck to superstars of yore, among them Henry Fonda and Frank Sinatra. Two of Hollywood's most famous characters, *King Kong* and *Mighty Joe Young*, made films in Hawai'i and helped propel the careers of future Academy Award®-winning actresses Jessica Lange and Charlize Theron. The Oscar®-winning directors who have brought their own unique vision of paradise to the screen include a high caliber selection of honored filmmakers, from the Golden Age of Hollywood's legendary Cecil B. DeMille and John Ford, to contemporary helmers such as Steven Spielberg, Clint Eastwood, and Alexander Payne.

The Shark God

1913 World's Fair Stock Co.–Universal Film Co./Champion Film Company

DIRECTED BY **John Griffith Wray**
PRODUCED BY **Mark Dintenfass**
CAST **Virginia Brissac, Evelyn Hambly, James Dillon, Rodney Brandt**

According to the May 5, 1913 edition of the film industry's trade journal *Moving Picture World,* the very first feature film shot on location in Hawai'i has "A slight plot located in Honolulu, with natives attired in breech clouts for actors. The scenes are artistic and well taken, but exhibitors catering to particular audiences will find perhaps that the close views of these almost naked natives are rather objectionable. The story has to do with certain superstitions in the islands and at the close, the wicked lover, goes out to sea and gives himself up to the shark god."

The storyline seems lifted straight out of the pages and canvases of South Seas Cinema's literary, painting, postcard, and photographic forebears. The suggestion of nudity, unbridled sensuality, sacrificial offering to a pagan deity, and the overall exotica shot on location in a Polynesian Isle appear to establish the genre's tropical tropes and template, its classic Kanaka clichés.

Like some of the later Hollywood moguls, Mark Dintenfass was an Eastern European immigrant, born in 1872 in what was then Galicia and is now part of Poland. Dintenfass headed the Champion Film Company, independent producers who first started making movies in 1910. Two years later, the company became part of the Universal Film Manufacturing Company (now Universal Studios) along with a variety of companies, including Éclair, Nestor, Gaumont, and Lux. A German Jewish émigré who became a movie-industry giant, Carl Laemmle founded the group on June 8, 1912, to resist the monopolistic Thomas Edison and the General Film Company, which secured distribution only to those producers who belonged to the Motion Pictures Patents Company and several interested parties. More than 2,000 theatrical feature films of 10 minutes in length were produced, and 99 percent of those films are now considered lost, possibly including some that were made in Hawai'i when

Virginia Brissac starred in both *Hawaiian Love* and *The Shark God* in 1913. Brissac resumed her career much later in the sound era as a character actress and is perhaps best remembered for playing rebellious James Dean's grandmother in *Rebel Without a Cause.*

32 Made in Paradise

a theatrical troupe traveled to Oʻahu in early 1913. According to Robert C. Schmitt's groundbreaking book *Hawaiʻi in the Movies, 1898-1959,* in between live shows at Honolulu's Bijou Theater, the visiting theatre company made *The Shark God* and *Hawaiian Love.* These are two of 1913 made-in-Hawaiʻi movies that later survived a fire at Universal Studios. In the same year, Mark Dintenfass also produced a film called *The Leper,* which was released May 19, 1913.

An American film director of the silent-movie era, John Griffith Wray worked with Douglas Fairbanks and Lillian Gish. Wray served as one of the leading directors for the Thomas Ince Company and directed the first film adaptation of Eugene O'Neill's *Anna Christie* (1923).

Hawaiian Love
1913 World's Fair Stock Co. –Universal Film Co./Champion Film Company

DIRECTED BY **John Griffith Wray**
PRODUCED BY **Mark Dintenfass**
CAST **Virginia Brissac (Labela), James Dillon (Kalike), Ray Hanford (The Chinaman)**

The second fiction film shot on location in Hawaiʻi debuted in theaters on May 10, 1913. Its single reel of 1,000 feet of film, when run through a movie projector at twenty-four frames per second, played a ten-minute movie. The trade publication *Moving Picture World* reported, "A story located in the Hawaiian islands, with some good scenic effects to help along its none too strong plot. The Captain of a trading vessel takes a native girl away from her Island lover. Their vessel is wrecked and they swim to shore. Later he sells the girl to a Chinaman. But a just fate awaits him as he falls from a cliff at the end. The photography in this might have been better."

Right at the beginning of Hawaiʻi feature filmmaking, one can see the incorporation of traditional themes derived from South Seas sources such as the eighteenth-century captains' logs. Virginia Brissac (1883-1979) was an accomplished stage actress by the time she made the films *The Shark God* and *Hawaiian Love* in 1913. She married the director of these two films, John Griffith Wray, and returned to the screen in 1935 as a character actress. *Hawaiian Love* was filmed at Honolulu, Windward Oʻahu, and Kapena Falls in Nuʻuanu in February 1913.

Made in Paradise

Bird of Paradise
1932 RKO

DIRECTED BY **King Vidor**

SCREENPLAY **adapted by Wells Root, Wanda Tuchock and Leonard Praskins from the play by Richard Walton Tully**

PRODUCED BY **David O Selznick**

CAST **Dolores Del Rio (Luana), Joel McCrea (Johnny Baker), John Halliday (Mac), Lon Chaney Jr. (Thornton), Napoleon Keloli'i Pukui (The King)**

Program book art for Bird of Paradise.

A schooner's crew drops in at a South Seas Isle, and one of the crewmen, Johnny "Bake" Baker (McCrea), stays behind and makes love to a beautiful native princess, Luana (Del Rio), despite her being betrothed to a prince of another island. Ignoring the native chief's warnings, Luana enters into the relationship with a playful sexuality to match Johnny's young and strapping red-blooded all-American passion and innocence. Johnny kidnaps her to a neighboring island and builds a Polynesian hut where they live uninhibited until a volcano erupts on her home island. The schooner with Baker's fellow crew members' returns for Johnny and his new found love—but Luana decides to stay at the Island and sacrifice herself to the Volcano.

In his book *A Tree is a Tree*, King Vidor claimed that when he was first offered the picture, David O. Selznick, new head of production at RKO, told him, "I don't care what story you use so long as we call it *Bird of Paradise* and Del Rio jumps into a flaming volcano at the finish."

After looking at travel brochures, it was decided to film the movie in Hawai'i, because it was closer to California. The trip to Tahiti would take several weeks by boat, and Hawai'i was only five days away by luxury liner steamship. When the Hollywood troupe arrived in Honolulu, Kona weather brought wind and rain for weeks on end. It was the worst weather Hawai'i had experienced in many years. If the skies cleared for a few hours, the troupe would gather over 100 extras and rush out with all the filming equipment to shoot as much footage as possible. Due to the inclement weather, Vidor asked producer David O. Selznick if he could return to Hollywood and finish the picture on nearby Catalina Island, off the coast of Los Angeles and at the RKO-Pathe studios in Culver City. Selznick agreed. However, there is still some stunning location photography in this black and white gem.

Dolores Del Rio, one of the most beautiful actresses to have ever graced the silver screen plays Luana in Bird of Paradise.
Far right photo: A young Joel McCrea on location in Kāne'ohe for *Bird of Paradise.*

34 Made in Paradise

Waikiki Wedding
1937 Paramount

DIRECTED BY **Frank Tuttle**
SCREENPLAY BY **Frank Butler, Don Hartman, Walter DeLeon and Francis Martin; based on a story by Butler and Hartman**
PRODUCED BY **Arthur Hornblow**
CAST **Bing Crosby (Tony Marvin), Bob Burns (Shad Buggle), Martha Raye (Myrtle Finch), Shirley Ross (Georgia Smith), Leif Erickson (Dr. Victor Quimby), Anthony Quinn (Kimo)**

In *Waikiki Wedding,* Crosby plays Tony Marvin, a public relations man for a pineapple company in Hawai'i, who strikes upon the idea of a contest to promote pineapples and tourism in Hawai'i. The winner of the contest arrives in Hawai'i and is not impressed with the Islands. Tony must make her see otherwise and, in so doing, falls in love with her.

Harry Owens (1902-1986) wrote "Sweet Leilani" on the occasion of his little daughter's birth (Oct. 19, 1934). Bing Crosby heard "Sweet Leilani" while in Honolulu in September

Popular singer/actor Bing Crosby on location in Waikīkī shooting background footage for *Waikiki Wedding.*

Made in Paradise

Garbed in grass skirts, "The Big Mouth" Martha Raye (on the left) and Shirley Ross flank costar crooner Bing Crosby in *Waikiki Wedding* (1937). Crosby warbles the hapa-haole hits "Sweet Leilani," which won band leader Harry Owen an Oscar®, and "Blue Hawaii." A quarter century later another pop singer, Elvis Presley, starred in a film that used one of the songs as its title, *Blue Hawaii*.

A young 22 year-old Anthony Quinn as Kimo in *Waikiki Wedding*. An accomplished painter and sculptor, the larger-than-life actor Quinn held the international premiere exhibition of his artwork at Center Art Galleries in Honolulu, Hawai'i in the eighties.

"Sweet Leilani" won the 1938 Academy Award® for Best Song. LeRoy Prinz was nominated for Best Dance Direction for "Luau."

1936 during a pre-production trip for *Waikiki Wedding*. Crosby and a small crew led by Robert C. Bruce went to Hawai'i to shoot backgrounds and process shots. Upon his return to Paramount Studios, Crosby insisted that "Sweet Leilani" be included on the film's soundtrack. He recorded the song on Feb. 23, 1937, with Lani McIntire and His Hawaiians. The song spent twenty-five weeks on the pop charts, becoming the first of Crosby's twenty-two million-selling gold records. The flip side of the record, "Blue Hawaii," was also a popular hit. Elvis Presley later made it even more famous by singing the tune and using the same title for his hit 1961 Technicolor movie filmed on location in Hawai'i. The soundtrack album became a million-selling gold record for the King of Rock and Roll.

At the beginning of his five decade-long career, internationally famous, future two-time Oscar®-winning actor Anthony Quinn (1952's *Viva Zapata* and 1956's *Lust For Life*, wherein he portrayed painter Paul Gauguin) plays a Hawaiian named Kimo in *Waikiki Wedding*, his fourth credited screen role. Born in Mexico and raised in Los Angeles, Quinn (1915-2001) played all kinds of ethnic characters that he became identified with, most notably the earthy peasant title character in 1964's *Zorba the Greek*.

Harry Owens was called "Mister Hawai'i" because he wrote hundreds of Hawai'i-themed songs, composing more than 300 songs and 140 recordings for Decca Records. Some of the songs include "To You, Sweetheart, Aloha," "Hawaiian Paradise," "Hawaii Calls," as well as some novelty numbers, "Princess Poo-poo-ly has Plenty Papaya" and "The Cockeyed Mayor of Kaunakakai."

Made in Paradise

Bird of Paradise
1951 Twentieth Century Fox

DIRECTED BY **Delmer Daves**
SCREENPLAY BY **Delmer Daves**
PRODUCED BY **Darryl F. Zanuck**
CAST **Jeff Chandler (Tenga), Debra Paget (Kalua), Louis Jourdan (Andre), Maurice Schwartz (Kahuna), Everett Sloane (The Akua), Prince Leilani (native chief), Jack Elam (The Trader), Otto Waldis (Skipper)**

In this Technicolor remake a nineteenth century Polynesian chief's son returns home with his college friend Andre, a Frenchman (Jourdan) who is tired of civilization and seeks paradise among the Natives. He falls in love with a chief's daughter, Kalua (Paget), against the wishes of the people's holy man, or Kahuna (Schwartz). Kalua's brother, Tenga (Chandler), encourages the romance and helps Andre to understand the ways of the Islanders, all the while threatening to kill him if he fails the girl. Try as he may, Andre cannot cope with the beliefs of the indigenous Islanders. He is shocked beyond belief when Kalua follows the traditional ritual of walking on fire, a feat she performs harmlessly because of her nature-worshipping faith. Unfortunately, he loses his dream of paradise and his pagan bride when she serenely sacrifices herself in a volcano to appease the goddess of fire.

Bird of Paradise was beautifully filmed in Technicolor by two-time Academy Award® winning cinematographer Winton Hoch (1949's *She Wore a Yellow Ribbon*, 1952's *The Quiet Man*) on various sites in Hawai'i, O'ahu and Kaua'i that included the Shipman Estate and the black sand beaches of Kaimū and Kalapana in the Puna District; the Garden Isle's Hanalei Bay and the area around Coco Palms Resort; plus Waikīkī. The director created a composite Polynesia for the movie, "telescoping" three Islands separated by 350 miles of Pacific Ocean and ten locations into a tightly compressed one-half square mile Polynesian village. To create one idyllic locale, Hoch photographed Jourdan and Chandler sailing a boat into Hanalei Bay on Kaua'i and jumping off to greet Natives swimming toward them who had been shot south of Hilo on the island of Hawai'i. From there the film cuts to surfing scenes at Waikīkī and sunset on the fabulous Kona Coast. Miss Paget's sacrifice to Mauna Loa appears only a hop, skip and jump away through a flowery jungle.

Colorful Spanish poster art for *Bird of Paradise*.

Jeff Chandler, a prematurely grey masculine, tall and ruggedly handsome leading man of the 1950s. After military service in WWII, he began his career in radio, which led to a contract at Universal. Chandler quickly became a film star after he was nominated for an Oscar® in 1950 as best supporting actor for his role as the noble Apache chief Cochise in the groundbreaking western *Broken Arrow* opposite James Stewart, directed by Delmer Davies. The director cast Chandler as Tenga in *Bird of Paradise*.

Debra Paget played a native American princess in *Broken Arrow* who falls in love with a white man who becomes a sacrificial lamb and played a similar role in *Bird of Paradise*.

Actual footage was taken of the 1950 Mauna Loa volcanic eruption. Two hundred Hawai'i inhabitants were cast as extras, several in important speaking, dancing and singing roles, which along with the scenic cinematography makes this Technicolor version of *Bird of Paradise* an enduring local favorite.

Hilo-born actor Prince Leilani traced his lineage to King Lunalilo. Leaving Hawai'i as a young man, Leilani toured the continental U.S. with his "Royal Samoans" and appeared as the Kahuna in the original stage version of *Bird of Paradise*. In the film, the tall, stately actor plays a native chief. Also featured is young Mary Ann Ventura, regarded as one of the most talented exponents of ancient Polynesian dancing in Hawai'i. Dance movements were created by Iolani Luahine, reputedly the greatest teacher of ancient Hawaiian dances at that time. The *Bird of Paradise* music score included indigenous tunes and chants by the elderly "Mama" Bray, wife of "Daddy" Bray, both of whom sang songs from memory. "Daddy" was well known and respected in Hawaiian society as one of the few men in the territory who knew the old religious chants.

Bird of Paradise was originally filmed in 1932 by RKO and starred Dolores Del Rio and Joel McCrea. In 1950, Darryl F. Zanuck, vice president in charge of production at Twentieth Century Fox, decided that the title, the locale and one dramatic highlight, the sacrifice of a maiden to a volcano, were the essential ingredients for a successful motion picture. The rest of the story he felt was too dated for modern audiences. He called on ace writer-director Delmer Daves to submit an original screenplay. Daves was coming off the hit film *Broken Arrow*, a story of Apaches and "palefaces," which starred Jimmy Stewart and Jeff Chandler as the dignified chief Cochise (a role that won him an Academy Award® nomination for Best Supporting Actor) and Debra Paget as the American Indian woman. Zanuck was so pleased with the script Daves turned in that he gave the production an immediate go ahead.

Made in Paradise

From Here to Eternity
1953 Columbia

DIRECTED BY **Fred Zinnemann**
SCREENPLAY BY **Daniel Taradash, based on the novel by James Jones**
PRODUCED BY **Buddy Adler**
CAST **Burt Lancaster (Sgt. Milton Warden), Montgomery Clift (Robert E. Lee "Prew" Prewitt), Deborah Kerr (Karen Holmes), Frank Sinatra (Angelo Maggio), Donna Reed (Alma "Lorene"), Philip Ober (Capt. Dana Holmes), Ernest Borgnine (Sgt. "Fatso" Judson)**

2013 marks the sixtieth anniversary of the screen version of *From Here to Eternity*. Few films have swept and scored cinema's highest acclaim as did *Eternity*, which also won kudos from the Cannes Film Festival, the Golden Globes®, the Directors Guild of America, the Writers Guild of America, et al. *Eternity's* Oscar® competition that year included *The Robe*, *Roman Holiday*, *Julius Caesar* and *Shane*. Sixty years later, *From Here to Eternity* is best remembered as one of the first post-1945 films to shoot on location in Hawai'i, containing one of the most romantic scenes ever put on celluloid and for its pivotal role in the legendary career of Frank Sinatra. This mature masterpiece also helped to establish the Hawaiian Islands as an exotic, romantic destination prior to the advent of the passenger jet and statehood in 1959. The film marked the acceptance of adult themes and influenced generations of filmmakers.

From Here to Eternity is the epic tale of pre-World War II enlisted men, their women, and the grim destiny that overtakes them in the days leading up to the Pearl Harbor sneak attack, which plunged them—and America—into the global conflagration. The best-selling 1951 James Jones novel, inspired by his own Army experiences, was widely considered to be un-filmable due to the era's film censorship (publishers even prevailed upon Jones to cut some of the pages with tabu subjects from his hefty manuscript). Based on his firsthand observations, *Eternity* indicts the pre-war U.S. Army, uses frank language, and has steamy sexual descriptions.

Columbia Pictures mogul Harry Cohn purchased the film rights in 1951 and assigned screenwriter Daniel Taradash to write the screenplay, which took almost a year to complete. Cohn first thought of casting Robert Mitchum, Joan Crawford, Aldo Ray, and Eli Wallach. Fresh from his success with the classic American Western

> *From Here to Eternity* is the only movie shot on location in Hawai'i to ever win the Best Picture Oscar®. The film version of James Jones' controversial novel about the peacetime Army stationed in O'ahu was nominated for thirteen Academy Awards®. In 1954, *Eternity* won eight Oscars®: Best Picture, Best Actor in a Supporting Role (Frank Sinatra), Best Actress in a Supporting Role (Donna Reed), Best Director (Fred Zinnemann), Best Adapted Screenplay (Daniel Taradash), Best Cinematography, Black-and-White (Burnett Guffey), Best Film Editing (William A. Lyon) and Best Sound Recording (John P. Livadary, Columbia SSD).

The three male stars of Fred Zinnemann's *From Here to Eternity* pose for a picture during a break in filming at Schofield Barracks on location in O'ahu. Montgomery Clift, Burt Lancaster and Frank Sinatra.

Made in Paradise

Cameraman Burnett Guffey sets up a shot (director Fred Zinnemann behind camera) with Frank Sinatra and Montgomery Clift on location at Schofield Barracks for *From Here to Eternity*.

Belgium French poster art for *From Here to Eternity*.

High Noon (1952), Director Fred Zinnemann wanted to cast against type and won many arguments over Cohn. Burt Lancaster was finally cast as 1st Sgt. Milton Warden, the tough career soldier, and Deborah Kerr as Karen Holmes, the unhappy captain's wife who has an affair with the lower-ranking but better-looking enlisted man. Frank Sinatra was cast as Pvt. Angelo Maggio, the scrappy Italian-American kid from Brooklyn and the only friend in Company "G" of Pvt. Robert E. Lee Prewitt. Montgomery Clift poignantly plays "Prew," the sensitive boxer and bugler who woos prostitute, Alma "Lorene" Burke (Donna Reed). Beefy Ernest Borgnine plays the sadistic Staff Sgt. "Fatso" Judson who tortures Maggio in the brig.

Eternity's other nominations went to Burt Lancaster and Montgomery Clift for Best Actor in a Leading Role; Deborah Kerr for Best Actress in a Leading Role; Jean Louis for Best Costume Design, Black-and-White and George Duning and Morris Stoloff for Best Music Scoring of a Dramatic or Comedy Picture.

With a $2 million budget, the cast and crew of 100 first filmed interiors in Hollywood at Columbia Studios. They then flew via chartered airplane to Hawai'i on March 2, 1953, for three weeks of location shooting at Schofield Barracks, Kolekole Pass, The Royal Hawaiian Hotel, Waikīkī Beach, Wai'alae Golf Course, and Hālona Cove.

Located at Wahiawā, Schofield Barracks remains relatively unchanged since the filming; the quadrangle buildings still stand. The Tropic Lightning Museum on base includes a small exhibit about the film. Although many fans thought the nearby period bungalows were used in the movie, they were actually recreated on a Hollywood sound stage. A group of planes from the 199th squadron of the

40   Made in Paradise

One of the most memorable scenes in film history. Burt Lancaster and Deborah Kerr in a passionate embrace on a Hawaiian beach as the waves crash over them in *From Here to Eternity*.

Hawai'i Air National Guard enacted the Japanese Zeros' strafing of Schofield Barracks for the film. Dogfaces of the Hawai'i Infantry Training Center participated as extras in the simulated attack that featured most of the major stars, and wherein an exuberant Burt Lancaster shoots down one of those planes bearing the "red meatball" on its wings.

The then-daring footage of Kerr and Lancaster kissing amidst the crash of ocean waves is powerful and lasts only eight seconds on screen, but took three days to film. The scene—arguably the most romantic one ever filmed—has been described by film critics as the "surf smooching scene," "watery embrace in the rolling surf of O'ahu," "clinching in the waves," "rolling passionately on a Hawaiian beach" and "the immortal beach clinch." In it Kerr unforgettably passionately purrs, "I never knew it could be like this."

The scene was shot at Hālona Cove (now also known as the "From Here to Eternity Beach") near the Blowhole on O'ahu's southeast coast. As shot by Zinnemann, the scene is immeasurably more evocative, vivid, and powerful onscreen than as rendered on the page in Jones' novel. In a 1963 interview with *The Hollywood Reporter,* Kerr recalled, "All I remember is that after a full day's filming of the scene, with all that sand in my bathing suit, my skin was rubbed raw. We had to time it for the waves, so that at just the right moment, a big one would come up and wash over us. Most of the waves came up only to our feet, but we needed one that would come all the way. We were like surfers, waiting for the perfect wave. Between each take we had to do a total clean up."

In a 1954 *L.A. Daily News* interview with Erskine Johnson, Burt Lancaster recalled, "It was a fine script, but none of us thought of the picture as really great while we were making it. It was just one of those films that added up when it was put together. It sticks with you."

But not all of the actors underestimated the screenplay's potential. "One of the most dramatic comeback stories in Entertainment history" is how daughter Nancy Sinatra describes the way her father turned his career around. The then-nearly washed up Frank Sinatra won his only Academy Award® for Best Supporting Actor for his role as Maggio in *Eternity*. When he read the novel, Sinatra related very easily to the character of the high-spirited Ital-

Made in Paradise

Cast and crew on location at Oʻahu's Hālona Cove filming that now iconic film moment. In an *LA Times* obituary of 10/19/2007, Kerr was quoted as saying in a 1982 *The Times* interview, of being drenched with water and sand: "The scene turned out to be deeply affecting on film, but, God, it was no fun to shoot."

ian-American G.I. Angelo Maggio. When Sinatra found out the book was going to be made into a film, he fought to get the part. "I was determined to land that role," Sinatra told Larry King in a 1988 CNN interview. The part was the chance for Sinatra—mainly known as a crooner who'd been idolized by "bobbysoxers," the 1940s equivalents of teenyboppers—to prove that he really could act. Most of *Eternity's* principal cast has passed on. The late Ernest Borgnine, who passed away in 2012 at age 95, played Staff Sgt. "Fatso" Judson, but he never made it to Hawaiʻi because all of his scenes were interiors filmed in a Hollywood studio. George Reeves, who became famous as *Superman* in the 1950's television series, had a small role as Sgt. Maylon Stark, but was severely edited out of the film when preview audiences were distracted by the Man of Steel's presence.

But the power of *From Here to Eternity*—with its themes of the individual up against the power structure, illicit sexual passion, and ultimately, patriotic self sacrifice when the chips are down and your country is under attack—will never be edited out of the viewing public's mind. Several of James Jones' other novels have been adapted for the screen, notably *The Thin Red Line*, which, in its 1964 and 1998 film versions, followed the infantry unit depicted in *Eternity* to the Battle of Guadalcanal. *From Here to Eternity* was adapted for the little screen as a miniseries in 1979 and as an episodic TV drama in 1980.

Sir Tim Rice and Lee Menzies are bringing a musical version of *From Here to Eternity* to the Shaftesbury Theatre, London, in the autumn of 2013. Stuart Brayson composed the music while Rice wrote the lyrics. Rice's other musicals for stage and screen include *Jesus Christ Superstar* and *Evita*. It seems that *Eternity's* appeal is, well, eternal.

Made in Paradise

Mister Roberts
1955 Warner Bros

DIRECTED BY **John Ford and Mervyn Leroy**

SCREENPLAY BY **Frank Nugent and Joshua Logan, from the play by Joshua Logan and Thomas Heggen and the novel by Thomas Heggen**

PRODUCED BY **Leland Hayward**

CAST **Henry Fonda (Lt. Doug Roberts), James Cagney (Capt. Morton), Jack Lemmon (Ensign Pulver), William Powell (Doc), Betsy Palmer (Lt. Ann Girard), Ward Bond (Chief Petty Officer Dowdy)**

Beneath the blazing Pacific sun, the USS *Reluctant* carries cargo along the forgotten sea lanes of World War II. The crew is going crazy. Somewhere beyond the horizon, the real war is passing them by. Mister Roberts struggles against a dictatorial captain onboard a supply ship in the South Pacific, all the while longing for more active duty.

Mister Roberts was one of the greatest successes in Broadway theatre history, and Henry Fonda became absolutely identified with the role, playing it over 1,600 times on the Great White Way and on a national tour. Fonda won Broadway's coveted Tony Award as Best Actor for the role in 1948. The actor had been away from movies almost seven years when producers began casting *Mister Roberts* and Warner Bros., which owned the screen rights, offered the role to William Holden, then a recent Oscar® winner and the hottest actor in films. Holden turned the part down on moral grounds that Fonda owned the part. Still believing that Fonda was too old and that the public had forgotten him, Warners gave the part to Marlon Brando, then the next biggest star in movies, who actually accepted the role.

In the meantime, however, four-time Academy Award® winner John Ford (1935's *The Informer*, 1940's *The Grapes of Wrath*, 1943's *How Green Was My Valley* and 1952's *The Quiet Man*) had been signed to direct the film adaptation of *Mister Roberts*. Remembering the many brilliant performances Fonda had given in their joint 1930s/1940s masterpieces—*Drums Along The Mohawk, Young Mr. Lincoln, The Grapes of Wrath, My Darling Clementine* and *Fort Apache*

> Jack Lemmon won a Best Supporting Actor Oscar® for his role as Ensign Pulver in *Mister Roberts*, which was also nominated for Best Picture and Best Sound Recording (William A. Mueller).

The principal cast of *Mister Roberts. Left to right:* James Cagney, Henry Fonda, (center) Jack Lemmon, William Powell.

Made in Paradise 43

(Fonda's last starring role before his long sojourn on Broadway)—Ford insisted that Fonda play Mister Roberts.

Warners wanted the stage play opened up for the screen and thus sought Navy cooperation to film at naval bases and on warships. The Navy refused on the grounds that the tyrannical Captain Morton character was detrimental to its image. Ford, who still had enormous influence due to his extraordinary documentary work during World War II, simply went to the chief of naval operations for help. The Navy immediately relented, giving Warners the use of the cargo ship USS *Howell* and permission to film at naval facilities on Midway and Hawaiʻi. Most of the film's exteriors were shot at Kāneʻohe Bay, Oʻahu, which included dockside shots of the then-U.S. Marine Air Corps Station, also located at Kāneʻohe. Former Olympic swimming champion Duke Kahanamoku is seen in a bit role as a Native chief who boards the ship when it enters an Island port. Interiors were filmed at Warner Bros. studios in Burbank, California.

Jack Lemmon on location in Kāneʻohe for *Mister Roberts*.

Though they were great friends and collaborators, Fonda and Ford clashed during the filming. Having become possessive of *Mister Roberts* after playing the title role onstage for seven years, Fonda had certain ideas about the direction of the movie that challenged the authoritarian director's vision. The differences came to a head one night on location after the day's work was completed, when Ford—who'd been drinking heavily—and Fonda came to blows, an incident that caused an irreparable break in their friendship. After *Mister Roberts*, Ford and Fonda never worked together again though Fonda participated in several late in life in-person tributes to the director. When illness sidelined Ford during the making of *Mister Roberts*, director Mervyn Leroy took over the direction, and Joshua Logan did some uncredited work on the film. Ford directed all of the outdoor location scenes.

Mister Roberts restored Fonda's star power, even though he rather inexplicably was not even nominated for a Best Actor Oscar® for the role. Fonda had received an Oscar® nomination for his memorable lead role as ex-con-turned-union-organizer Tom Joad in Ford's 1940 screen adaptation of Steinbeck's *The Grapes of Wrath*. Over the next three decades Fonda cemented his iconic image in film, television and on the stage. Before dying in 1982 he finally won a Best Actor Oscar® in 1981 for his last screen portrayal as an ailing old man in the film version of the stage play *On Golden Pond*, appearing opposite his daughter Jane Fonda, who won two acting Oscars® and was nominated for five more. Henry's son, Peter Fonda, is also an actor who is best known for the hip 1969 biker flick *Easy Rider*.

A young Jack Lemmon won his first Academy Award® for his supporting role as Ensign Pulver. He was cast by John Ford from a previous screen test. By this time, with his fourth film role, Lemmon had mastered the comic delivery, timing and mannerisms that would become his trademark urban American everyman and serve him well for the rest of his career in films such as *Some Like It Hot, The Apartment, The Odd Couple* and Costa-Gavras' 1982 chilling Chile coup drama *Missing*. Lemmon was nominated seven times for an Oscar® and won a Best Actor Oscar® in 1973, for his dramatic turn in the film *Save the Tiger*. Lemmon returned to Oʻahu and Kauaʻi for the service comedy drama *The Wackiest Ship In The Army* in 1961. Lemmon passed away in 2001.

South Pacific
1958 Magna/Twentieth Century Fox

PRODUCED BY	**Buddy Adler**
DIRECTED BY	**Joshua Logan**
SCREENPLAY BY	**Paul Osborn**
CAST	**Mitzi Gaynor (Nellie Forbush), Rossano Brazzi (Emile De Becque), Ray Walston (Luther Billis), Juanita Hall (Bloody Mary), John Kerr (Lt. Cable), France Nuyen (Liat)**

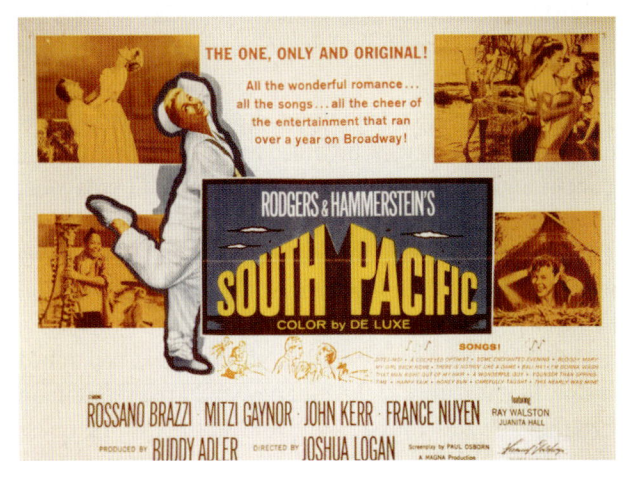

South Pacific won the Oscar® for Best Sound, which was awarded to Fred Hyner, Todd AO SSD. It was also nominated for Best Cinematography, Color and Best Music, Scoring of a Musical Picture.

In this overblown translation to the big screen of the Richard Rogers and Oscar Hammerstein Pulitzer Prize-winning Broadway musical *South Pacific*, director Joshua Logan, also the co-author, co-producer, and director of the musical play, kept with Hollywood tradition by replacing original musical actors with screen stars. MGM musical talent Mitzi Gaynor and Italian heart-throb Rossano Brazzi took over the roles of Nellie Forbush and Emile De Becque. Only Juanita Hall as Bloody Mary and Ray Walston as Luther Billis were retained from the stage.

The music of *South Pacific* constitutes a unique part of American musical stage history and has been recorded by major recording artists the world over. The movie soundtrack recording album has sold millions of copies. All the great songs of the stage success are present in the film version: "Some Enchanted Evening," "Bali Hai," "I'm Gonna Wash That Man Right Out of My Hair," "Younger than Springtime," "I'm In Love With a Wonderful Guy," and "Happy Talk."

A large movie troupe of 178 cast members went to Kauaʻi for nine weeks to film most of the $6.5 million production. Four shiploads of cameras, lights, grip equipment, costumes, rolling stock, construction material, and props were brought there. Although the beautiful Garden Isle proved to be scenically ideal, a tidal wave on March 10, 1957, and rainy weather posed numerous production problems. Exteriors, notably aerial shots, were also filmed at Fiji, which like Vanuatu is part of Melanesia.

At Hāʻena Beach, which was used as the Bali Hai village, a pier was built for the landing of Lt. Cable and Billis—but only after dynamiting the solid coral bottom of the harbor could piles be driven to anchor the pier. The Bali Hai seen on the screen is a composite of numerous Fiji and Kauaʻi scenic

Poster art for the film *South Pacific*.

Racism is a recurring theme in *South Pacific*, based on the James Michener's Pulitzer Prize winning novel, *Tales of The South Pacific*. Mitzi Gaynor stars as the U.S. nurse Nellie Forbush and Italian screen idol Rossano Brazzi as the French planter Emile DeBecque. They are at his plantation, located at a Promontory near Hanalei Bay, Kauaʻi.

In this scene Nellie rejects DeBecque because the widower has half Polynesian children, a racial taboo for the nurse from Little Rock, Arkansas (ironically, a huge integration struggle took place at Little Rock in the 1950s).

Made in Paradise

spots, plus the beautiful Allerton Gardens. Robert Allerton and John Gregg had developed their estate into a fabulously beautiful place complete with canyons, formal gardens, running water streams, bamboo forests, walls of maidenhair ferns, and vines with turquoise orchid-like blooms. The grounds originally served as a country estate for Hawai'i's Queen Emma. The Bali Hai sequence was filmed in nine days and required 350 local people as extras.

The first two days at Lumahai Beach, which was used as the nurses' beach where Mitzi Gaynor washes that man right out of her hair, were unbelievably hot and humid, followed by rainy weather lasting three weeks. Director Josh Logan and cameraman Leon Shamroy shot scenes between downpours and lost only one day due to a storm. That torrential rain, however, eventually complicated the moving of equipment from Lumahai Beach to the Birkmyre Estate. Assistant director Ben Kadish hired five airline stewardesses, who happened to be visiting Kaua'i, on the spot to act as Nellie Forbush's nurses, and they took a short leave of absence from their jobs to appear in the film. For years, these unknown nurses were prominently featured in the poster art for the film, especially in England.

The Birkmyre Estate served as the De Becque plantation home. Situated on a promontory above Hanalei Bay with a commanding, fabulous view, it provided an ideal setting for the "Some Enchanted Evening" romantic scene and others between Nurse Nellie and De Becque. The company transformed a tin-roof home here by adding a thatched roof, widening the verandahs, adding lush trees and foliage and creating a rock pool and rock-terraced levels at the promontory's edge. The Birkmeyre estate no longer exists; the filming site is now the location of the present-day St. Regis Princeville Resort.

During the talent-show sequence, 1,000 Marines and several hundred sailors had a field day acting as an audience for Mitzi Gaynor, Ray Walston, Jack Mullaney, and Fred Clark in an amphitheater on the forty-acre campground. The director had Mitzi and all the cast members don their costumes and perform the show, so he could get reaction shots. A war sequence in the film's story line featured actual Marine and Naval maneuvers near Barking Sands on Kaua'i. The entire company was quartered at the Coco Palms Resort on Kaua'i, situated beside a lagoon and a grove of coconut trees. Getting to every location required a minimum of an hour's drive from the hotel, and shooting ran from sunup to sundown. The cast and crew had calls as early as 4:30 AM. Logan wanted his screen Liat (France Nuyen) to slide down the Waipahe'e slippery slide, swim underwater in the pool with Lt. Cable and come to the rocky shore for the "Happy Talk" number. The construction crew however could not think of a way to get the studio's heavy camera equipment down the torturous three-mile narrow trail through dense brush to Waipahe'e. The art director found a more accessible waterfall above the Kīlauea River, with access to it requiring construction of only a half-mile road. The construction

In this scene from the World War II musical *South Pacific*, Lt. Cable (John Kerr) and Luther Billis (Ray Walston) are greeted at the pier as they arrive for the exotic boars tooth ceremony at "your special island... where the sky meets the sea; Bali Ha'i," a mythic Pacific paradise. This scene was shot on location at Hā'ena Beach, Kaua'i.

Mitzi Gaynor, star of *South Pacific* on the lawn of the St. Regis Princeville Resort during a return visit to Kaua'i in 2009. The hotel and resort overlooks Hanalei Bay and was built on a promontory near the location site of the De Becque plantation from the movie *South Pacific*.

crew and art department built a water slide to the directors' specifications.

The only interiors in the film include the service headquarters and Liat's hut, both built and filmed at the Twentieth Century Fox studio, along with the camp and bamboo forest for the Boar's Tooth ceremony.

Logan came up with the idea of the subtle change in color during the musical numbers to duplicate the lighting changes that occur in the theater onto celluloid. Logan attached a crank with a piece of colored glass across the lens of the camera during the shooting. The color was shot as is, right on the camera negative. Producer Buddy Adler tried to convince Logan to light the scene as it would look normally, arguing that the special color filter effects could be done in post-production in the film laboratory. But Logan would not budge. Since he was coming off of the hit 1956 movie *Bus Stop* starring Marilyn Monroe, he had the power to get what he wanted. Ultimately, the controversial effect marred the film. Logan did not quite grasp the suggestive power of the art of cinematography in the hands of a master craftsman, as well as the differences between stage and film.

In October 2009, Mitzi Gaynor returned to Kaua'i for the first time since the making of *South Pacific*. In the Hawai'i Magazine blog, she reminisced about filming the "I've got to Wash That Man Out of My Hair" musical number and having to stop the scene when the shampoo created an eye irritation. She remembered seeing No Tears Baby shampoo at Lihu'e General Store, and someone drove one hour each way from the location for a bottle, so filming could continue. She concluded that the filming on the island "was a hoot," for which she rather deservedly earned a Hollywood Foreign Press Golden Globe® Nomination for Best Actress in a Musical for her role as Nurse Nellie Forbush. *South Pacific* was also nominated for the Golden Globe® Best Motion Picture—Musical, while Alfred Newman was likewise nominated for the Grammy Award for Best Soundtrack Album, Dramatic Picture Score or Original Cast.

Originally taken from the pages of James Michener's novel, *South Pacific* has proven to be so popular that it has been reincarnated in other formats, including a made-for-TV movie starring Glenn Close as Nurse Nellie, the Croatian-actor Rade Serbedzija as the suave Planter De Becque and Harry Connick Jr. as dashing Lt. Cable. Shot at Carnegie Hall, a concert performance that was aired on PBS in 2006 featured CW singer Reba McEntire as Nellie, Brian Stokes Mitchell (who depicted Duke Kahanamoku in the 1999 TV movie *Too Rich: The Secret Life of Doris Duke*) as De Becque and Alec Baldwin as Luther Billis.

Like Bali Hai, *South Pacific's* South Seas siren song continues to call viewers to "come away, come away" to their own special production. In 2013, the TCM Classic Film Festival in Hollywood included a special screening of the 1958 musical, with Mitzi Gaynor and France Nuyen making personal appearances. In 2008, the Rodgers and Hammerstein play returned to Broadway, with "local girl" Loretta Ables Sayre, who went from the cane fields of Mililani to Manhattan's Lincoln Center to co-star in a revival of *South Pacific*, playing Bloody Mary.

Made in Paradise

Hawaiian Eye
1959-1963 ABC Television Series

PRODUCED BY **Warner Bros.**

CAST **Robert Conrad (Tom Lopaka), Anthony Eisley (Tracy Steele), Grant Williams (Greg Mackenzie), Connie Stevens (Cricket Blake), Poncie Ponce (Kazuo Kim), Mel Prestidge (Lt. Danny Quon), Troy Donahue (Philip Barton), Doug Mossman (Moke)**

Actor, director, and producer Robert Conrad is the best known of the *Hawaiian Eye* cast members, as he found television fame as 1870s secret service agent James T. West in the outlandish action spy series with an old west setting *Wild Wild West* (the 1965-1969 included episodes written by Samoan screenwriter Johnny Kneubuhl) and as Pappy Boyington on the NBC WWII series *Baa Baa Black Sheep,* aka *The Black Sheep Squadron* (1976-78). He scored a personal and critical triumph with his role as the wily French fur trader Pasquinel in the acclaimed television miniseries *Centennial* (1978-79), based on James Michener's novel. Conrad solidified his tough guy image with a series of high profile battery commercials in the '80s that showed him with a battery on his shoulder as he dared anyone to "Knock it off."

"I guess there were too many people in *Hawaiian Eye* for any one person to get all the attention," Conrad remarked in a 1965 interview with Jack Major of the *Akron Beacon Journal*. "Besides I was under contract to Warner Bros. and they operate on a seniority system." In an April 2007 radio interview with Shade Steel, Conrad reminisced: "I embraced the roles in my three television series with equal enthusiasm. When I was doing *Hawaiian Eye*, I learned to surf in Hawai'i and learned to mingle with the Hawaiian population. And when I did the *Wild Wild West*, I learned to do stunts and I ended up doing all my own stunts, which I enjoyed. And when I did *Baa Baa Black Sheep* or *Black Sheep Squadron*, I learned to fly and became a pilot. And subsequently every role I had, I tried to be as close to what I was portraying as possible."

Connie Steven's endearing and classic role as Cricket Blake on *Hawaiian Eye* made her a household name. To this day Connie is amazed at the craze that her character and image created, becoming one of America's teen idols of the '60s. Connie's career as an actress began with roles in youth-oriented films and was introduced by Jerry Lewis in Frank Tashlin's *Rock-a-Bye Baby*. Under contract to Warner Bros., Connie appeared with heartthrob Troy Donahue in a series of films that included *Parrish* and *Palm Springs Weekend,* which also co-starred Robert Conrad. She has worked in episodic television in guest star roles on such popular shows as *Love Boat* and *Titus* and has performed on Broadway and in Las Vegas. Stevens has experienced phenomenal success in the business arena having created one of America's most successful beauty skin cosmetic care lines, "Forever Spring, The Beauty System."

Connie Stevens as singer Cricket Blake and Robert Conrad as Tom Lopaka pose for a publicity still on the Shell Bar set of *Hawaiian Eye*, the first television series set in Hawai'i but filmed almost entirely at the Warner Bros. studios and backlot in Burbank, California.

Made in Paradise

Blue Hawaii
1961 Paramount

DIRECTED BY **Norman Taurog**
SCREENPLAY BY **Hal Kanter, based on a story by Allan Weiss**
PRODUCED BY **Hal Wallis**
CAST **Elvis Presley (Chad Gates), Joan Blackman (Maile Duval), Angela Lansbury (Sarah Lee Gates), Roland Winters (Fred Gates), Frank Atienza (Ito), Jose de Vega (Ernie Gordon)**

Blue Hawaii, Elvis as tour guide Chad Gates leads four girls on a horseback trail ride up Kuamoʻo Road on Kauaʻi.

Just out of the U.S. Army, Chad Gates (Presley), the rebellious son of a pineapple tycoon, and his Southern wife, wants to make his own way in life. Undaunted by his father, the independent-minded Chad sets up a tour-guide service and takes a group of pretty school girls and their chaperone around the archipelago. Romantic complications ensue out of misunderstandings between Gates and his Hawaiian–French girlfriend, Maile (Blackman), who is also a business partner.

Elvis Presley shared starring honors with the natural wonders of the Fiftieth State in his eighth film and his fourth for producer Hal Wallis. *Blue Hawaii* was Elvis's biggest box office hit, grossing $4.7 million in 1962. The soundtrack album

Elvis goes Hawaiian in *Blue Hawaii*. Although it was made on location on Oʻahu and Kauaʻi, this is a studio shot of Elvis Presley with a Diamond Head backdrop.

Made in Paradise

Elvis: Aloha From Hawai'i, was the first televised concert program in history that was broadcast around the globe via satellite and seen in over 40 countries by close to 1.5 billion people held at Hononlulu International Center arena (now the Neal Blaisdell Center). The concert served as a fundraiser for the Kui Lee Cancer Fund. Lee was a Hawaiian composer and entertainer who wrote the song "I'll Remember You" and died of throat cancer in 1966 at the young age of 34.

Elvis Presley rocks in a musical number filmed at the Polynesian Cultural Center in O'ahu for *Paradise Hawaiian Style* (1966).

marked the singer's thirteenth gold record and eventually passed the 5 million mark in sales. Famed singer and actor Bing Crosby introduced the song "Blue Hawaii" in the 1937 Paramount film *Waikiki Wedding.*

Hawai'i had just joined the Union in 1959 and was as eager for the exposure of a major Hollywood film as the producers and actors were to shoot there. Among the O'ahu locations used were Waikīkī Beach, Mount Tantalus, Diamond Head, Ala Moana Park, Lydgate Park, Hanauma Bay, Punchbowl, and on Kaua'i, the Wailua River, and the Coco Palms Resort. Further filming took place at Paramount Studios.

Presley made two other features in Hawai'i: *Girls, Girls Girls* in 1962, co-starring Stella Stevens in a romance about a tuna-boat skipper who moonlights as a nightclub entertainer, and *Paradise Hawaiian Style,* in 1966, a musical about an out-of-work helicopter pilot who starts his own chopper charter service. Neither film succeeded as much as *Blue Hawaii*, which was originally titled *Hawai'i Beach Boy.* The hip-swiveling, lei-wearing "the King" also headlined the 1973 concert *Elvis: Aloha From Hawai'i,* taped at Honolulu International Center (now known as the Neal S. Blaisdell Center)—the first televised concert program in history that was broadcast around the globe via satellite. Elvis died at the early age of 42 in 1977.

Location filming for *Blue Hawaii* commenced on March 27, 1961, and ended on April 17, 1961. Just before the start of production, Elvis held a special concert in Honolulu that raised $67,000 for the USS *Arizona* Memorial in Pearl Harbor.

Elvis Presley's special relationship with Hawai'i came at a turning point in Hawai'i's history, when Hawai'i was moving from territorial status to statehood. These majestic islands filled with ancient Polynesian lore of gods and kings made a fitting setting for the future King of Rock 'n' Roll. Elvis and his music symbolized the restless American spirit of manifest destiny, strength and youth. Presley's presence in Hawai'i functioned as a commercial for what is now the Hawai'i Visitors and Convention Bureau, inspiring a generation of Depression-era children and baby boomers to visit Hawai'i.

Made in Paradise

Donovan's Reef
1963 Paramount

DIRECTED BY **John Ford**

SCREENPLAY BY **Frank Nugent and James Edward Grant from a story by Edmund Beloin**

PRODUCED BY **John Ford**

CAST **John Wayne (Michael Patrick "Guns" Donovan), Lee Marvin (Gilhooley), Jack Warden (Dr. Dedham), Elizabeth Allen (Amelia), Cesar Romero (French Governor), Dorothy Lamour (Fleur)**

Two ex-Navy men, "Guns" Donovan (Wayne) and Dr. Dedham (Warden), have remained on the fictionalized French Polynesia Island of Haleakaloha following World War II. Donovan operates a bar and nightclub known as Donovan's Reef, and widower Dr. Dedham, who had married a lovely Pacific princess, raises a family and carries on a medical practice. Another shipmate, "Boats" Gilhooley (Marvin) arrives later, and he and Donovan continue their brawling friendship.

Trouble comes to paradise in the form of the unexpected arrival of a beautiful but proper, haughty Bostonian, Amelia Dedham (Allen). She is trying to find her father and uncover information that might warrant his being left out of the family will. Doctor Dedham's friends, including sultry singer Fleur (Lamour), an entertainer at Donovan's Reef, and the French Governor (Romero), plot to save his moral reputation. The results are dynamic, often hilarious, and always heartwarming. The film is a fast-moving, nonstop-action buddy comedy in which a strong ensemble cast matches and supports John Wayne and Lee Marvin.

Advertising poster art from *Donovan's Reef*.

> When not working, Lee Marvin went out on drunken binges. In one instance, he was so drunk that he reportedly stripped naked and danced at a bar in Nāwiliwili Harbor.

Lee Marvin as Gilhooley and Dorothy Lamour as Fleur in *Donovan's Reef*.

Made in Paradise

Lee Marvin as Gilhooley, John Wayne as Guns Donovan and Elizabeth Allen as Amelia Dedham meet at the native village built by Paramount at Hanamā'ulu Beach on Kaua'i.

Although set in a made-up French Polynesian Island of Haleakaloha, in fact, Imperial Japan never invaded this French-administered overseas territory during World War II. Thus, the military action and Japanese occupation spoken of by Wayne as Guns Donovan never occured. As in *Guadalcanal Diary, South Pacific,* and *Windtalkers*, the Pacific Theater's Island-hopping campaign primarily took place in Melanesia and Micronesia.

Donovan's Reef's exteriors were filmed during four weeks on Kaua'i. Thanks to Ford's peripatetic filming, approximately two thirds of Kaua'i's fascinating coastal areas enhance *Donovan's Reef*. Such tourist attractions as the Wailua River, Hanamā'ulu Beach, Makahū'ena Point, Nāwiliwili Harbor, Waimea Canyon, and Kalihiwai Bay are prominent in the backgrounds. Paramount construction crews built a native village of thirty-one grass shacks among the palm trees at Hanamā'ulu Beach, where the company worked for three days. Haleakaloha's town exteriors were filmed in a corner of the standing nineteenth century Western town set at Paramount studios in Hollywood (used in countless Westerns and as Virginia City on TV's *Bonanza* series), along with interiors.

> Making her screen debut in *Donovan's Reef* is John Ford's 110-foot Ketch-rigged, *Araner*, portraying John Wayne's trading ship in the picture. The sailing vessel was made available by Ford to the U.S. Navy during World War II. Ford served in the U.S. Navy Field Photographic Unit during the war and actually filmed the Battle of Midway under combat conditions and was wounded by shrapnel. Actor Lee Marvin saw duty as a U.S. Marine in the South Pacific during the Second World War. After surviving the horrors of war, some American servicemen chose to stay and live a more peaceful lifestyle in the South Pacific Isles.

52 Made in Paradise

Hawaii
1966 United Artists

DIRECTED BY **George Roy Hill**
SCREENPLAY BY **Dalton Trumbo and Daniel Taradash, based on the book by James A. Michener**
PRODUCED BY **Walter Mirisch**
CAST **Julie Andrews (Jerusha Bromley Hale), Max Von Sydow (Abner Hale), Richard Harris (Rafer Hoxworth), Gene Hackman (Rev. John Whipple), Carroll O'Connor (Charles Bromley), Jocelyn LaGarde (Queen Malama), Manu Tupou (Keoki), Ted Nobriga (Kelolo), Elizabeth Logue (Noelani)**

Hawaii is filled with dramatic conflicts and love affairs that grew out of the contact between two very different cultures, the Hawaiians and the White Anglo-Saxon Protestant missionaries from New England. From the beginning, the major challenge in bringing *Hawaii* to the screen evidently sprang from the sprawling James A. Michener novel itself. Michener liked to track the origins of the subjects of his various tomes, and *Hawaii* begins with the geological formations of the Islands, and with Bora Bora, where Michener claims the aboriginal Hawaiians came from. The monumental best-selling book by Michener contained such a wealth of potential film fare in the 946 pages with multiple stories. Thus, it was soon determined that filming the entire novel would take at least eleven hours.

> The big-screen epic *Hawaii* was nominated in seven Academy Award® categories, including Best Supporting Actress (Jocelyn LaGarde), Best Musical Score (Elmer Bernstein), Best Original Song ("My Wishing Doll"), Best Color Cinematography (Russell Harlan), Best Costume Design (Dorothy Jeakins), Best Visual Effects (Linwood G. Dunn) and Best Sound (Gordon Sawyer Samuel Goldwyn SSD).

Academy Award® winners Dalton Trumbo and Daniel Taradash wrote *Hawaii's* screenplay and wrote respectively *The Brave One* and *From Here to Eternity*. The screenplay aimed at retaining the novel's essential flavor while concentrat-

Advertising poster art work for the epic film *Hawai'i*

Made in Paradise

Jocelyn LaGarde, a Tahitian, played Malama, the Alii Nui and chief spokesperson for the Hawaiian people, and Hawaiian-born Ted Nobriga played Kelolo in *Hawai'i*.

ing on the heart of the novel: The early missionaries traveling across stormy seas from New England to far off Hawai'i circa 1820 to bring Christianity to "pagan" Polynesians.

The task of transforming the book into a movie spread out to four parts of the world. Costumes and props came from such diverse places as Hong Kong, Denmark, Australia, Japan, and the Philippines. An international cast was assembled, including the British Julie Andrews *(The Sound Of Music* and *Mary Poppins)*, the Swedish Max Von Sydow (star of many Ingmar Bergman classics such as *The Seventh Seal* and *The Greatest Story Ever Told*) and Irishman Richard Harris *(This Sporting Life* and *A Man Called Horse)*.

To play the pivotal Polynesian parts, the filmmakers went directly to the Pacific Islands, selecting personalities to accurately portray the kanaka characters. Many had never acted before, and one spoke no English, making the filming more difficult. Jocelyn LaGarde, a 300-pound Tahitian of royal blood, played Malama, the Ali'i Nui and chief spokesperson for the Hawaiians. Her vivid performance received a Golden Globe® for Best Supporting Actress, as well as a Best Supporting Actress Academy Award® nomination, and she was the only Polynesian to be so honored. A Polynesian from Fiji of Tongan ancestry, Manu Tupou, who was employed in London by the BBC, became Keoki. The role of Malama's daughter, Noelani, went to Elizabeth Logue, the Hawai'i Visitors Bureau's poster girl and former employee of Hawaiian Airlines. Another Hawaiian, Ted Nobriga, played Kelolo.

In June 1965, the troupe flew to Hawai'i for the fourth and lengthiest phase, which required some four months of filming, principally at Mākua Beach on the Leeward Coast forty miles from Honolulu. A quarter-mile-long village consisting of 107 buildings was constructed and continuously aged to represent the town of Lahaina on Maui as it existed from 1820 to 1848. Film technicians converted a former Navy warehouse at Pearl City into a fully equipped sound stage. Research continued, much of it at the Bishop Museum in Honolulu, to ensure the authentic look of the area during the time depicted. At the newly constructed replica of 1820 Lahaina, 150 mainly indigenous extras formed a village population. Kids played hide and seek in some two dozen grass huts constructed for the film. Nevertheless, despite the efforts at historical accuracy, reminders that the production date was actually 1965, not 1820, were evident: an elderly Hawaiian leaning comfortably against a grass shack reading the *Honolulu Advertiser,* the ever present taro patch sporting plastic plants and black wigs covering modern hair chuts.

The film features actor Carroll O'Connor as Jerusha's father in a role prior to his success as television's iconic Archie Bunker on *All in the Family* (1969-1979). Two-time Oscar® winning actor Gene Hackman plays Rev. John Whipple in an early role prior to his Best Supporting actor Oscar® nomination for *Bonnie and Clyde* (1967).

Born and raised in Hawai'i, singer/actress/entertainer Bette Midler, an Oscar® nominee for 1979's *The Rose*, made her film debut as an extra in a shipboard sequence. Midler portrays a seasick passenger on a ship who listens to a preacher and performs a small speaking role

Made in Paradise

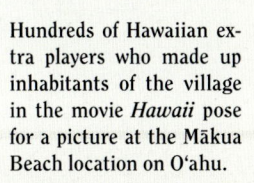

Hundreds of Hawaiian extra players who made up inhabitants of the village in the movie *Hawaii* pose for a picture at the Mākua Beach location on Oʻahu.

in the film in a Los Angeles studio. While her scenes did not make the final film, Midler used the money she earned to move to New York and launch her career. The rest, as they say, is show biz history, as "Bathhouse Betty" morphed into a true superstar.

In 1970, Fred Zinnemann's vision of filming a multi-part adaptation of the literary source for *Hawaii* was partially fulfilled, when United Artists released what its publicity poster called "The Continuation of James A. Michener's Epic Novel, *Hawaii*." *The Hawaiians* carried on with Michener's sprawling generational saga, starring Charlton Heston, Geraldine Chaplin, Mako, Tina Chen,

Julie Andrews as Jerusha Bromley and Max Von Sydow as Abner Hale bid farewell to the ship that brought them to the islands in *Hawaii*.

Made in Paradise 55

Charlton Heston, Tina Chen and Mako starred in the 1970 unofficial sequel continuation of *Hawai'i* called *The Hawaiians* also known as Master Of The Islands in its international release.

Keye Luke, Khigh Dhiegh, and John Phillip Law. In addition to bringing the Chinatown fire to the big screen, this is one of the few features to depict the overthrow of Queen Lili'uokalani (played by New Jersey-born character actress Naomi Stevens, who specialized in ethnic roles).

At the leper colony on Molokai, Mun Ki (Mako) and Nyuk Tsin (Tina Chen) give their baby daughter Mei Li to Whip (Charlton Heston) to carry home to safety

Hawaii Five-O
1968-1980 CBS

CREATED BY **Leonard Freeman**

CAST **Jack Lord (Steve McGarrett), James MacArthur (Danny Williams), Kam Fong (Chin Ho Kelly), Zulu (Kono Kalākaua), Richard Denning (The Governor), Khigh Dhiegh (Wo Fat)**

Jack Lord (1920-1998)

Jack Lord achieved worldwide television stardom with his role as Steve McGarrett, the stern, no-nonsense head of the elite police investigations unit, *Hawaii Five-O*. When *Hawaii Five-O* ended its twelve-year run on CBS in 1980, Lord directed and starred in a television pilot *M Station Hawaii*, that was not picked up by the network. Lord went into semi-retirement but remained active in Hawai'i civic affairs. The actor died on January 21, 1998, from congestive heart failure after a long battle with Alzheimer's disease.

James MacArthur (1937-2010)

MacArthur is best known for his role as Danny "Danno" Williams, McGarrett's trusted young lieutenant on the long-running *Hawaii Five-O* television series. The adopted son of famous parents—actress Helen Hayes and newspaperman, playwright, and screenwriter Charles MacArthur—James was raised in an environment of creative people and made his acting debut at the age of eight in *The Corn*

Jack Lord as Steve McGarrett, Lord of the Islands, who answers only to the governor on *Hawaii Five-O*.

Made in Paradise

is Green, in summer stock. By the time he was sixteen, he decided on acting.

In 1960, MacArthur appeared in the Broadway production of *Invitation to a March,* with Celeste Holm and Jane Fonda. His film credits include *Kidnapped, Spencer's Mountain, Swiss Family Robinson, The Light in the Forrest, The Interns, To Be a Man, The Battle of the Bulge,* and *The Love–Ins. Hawaii Five-O* producer Leonard Freeman remembered MacArthur, who had a small role in Freeman's theatrical feature, *Hang 'Em High,* with Clint Eastwood, and cast him as Danny Williams, after the original actor in the pilot was rejected by test audiences and the network.

MacArthur had expressed interest in doing a guest-starring role on the new *Hawaii Five-0* Reboot, and the producers were receptive to the idea, but unfortunately MacArthur passed away before it could be realized.

James MacArthur had his first association with the South Seas with his role in Disney's *Swiss Family Robinson.*

Kam Fong (1918-2002)

Kam Fong Chun was born in Kalihi and attended Honolulu's Fern Elementary School, Kalākaua Intermediate School and McKinley High School. Although he appeared in school plays in both intermediate and high school, it was only after working for seventeen years as a Honolulu policeman that Kam Fong decided on a full-time acting career. When not in front of the *Hawaii Five-O* cameras as Chin Ho Kelly, Kam spent much of his time working as an actor and master of ceremonies for the Honolulu Community Theatre, the Honolulu Theatre for Youth and charitable organizations. His film credits include movies filmed in Hawai'i such as *Gidget Goes Hawaiian, Ghost of the China Seas, Seven Women From Hell,* and *Diamond Head.* Kam Fong appeared regularly on Hawai'i radio and television stations and was once billed as "Hawai'i's only Chinese Disk Jockey." On television he conducted a series of children's programs called *Kam Fong's Comedies.* Kam Fong Chun's son, actor Dennis Chun, has a recurring role as HPD officer Sgt. Duke Lukela in CBS' *Hawaii Five-0* revival.

Zulu (1937-2004)

Zulu, who played Kono on *Hawaii Five-O,* was born Gilbert Francis Lani Damian Kauhi in Hilo on the Big Island of Hawai'i. When he was eleven, the family moved to Honolulu, where he attended Kamehameha Schools. Zulu, three quarters Hawaiian and one quarter English, grew up loving water sports. At age twelve, he became a beach boy in his free time, giving surfing lessons and outrigger rides to tourists at Waikīkī Beach. At seventeen, he joined the U.S. Coast Guard and served for four years in Atlantic and Pacific ports. He toured with a Polynesian revue in Japan. Zulu appeared in many movies made in Hawai'i including *Rampage, Hawaii, Gidget Goes Hawaiian,* and *Diamond Head.* Zulu became one of Hawai'i's most popular disk jockeys and performed in nightclubs throughout the Islands. Zulu left *Hawaii Five-O* at the end of the fourth season after a disagreement with series star Jack Lord and faded into obscurity.

Made in Paradise

Richard Denning (1914-1998)

Though perhaps best known today for his role as the Governor on 12 seasons of *Hawaii Five-O*, Denning's career includes more than 150 movies, 300 television shows, a radio series and four TV series. The actors' association with tropical Islands began with his co-starring role as Jacka the Magnificent opposite Dorothy Lamour in 1942's *Beyond the Blue Horizon*, followed by 1948's *Unknown Island*, about an uncharted South Pacific isle inhabited by dinosaurs. Denning later appeared in the 1954 horror classic *Creature from the Black Lagoon* (co-starring Tahitian actor Benny Chapman as the Gill-man in the land sequences) and starred for Roger Corman in 1957's in *Naked Paradise*, filmed entirely on Kauaʻi. On television he starred in the series *Flying Doctor*, about a physician in the Pacific. In the mid-1960s, Denning made his home on Maui with his wife, former actress Evelyn Ankers.

Khigh Dhiegh (1910-1991)

Red Chinese master criminal Wo Fat was played by Khigh Dhiegh, who was Steve McGarrett's nemesis over the 12 seasons of *Hawaii Five-O*. Dhiegh was born in New Jersey of Anglo-Egyptian-Sudanese descent. He was cast by series creator Leonard Freeman, who remembered him from his memorable role in John Frankenheimers' feature film, *The Manchurian Candidate* (1963), opposite Frank Sinatra and Laurence Harvey. Dheigh began his career in early television productions such as Studio One in the fifties and went on to guest star on such shows as *Naked City, Wild Wild West,* and *Mission Impossible* and made his last guest appearance on an episode of the Hawaiʻi-filmed TV series *Jake and The Fatman* in 1989. Among his other feature film credits are *The Hawaiians, Seconds, How to Murder Your Wife,* and *Goin' Coconuts*.

Khigh Dhiegh as Wo Fat, McGarrett's arch nemesis on Hawaii Five-0, who was captured in the final episode of the series' twelve-year run. The New Jersey-born actor of Egyptian heritage also played a Maoist secret agent in John Frankenheimer's feature film The Manchurian Candidate (1962), and Dhiegh starred in his own short-lived television series about a Chinese-American San Francisco police detective called Khan.

Leonard Freeman (1920-1974)

Freeman was born on October 31, 1920, in Sonoma County, California. He studied acting at the Pasadena Playhouse, where he appeared beside the woman who would become his wife, Rose Emma, (known professionally as Joan Taylor). In 1951 he began his career as a television actor. He soon began writing for television in 1952. He had over 300 television scripts to his credit and once held the position of President of the Writers Guild of America. In 1961, Freeman produced an episode of the ground-breaking, on-location series *Route 66*. Over the next decade, he produced or served as executive producer for such television series as *The Untouchables, Naked City, Cimarron Strip,* and *Storefront Lawyers*. He wrote and produced Clint Eastwood's first stateside western feature film, *Hang 'Em High*. In 1968, Freeman created and was executive producer of the CBS television series *Hawaii Five-O*.

Freeman was nominated three times for television's coveted Emmy® Awards: In 1955, for Best Written Dramatic Material for *Four Star Playhouse*; in 1965, for Outstanding Program Achievements in Entertainment for *Mr. Novak*; and in 1973, for Outstanding Drama Series-Continuing for *Hawaii Five-O*.

Freeman died on January 20, 1974, at the age of 53, soon after filming was concluded for the sixth season of *Five-O*, in Palo Alto, California, as the result of complications from heart surgery. After the death of her husband, Rose Freeman managed the *Hawaii Five-O* property and was active in the management of the new *Hawaii Five-0* Reboot in 2010. Rose passed away on March 4, 2012.

Morton Stevens (1929-1981)

Stevens composed the memorable title theme music for *Hawaii Five-O*. Stevens won an Emmy® Award for his musical compositions on the series in 1974 for the *Hook Man* episode.

Made in Paradise

Tora! Tora! Tora!
1970 Twentieth Century Fox

DIRECTED BY	**Richard Fleischer**
PRODUCED BY	**Elmo Williams**
SCREENPLAY BY	**Larry Forrester, Hideo Ogami, Ryuzo Kikushima, based on *Tora, Tora, Tora* by Gordon W. Prange and *The Broken Seal* by Ladislas Faragó.**
CAST	**Martin Balsam (Admiral Kimmel), Jason Robards Jr. (Gen. Walter C. Short), Joseph Cotton (Henry L. Stimson), E.G. Marshall (Lt. Col. Bratton), James Whitmore (Admiral William F. Halsey), Soh Yamamura (Yamamoto), Tatsua Mihashi (Cmdr. Genda), Takahiro Tamura (Lt. Cmdr. Fuchida)**

Tora! Tora! Tora! masterfully recreated the events leading up to the actual attack on Pearl Harbor. The movie filmed on location where the attack happened at Pearl Harbor at a final production cost of $25 million in 1970 dollars. Producer Elmo Williams and his director Richard Fleischer pioneered the docudrama as a new fact-based film form, a narrative technique stressing authenticity and credibility.

Almost thirty years after the attack, the Japanese in the film were shown as intelligent human beings (not as vicious, or even subhuman, WWII-era Asian stereotypes) who shared misgivings about their audacious, brilliant surprise attack. The film showed the differences in the American and Japanese military cultures of the time. The Japanese side is intercut with the American side, and Japanese characters speak in Japanese with English subtitles onscreen. The 144-minute film is logically divided into a 79-minute first act, which crosscuts between Japan and American locales, and a 65-minute act two, which consists mostly of the reenactment of the attack. The title was taken from the Japanese code signal "Tiger! Tiger! Tiger!" which was sent by Lt. Cmdr. Fuchida to communicate that maximum surprise had been achieved.

The Hawai'i production of *Tora! Tora! Tora!* required logistics nearly as complicated as a war. American airplanes of pre-World War II vintage were acquired from all over the world. Japanese planes had to be converted from other models, because no real ones had survived the war. The company rented five old destroyers from the Navy, but hired the Marine Services Division of the Dillingham Corporation in Honolulu to build a full-scale section of the USS *Arizona* at a cost of $1.5 million. Mounted on two steel barges, the 309-foot steel superstructure, fully fitted, was towed to Battleship Row to play her historic role.

Filming began in December 1968 aboard the aircraft carrier USS *Yorktown* doubling as the Japanese carrier Akagi. On Jan. 20, 1969, the planes came in low over the serene, silent monument that covers the USS *Arizona* and dipped their wings in tribute to the men

> *Tora! Tora! Tora!* deservedly won the Oscar® for Best Visual Effects for A.D. Flowers and L.B. Abbott. It was nominated for four other Academy Awards®: Best Art Direction-Set Decoration, Best Cinematography, Best Editing and Best Sound.

Made in Paradise

entombed there. This time, though, the planes were there to mark the opening of principal photography of the film—not drop lethal payloads.

Second Unit Director Ray Kellogg, whose credits include *The Alamo* and *The Tall Men,* headed the weeks of aerial and ground second unit photography. The aircraft, tested in California, were flown almost continuously from mid-December 1968 to late April 1969. Forty-seven experienced pilots, mostly on leave from the Air Force and Navy, comprised what came to be affectionately called the "Fox Air Force."

"There were so many elements involved in each scene that we were lucky to get one shot a day," said director Richard Fleischer to Associated Press writer Bob Thomas in the June 14, 1969 *Los Angeles Herald Examiner.* "For instance we had twenty-eight planes in the sky, and they had to maneuver so they could be seen on every camera. On the ground we had special effects men providing fire and smoke, and a sudden shift of wind could send the smoke right into the cameras, so we'd photograph nothing, or the sun would go behind the clouds and ruin the scene. We had the planes circling for an hour and a half before getting a shot."

"It had been a rather strange war, this second air battle of Hawai'i, chilling at times," commented *Honolulu Advertiser* editor Buck Buchwach in December 1968, while watching the filming of *Tora! Tora! Tora!* "Sometimes it seemed too real. It was comforting to know those were American pilots up there this time."

Tora! Tora! Tora! was photographed on the actual locations in Hawai'i where the historic events all took place: Ford Island, Kolekole Pass, Schofield Barracks, Waikīkī, Aloha Tower, the Kalihi District of Honolulu, Koko Head, 'Ōpana Point, Fort Shafter, Chinaman's Hat, and Hickam and Wheeler Fields.

Business on the island boomed during production. More than 250 carpenters, painters, steelworkers, scenic artists, and cabinet makers, mostly Hawai'i residents, were employed. The huge Hangar 79, marked with holes from the real attack on Pearl Harbor, was turned into a mini-film studio that became the hub of construction and storage facilities. *Tora! Tora! Tora!* opened to lukewarm critical and audience response in the U.S., but was a big hit in Japan.

Tora! Tora! Tora! press book.

Airmen scramble to get out of the line-of-fire of marauding Japanese Zeros hittng the U.S. Army Air Corps Base at Wheeler Field in this scene from *Tora! Tora! Tora!*

Made in Paradise

King Kong
1976 Paramount

DIRECTED BY **John Guillermin**
SCREENPLAY BY **Lorenzo Semple Jr.**
PRODUCED BY **Dino De Laurentiis**
CAST **Jeff Bridges (Jack Prescott), Jessica Lange (Dwan), Charles Grodin (Fred Wilson)**

In this 1976 remake, an exploration team (instead of a camera crew) is sent to the South Pacific to find an underwater oil shelf on Skull Island. Instead the team finds a giant forty-foot ape, King Kong. Realizing the commercial value of the find, the leader of the team subdues the beast and makes off with Kong to New York. With a plot similar to that of the original, this updated version is a $22 million Dino De Laurentiis retelling of the classic "Beauty and The Beast" story filmed in Technicolor.

Being carried off in the hand of Kong and screaming at every turn would have killed the career of a lesser actress, but Jessica Lange proved she had more than just a pretty face and sultry body. Lange went on to win two Best Actress Academy Awards® for 1982's *Tootise* and 1994's *Blue Sky*. In 1982, Lange received another Best Actress nomination for playing the title character in *Frances* (about the life of actress Frances Farmer, whose nephew, David Farmer, worked as a Honolulu attorney and actor).

Jeff Bridges, who co-starred with Kong and Lange, also went on to a bright career as one of America's finest actors, winning that coveted golden statuette as a country singer in 2009's *Crazy Heart* opposite Harry Zinn. The son of actor Lloyd Bridges received five more Oscar® nominations, including for 2010's *True Grit*.

> Carlo Rambaldi, Glen Robinson and Frank Van der Veer were each awarded a special achievement Academy Award® for Visual Effects for their work on *King Kong*. It was nominated for two Academy Awards, Best Cinematography (Richard H. Kline) and Best Sound (Jack Solomon, Aaron Rochis, Harry W. Tetrick and William McCaughny).

King Kong was filmed on locations ranging from Kaua'i to sets on Hollywood sound stages and to the streets of New York at Lower Manhattan's World Trade Center. In what may be an eerie motion-picture prediction of disaster, Kong makes his last stand at the Twin Towers destroyed twenty-five years later during the terrorist attack of September 11, 2001.

Up until *King Kong*, no major commercial film company had gone into the rugged terrain of northern Kaua'i, an incredibly remote area with beautiful valleys and mountains, the area used as a location for Skull Island. Four helicopters daily airlifted the fifty-member cast and crew over the beautiful valleys and mountains of the Nā Pali Coast to the Honopū Valley location.

PARAMOUNT PICTURES

Two-time Oscar®-winning actress Jessica Lange made her auspicious film debut in the hands of Hollywood's biggest star, *King Kong*, in the Dino DeLaurentiis 1976 remake of *King Kong*.

Made in Paradise

Magnum P.I.
1980-1988 CBS

CREATED BY   **Glen Larson and Don Bellisario**

CAST   **Tom Selleck (Thomas Magnum), John Hillerman (Jonathan Q. Higgins), Roger E. Mosley (T.C.), Larry Manetti (Rick Wright)**

Tom Selleck (Thomas Sullivan Magnum)

Tom Selleck's versatility in both television and film is well known, but prior to his starring role as Police Commissioner Frank Reagan on the current multigenerational New York -based police drama series *Blue Bloods* (2010-), he was best known for his portrayal of Thomas Magnum in the '80s CBS television hit series *Magnum P.I.* Since 2003, over a span of eight years Selleck established a new following due to the success of his series of eight made-for-television movies based on the Robert B. Parker mystery novels, Jesse Stone. His portrayal of down-on-his-luck, small-town New England police chief *Jesse Stone,* who investigates a string of murders, garnered Selleck an Emmy® Award nomination.

Selleck's motion-picture acting career has featured him in a variety of roles for such films as *Three Men and a Baby* and its sequel *Three Men and a Little Lady, Quigley Down Under, In and Out, Mr. Baseball, Her Alibi, The Love Letter, Broken Trust, Folks, An Innocent Man, Runaway,* and *High Road To China.*

The actors' additional television credits include the series *Las Vegas* and the recurring role of Candice Bergen's lovable rogue ex-husband on *Boston Legal.* His memorable guest starring role on *Friends* as Courteney Cox's love interest earned him an Emmy® Award nomination in 2000 for Outstanding Guest Actor in a Comedy Series.

Making his Broadway stage debut in 2001, Selleck starred in a revival of *A Thousand Clowns* that broke box office records at New York's Longacre Theatre.

On cable television the actor starred in the films *Ike: Countdown to D-Day, Louis L'Amour's Crossfire Trail, Last Stand at Saber River,* and a remake of *Monte Walsh.*

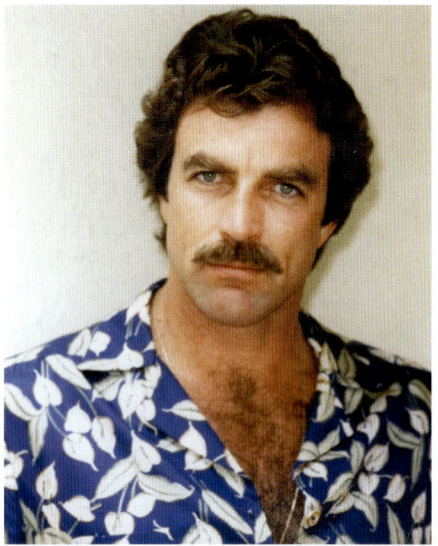

Tom Selleck as Magnum P.I.

Tom Selleck as Magnum walks along Waimānalo Beach, Oʻahu. Twin-peaked Olomana is in the background.

Made in Paradise

Raiders of the Lost Ark
1981 Paramount

DIRECTED BY **Steven Spielberg**
SCREENPLAY BY **Lawrence Kasdan**
PRODUCED BY **George Lucas**
CAST **Harrison Ford (Indiana Jones), Karen Allen (Marion Ravenswood), Denholm Elliott (Dr. Marcus Brody)**

In the opening scene of *Raiders of the Lost Ark*, set in a South American jungle, Indiana Jones pillages a temple full of boobytraps and blowguns. Then, he runs just ahead of a huge rolling boulder. Having averted a disastrous fate, Jones is chased by the fierce Indians of Chachapoyan through a marsh grove, where an awaiting plane whisks him off to safety. These are only a few of the many adventures of Indian Jones.

The South American scenes of this movie were shot on Kauaʻi. The first location, where the temple exterior was shot, was reached via a narrow dirt track that led down a cliff face into a hole full of mosquitos. Other locations included Nā Pali coastal mountain shots, for which donkeys were transported by helicopter, and the Huleʻia River on the east side of the Garden Island.

> Inspired by the filmmakers' love of the movie serials of the 1930s and 1940s, this blockbuster won five Academy Awards and was nominated for another four. *Raiders of the Lost Ark* won for Best Art Direction-Set Decoration; Best Effects, Visual Effects; Best Film Editing; Best Sound and a Special Achievement Award Oscar® for sound effects editing. *Raiders* was also nominated for Best Picture and Spielberg for Best Director while composer John Williams was nominated for Best Music, Original Score and Douglas Slocombe for Best Cinematography.

Left: Poster advertising art from the original release of *Raiders of the Lost Ark*.

Below: Producer George Lucas and director Steven Spielberg with local actors playing South American Indians on location on Kauaʻi, which doubles for a South American jungle.

Made in Paradise

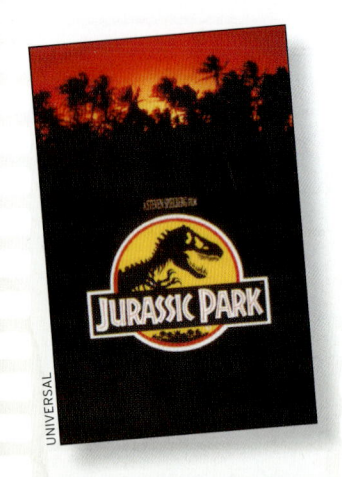

Jurassic Park
1993 Universal

DIRECTED BY **Steven Spielberg**

SCREENPLAY BY **Michael Crichton and David Koepp, based on the novel by Michael Crichton**

PRODUCED BY **Kathleen Kennedy and Gerald R. Molen**

CAST **Sam Neill (Dr. Allen Grant), Laura Dern (Ellie Sattler), Jeff Goldblum (Ian Malcolm), Richard Attenborough (John Hammond), B.D. Wong (Henry Wu), Samuel L. Jackson (Ray Arnold), Wayne Knight (Dennis Nedry)**

Jurassic Park became the highest-grossing movie in the world up to that time and spawned two sequels. Kaua'i, which played a starring role in this record-breaking box-office hit, reveled in the worldwide attention the film garnered. To mark the occasion of the film's twentieth anniversary, Steven Spielberg introduced it in a state-of-the-art 3D format and IMAX theaters re-release in April 2013.

Engineering DNA to recreate dinosaurs on a remote island near Central America was the scientific basis for the popular Michael Crichton novel, which intrigued Director Steven Spielberg. According to the press note: "When *Jurassic Park* began principal photography on the island of Kaua'i on August 24, 1992 exactly two years and one month had passed since the start of pre-production. For more than eighteen months before filming began, an award winning design team had been conceiving and creating the live-action dinosaurs that would inhabit the unique park."

An unparalleled level of special effects was developed for this film to make the dinosaurs as lifelike as possible.

> The film developed an unparalleled level of special effects and earned three Academy Awards® for its groundbreaking technical achievements: Best Sound Effects Editing, Best Visual Effects and Best Sound.

Along with King Kong, Godzilla and Moby Dick, the dinosaurs of *Jurassic Park* are the most popular creatures associated with South Seas Cinema. Here Laura Dern, Martin Ferrero, Jeff Goldblum, Sam Neill and Richard Attenborough begin a tour of the dinosaur theme park.

Made in Paradise

Laura Dern and Sam Neill examine a dinosaur in a scene from Jurassic Park filmed at Kualoa Ranch on Oʻahu.

Ariana Richards, Joseph Mazzello and Sam Neill in *Jurassic Park*.

The movie's production notes state that following three weeks of filming in the tropics sun, a real-life disaster overtook the movie: Hurricane Iniki, the strongest hurricane to hit the Islands in over a century, slammed into Kauaʻi on September 11. Spielberg and the film's stars Richard Attenborough, Laura Dern, and Jeff Goldblum, along with the rest of the cast and crew, sat out the storm together in the ballroom of the Westin Kauaʻi Resort Hotel.

Upon the production's return to Los Angeles, *Jurassic Park* resumed filming at Universal Studios, returning only once more to Oʻahu to complete one day of location filming at Kualoa Ranch. Revenues totaling $4.5 million were spent in Hawaiʻi on the production of *Jurassic Park*.

Made in Paradise

Waterworld
1995 Universal

DIRECTED BY **Kevin Reynolds**
SCREENPLAY BY **Peter Rader and David Twohy**
PRODUCED BY **Kevin Costner, Charles Gordon, John Davis**
CAST **Kevin Costner (Mariner), Dennis Hopper (Deacon), Jeanne Tripplehorn (Helen), Tina Majorino (Enola), Jack Black (Pilot), Zakes Mokae (Priam), Henry Kapono (Gatesman)**

When *Waterworld* was released in 1995, its storyline—about a dystopian future wherein the polar ice caps have melted and the planet has been flooded—seemed like a mere Tinseltown science-fiction flight of fancy. But with the exponential increase in extreme weather since then, science fiction now appears to becoming scientific fact, and what was perceived as fantasy then now looms as motion-picture prophecy. The 2012 *National Geographic* documentary *Chasing Ice* reveals in graphic detail, through startling time-lapse cinematography, the melting of glaciers in Greenland, the Arctic, and elsewhere, illustrating that climate change is more than mere movie whimsy.

Waterworld received a Best Sound Oscar® nomination.

Since global warming affects the Pacific Islands, it's therefore all the more fitting that *Waterworld* was shot on location in—and around—the Big Island. The watery scenes were lensed near Kawaihae in the South Kohala district from June 1994 through February 1995. At the height of his post-*Dances with Wolves* fame, with that Western scoring seven Academy Awards®, including for Best Picture and Best Director, Kevin Costner was Tinseltown's golden boy who could do no wrong.

In *Waterworld*, Costner played Mariner, a part-amphibian, part-human with gills behind his ears and webbed feet who sails his jerry-rigged trimaran around the waterlogged globe. (Renowned surfer Laird John Hamilton actually depicts the nautically nimble Mariner in some sea scenes.) Instead of a collection of sandy, palm-fringed islets as in the South Seas, *Waterworld's* so-called atoll is a series of interconnected manmade rusty ramshackle dwellings and towers enclosed by a wall. This elaborate, exorbitantly expensive set was located off the Kona Coast, where land could not be seen in any of the shots. The final sequence of *Waterworld* was shot at Waipio Valley, that extravagantly exquisite indigenous enclave on the Big Island. Everest's once-snowy peak has become tropical in this epic's post-global warming planet. Although he has found domestic bliss and solid Earth, in classic cowboy style, Mariner rides off into the sunset on not his trusty steed, but a boat, sailing ever onwards towards the beckoning horizon.

Built before CGI (computer-generated imagery) became the norm, *Waterworld's* 1,000-ton, quarter-mile-in-circumference atoll set was constructed at an extravagant cost of $5 million, substantially adding to the movie's reported $175 million budget. Adding to the expenses, Kona winds and weather conditions—which the filmmakers reportedly had not looked into prior to the lengthy shoot—repeatedly caused the floating set to change position, necessitating reshoots.

Waterworld belongs to that select group of movies with budgets overshadowing the pictures themselves, which the press portrays as filmic fiscal fiascoes. This handful of epics also includes Michael Cimino's 1980 Western *Heaven's Gate*, co-starring part-time Maui resident Kris Kristofferson, and Elaine May's 1987 Arabia-set *Ishtar*, starring Warren Beatty and Dustin Hoffman. The former even inspired an entire 1985 nonfiction book by film historian Steven Bach, *Final Cut, Dreams and Disaster in the Making of Heaven's Gate*.

Prior to James Cameron's 1997 mega-movie *Titanic*, *Waterworld* was the most expensive

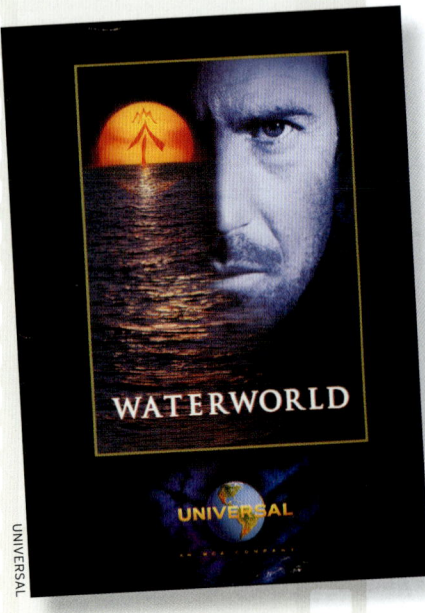

Poster art for Universal's *Waterworld* with star Kevin Costner shown prominently as Mariner.

movie ever made. According to BoxOfficeMojo.com, as of this writing *Waterworld* has made only $88,246,220—meaning that it lost approximately $100 million. IMDB says it is "Widely considered to be one of the biggest box-office bombs of all time. Although it grossed $255 million from a $175 million production budget, this does not factor in marketing and distribution costs, or the percentage of the gross that theaters keep (which is up to 45% of a film's box office takings)."

Movies should be judged by their quality and meaning, not by their budget, and *Waterworld* deserves to be reevaluated. Not only is it an action-packed, exciting, eye-popping, big-screen 135-minute extravaganza, but it prophetically forecasts the cataclysmic effects of climate change that we may now be witnessing and experiencing. Instead of a disaster, the movie just might be an environmental masterpiece that had the misfortune of being made ahead of its time, but in our post-Hurricane Sandy world is, alas, more timely than ever. While *Waterworld* is set at some unspecified time in the future, the catastrophic realities of extreme weather are becoming more relevant today.

Nonetheless, thanks to Kevin Costner and *Waterworld's* steep price tag, lots of Big Island and other Fiftieth State residents got plenty of work out of it. Almost 500 people worked in production on the first and second unit filming crews and as extras. The production filmed in Kawaihae in the south Kohala district of the Big Island over a seven-month-long shooting schedule, which began on June 27, 1994, extending to February 1995.

Picture Bride
1995 Miramax

DIRECTED BY **Kayo Hatta**
SCREENPLY BY **Kayo Hatta and Mari Hatta**
PRODUCED BY **Lisa Onodera and Diane Mei Lin Mark**
CAST **Youki Kudoh (Riyo), Akira Takayama (Matsuji), Tamlyn Tomita (Kana), Cary-Hiroyuki (Tagawa Kanzaki), Toshiro Mifune (Benshi)**

Inspired by the true stories of Hawai'i's pioneers during the early years of the twentieth century, *Picture Bride* is about Riyo (Youki Kudoh), a spirited young Japanese woman who ventures to Hawai'i as a "picture bride." In her attempts to leave behind a troubled past in Japan, Riyo exchanges photographs and letters with Matsuji (Akira Takayama), a Japanese sugarcane worker in Hawai'i, and a marriage is arranged. Upon her arrival in Hawai'i, Riyo discovers that her new husband bears little resemblance to the handsome young man in the photo while her new world is not the paradise she expected—plantation life is grueling and hard.

A friendship with an enigmatic woman she meets in the canefields helps Riyo through her first year, a time of struggle and unexpected joy. *Picture Bride* is the inspiring story of the pioneers who came to Hawai'i as plantation workers and stayed, creating a multi-ethnic society.

Produced by Thousand Crane Filmworks, *Picture Bride* is one of the first modern local Hawai'i theatrical film productions. Hawai'i-born director Kayo Hatta and her sister Mari Hatta wrote the script. They teamed up with Lisa Onodera, a UCLA classmate, and Diane Mei Lin Mark, a Hawai'i-based writer and media specialist, who moved the film forward as producers. Legendary Japanese film-star Toshiro Mifune (the lead in numerous Akira Kurosawa sword and kimono sagas, including *Rashomon, Seven Samurai, Throne of Blood,* and *Yojimbo*) signed on for a cameo role as the "benshi," or silent movie narrator, through the assistance of Kaua'i business man Art Umezu, a friend of the actor.

Made in Paradise

Riyo (Youki Kudoh) works in the cane fields of Hawaiʻi in Hawaiʻi-born Kayo Hatta's *Picture Bride*. Hatta captured a period of history in Hawaiʻi through the experiences of a Japanese picture bride, which was greatly enhanced by the location cinematography by Claudio Rocha *(Like Water For Chocolate)*. Berkeley professor Ronald Takaki, author of *Pau Hana: Plantation Life and Labor in Hawaiʻi* remarked in an article that appeared in the spring 1995 issue of Visual Communications' *In Focus*, "It was the intercultural weave between many ethnicities that contributed to Hawaiʻi's development."

Picture Bride was filmed primarily on an actual working sugarcane plantation (currently a coffee plantation) at Waialua on the North Shore of Oʻahu, as well as on the Hāmākua Coast of the Big Island. In addition to the canefields, on-location shooting included the Kanraku Tea house in Kapalama (for the Japan scenes), Honolulu Harbor as well as in the Hawaiʻi Film Studio at Diamond Head.

The local branches of the IATSE, Screen Actors Guild and Teamsters unions greatly supported *Picture Bride*. Longtime Hawaiʻi residents donated family heirlooms and artifacts to the production, helping to bring the plantation era back to life. Many of Hawaiʻi's businesses backed the film through providing hotel rooms, catering, meals, vehicles, and services. Some of the organizations that supported the production included the Hawaiʻi State Legislature, State Foundation on Culture and the Arts, National Endowment for the Humanities, National Endowment for the Arts, American Film Institute, National Asian American Telecommunications Association, Cecile Company, and numerous other organizations.

Picture Bride won the Audience Award for Dramatic Film at the eleventh annual Sundance Film Festival in 1995. The film had a limited national theatrical release through Miramax and is available on DVD. The gifted filmmaker Lori "Kayo" Hatta passed away at the age of 47 in 2005 in a drowning accident in Encinitas, California.

THOUSAND CRANE FILMWORKS

Outbreak
1995 Warner Bros.

DIRECTED BY	**Wolfgang Petersen**
SCREENPLAY BY	**Lawrence Dworet, Robert Roy Pool**
PRODUCED BY	**Arnold Kopelson, Ann Keelson, Wolfgang Petersen, Gail Katz**
CAST	**Dustin Hoffman (Col. Sam Daniels), Rene Russo (Robby Keough), Morgan Freeman (General Billy Ford), Patrick Dempsey (Jimbo Scott), Cuba Gooding Jr. (Major Salt), Donald Sutherland (General Donald McClintock)**

This film starts off at an African village that gets incinerated with a firebomb to prevent the spread of a deadly virus. Thirty years later, the story moves from the jungles of Zaire to the fictional city of Cedar Creek in Northern California, which has a deadly virus outbreak. It's discovered that a test monkey from the African village carried over the virus to the city.

The Africa scenes were filmed at a site along the Wailua River on Kauaʻi where the faux village was constructed.

African Village set for *Outbreak* along the Wailua River on Kauaʻi.

ANGELA TILLSON

Made in Paradise

Race the Sun
1995 Tri Star

DIRECTED BY **Charles T. Kanganis**
SCREENPLAY BY **Barry Morrow**
PRODUCED BY **Barry Morrow, Beau St. Clair, David Nichols, Herb Squires, Richard Heus**
CAST **Halle Berry (Miss Sandra Beecher), Jim Belushi (Frank Machi), Casey Affleck (Daniel Webster), Eliza Dushku (Cindy Johnson), Anthony Michael Ruivar (Eduardo Bame), Kevin Tighe (Jack Fryman), Steve Zahn (Hans Kooiman), Dion Basco (Marco Kito), Joseph Moki Cho (Gilbert Tutu), Nadja Pionilla (Oni Magano), Adriane Napualani Uganiza (Luana Kanahale), Sara Tanaka (Uni Kakamura)**

Based on a true story, *Race the Sun* is about a new science teacher at Hawai'i's Kona Pali High School (in reality, Konawaena High School), Miss Sandra Beecher (Berry), who takes on a bunch of bored and disillusioned students. When she inspires her pupils to design and build a solar-powered car, Sandra brings hope back to their world. They enter the car in a race in Hawai'i and win. This victory leads to a chance to compete in a championship race in Australia. *Race the Sun* is an inspirational, feel-good film about a bunch of disadvantaged youth from a school in Hawai'i who, against all odds, secure a spot in the annual Darwin-to-Adelaide international solar car race and finish first in the high school division. Believable acting from the kids and strong leading performances from Berry, Belushi, and Affleck give *Race the Sun* a different contemporary look at life in Hawai'i. Though the film takes place at Kona on the Big Island, it was shot in Waialua on O'ahu's North Shore.

Oscar®-winning actress Halle Berry went local and donned a flower lei and a bikini for her role as Sandra Beecher, an English teacher who is determined to teach science to a class filled with kids who have long given up on school in *Race The Sun*.

Sandra Beecher (Halle Berry, 2nd from left) and Frank Machi (Jim Beluchi, far right) help a group of bored and disillusioned high school kids. *Left to right:* Casey Affleck, Dion Basco, Andriane Napualani, Nadja Pionilla, Joseph Moki Cho, Sara Tanaka, Anthony Michael Ruivivar, and Eliza Dushku enter in the World Solar Car Challenge competition that takes them across the Australian desert in *Race the Sun*, a Tristar Picture release.

Made in Paradise

A Very Brady Sequel
1996 Paramount

DIRECTED BY	**Arlene Sanford**
SCREENPLAY BY	**Harry Elfont, Deborah Kaplan, James Berg, Stan Zimmerman**
PRODUCED BY	**Sherwood Schwartz, Loyld J. Schwartz, Alan Ladd Jr.**
CAST	**Shelly Long (Carol), Gary Cole (Mike), Tim Matheson (Roy), Christopher Daniel Barnes (Greg), Christine Taylor (Marcia), Paul Sutero (Peter), Jennifer Elise Cox (Jan), RuPaul (Ms. Cummings)**

In this second silver screen spoof of the popular '70s TV sitcom, Shelly Long and Gary Cole reprise their roles as Carol and Mike Brady, which they originally performed in 1995's *The Brady Bunch Movie*. *A Very Brady Sequel* reunites the cast as they portray their moral, sunny '70s attitudes in the more cynical '80s. This time, a young man shows up claiming to be Carol's long-lost husband Roy (Tim Matheson), and Carol and Mike invite him in as a house guest. However, Roy is not on the level—he steals an ugly family heirloom, kidnaps Carol, ties up the children and jets off to Hawai'i, where he tries to sell the antique for millions of dollars to a dealer. Mike packs the family up and heads off in pursuit. En route the children perform a musical number on the plane to the Islands, where they arrive safely and foil Roy's caper.

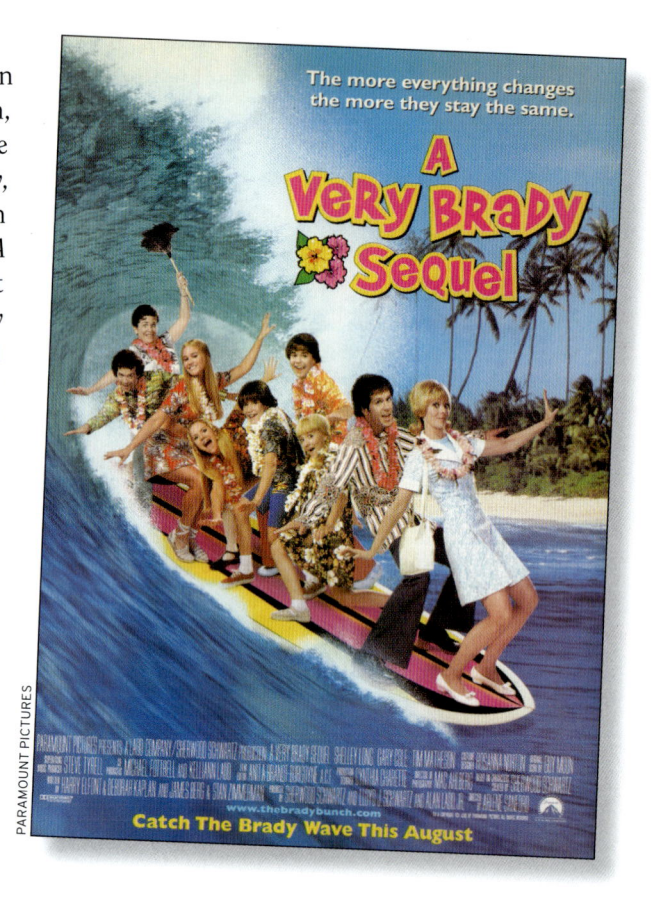

Producer Sherwood Schwartz also created the popular television series *Gilligan's Island* (1964-1967); its pilot episode was filmed on Kaua'i and O'ahu.

Poster for the Paramount Pictures movie *A Very Brady Sequel* featured Island motifs and the family riding a surfboard in this comedy.

Made in Paradise

The Lost World: Jurassic Park II
1997 Universal

DIRECTED BY **Steven Spielberg**
SCREENPLAY BY **Daniel Koepp**
PRODUCED BY **Kathleen Kennedy**
CAST **Jeff Goldblum (Ian Malcolm), Julianne Moore (Sarah Harding), Pete Postlewaite (Richard Tembo), Arliss Howard (Peter Ludlow), Richard Attenborough (John Howard), Vince Vaughn (Nick Van Owen), Thomas Rosales Jr. (Carter)**

Recounting events on a Costa Rican Island, something has survived on Isla Sorna, a second isle known as Site B where the dinosaurs are thriving. Hammond is well aware of the commercial potential in Site B, while Ian Malcolm realizes that his girlfriend is alone there, and he must rescue her.

For the film's opening sequences, Spielberg returned to Kaua'i where he'd previously shot portions of *Jurassic Park* and *Raiders of the Lost Ark*. While Eureka, California, and Hawai'i provided the Isla Sorna exteriors, most of the film was shot in Southern California at Universal Studios sound stages and backlot.

The Lost World: Jurassic Park II earned an Academy Award® nomination for Best Visual Effects.

Steven Spielberg directs Sam Neill in *The Lost World*.

Far left photo, left to right: Ian Malcolm (Jeff Goldblum), Kelly (Vanessa Lee Chester), Nick (Vince Vaughn), Sarah (Julianne Moore) and Eddie (Richard Schiff) carefully plan their next move after discovering that they are not the only people on Site B.

Four years after dinosaurs broke loose at Jurassic Park, Ian Malcolm (Jeff Goldblum, *third from the left*), along with, *left to right*, Eddie (Richard Schiff), Sarah (Julianne Moore) and Nick (Vince Vaughn) explore reports that "something has survived" on another island.

Made in Paradise

Walt Disney Pictures live-action updating of the popular comedy cartoon series *George of the Jungle*, Brendan Fraser stars in the title role, and Leslie Mann is his beautiful friend Ursula.

George (Fraser) and Ursula (Mann) ride through the jungle on George's lovable pet elephant Shep in *George of the Jungle*.

George of the Jungle
1997 Walt Disney

DIRECTED BY	**Sam Weisman**
SCREENPLAY BY	**Dana Olsen, Aubrey Wells**
PRODUCED BY	**David Hoberman, Jordan Kerner, Jon Avnet**
CAST	**Brendan Fraser (George), John Cleese (voice of Ape), Leslie Mann (Ursula), Thomas Haden Church (Lyle Van de Groot)**

Jay Ward's groovy "cooltoon" of the 1960s, a cartoon takeoff on the Tarzan character, inspired *George of the Jungle*. The movie version tells the story of George (Fraser), an earnest young man brought up in the jungle with a propensity for swinging from vines and smacking, face first, into trees. When George valiantly saves beautiful San Francisco socialite Ursula (Mann) from the clutches of a fierce lion, he falls head over heels in love with her, despite Ursula's not-so-thrilled and utterly ruthless fiancé, Lyle (Church). George and Ursula head for the comforts of modern life, leaving behind George's closest friends, a noble gorilla cleverly named Ape (Clese); Shep, an elephant who frolics through the jungle like a puppy dog; and Tookie Tookie Bird, a wise and eagle-eyed Toucan. But things are amiss in the jungle, and George returns to his tree-top abode to fight off loathsome poachers and save his lifelong buddies. In the end, George finds that love conquers all and regains his rightful position as king of the jungle.

George of the Jungle is a wacky, heartfelt comedy that works from beginning to end, with an engaging cast led by Brendan Fraser, loaded with laughs, action, and romance. The beloved and timeless theme song recognized by the pounding of its very first drum—"George, George, George of the Jungle, watch out for that tree!"—is used extensively and sets the tone for the film.

One of the best effects in the feature is *George's* jungle settings. While some of the movie was shot at Kualoa Ranch on Oʻahu, Hawaiʻi, many months were spent on a jungle set inside an enormous Hughes Aircraft facility in California that became George's jungle home.

Made in Paradise

Mighty Joe Young
1998 Walt Disney Pictures, RKO Pictures

DIRECTED BY	**Ron Underwood**
SCREENPLAY BY	**Merian C. Cooper, Ruth Rose, Mark Rosenthal, Lawrence Konner**
PRODUCED BY	**Gail Katz, Ted Hartley, Tom Jacobson**
CAST	**Charlize Theron (Jill Young), Bill Paxton (Gregory O'Hara), Rade Serbedzija (Andre Strasser), Peter Firth (Garth), Regina King (Cecily Banks), David Paymer (Harry Ruben)**

Mighty Joe Young is a rip-roaring adventure yarn in the classic Hollywood tradition—and it's no wonder, considering *Mighty's* motion picture pedigree. This exciting 1998 version is a remake of the 1949 original of the same name, in which the iconic John Ford served as executive producer, Merian C. Cooper wrote and produced and Ernest B. Schoedsack directed (his wife Ruth Rose co-wrote the script).

> *Mighty Joe Young* was nominated in the Best Effects, Visual Effects Oscar® category.

Tinseltown often remakes popular movies to cash in on established brand names, which enables recycled titles to standout in a crowded media marketplace. However, half a century of advances in film technology from the late 1940s to the late 1990s justifies a *hana hou* for *Mighty Joe Young*. The black and white (with a few sepia-tone sequences) original deservedly won a Special Effects Academy Award® for the 1949 movie, which used stop-motion animation by *King Kong's* venerable Willis O'Brien (assisted by Ray Harryhausen) and a model crafted by Marcel Delgado, who'd previously built *King Kong*. But by 1998, special effects had dramatically evolved, with computer-generated imagery, Industrial Light & Magic, Dream Quest Images, makeup artist Rick Baker (who reportedly made full-scale animatronic puppets and a man-sized costume for Joe) plus an army of artistes making movie miracles. According to the Visual Effects Headquarters (VFX-HQ.com), "*Mighty Joe Young* features some of the most advanced character animation and computer generated hair ever made."

In addition to a more realistically rendered cinematic simian, another *raison* d'etre for giving *Mighty Joe Young* a re-makeover was—like the subsequent 1976 *King Kong* remake—shooting on location in Hawai'i. The first scenic shot in *Mighty* is of Ka'a'awa Valley, which here doubles for Africa (in particular probably Botswana, a landlocked nation in the continent's southern end). As the movie opens, Dr. Ruth Young (Linda Purl) and her daughter, Jill (portrayed as a child by Mika Boreem), observe Joe, as a baby gorilla, climbing a pandanus tree amidst other gorillas. After around forty minutes, the movie—shot largely near Kualoa Ranch in an O'ahu doubling as "deepest, darkest" Africa—jump cuts to southern California.

Near the end of the film, our hero Joe returns to Africa—or rather to Ka'a'awa Valley—to live happily ever after (it is a Disney picture after all!) in the newly founded "Joe Young Wildlife Park." Joe romps around his Kualoa Ranch stomping grounds as the camera pans, revealing the Ko'olau Mountains' exquisite peaks, and the credits roll, bringing the curtain down on a highly entertaining motion-picture experience.

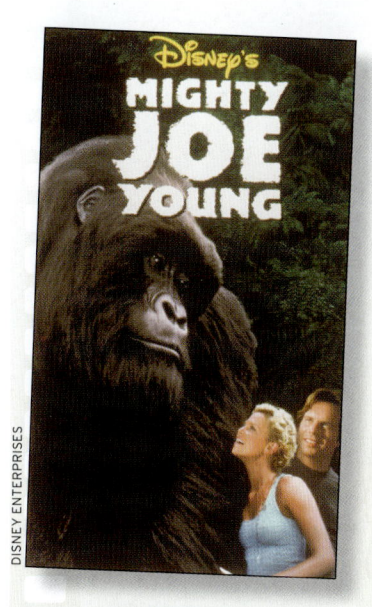

Mighty Joe Young, an enormous, heroic gorilla, joins his friends Jill (Charlize Theron) and Zoologist Gregg O'Hara (Bill Paxton) in *Mighty Joe Young*.

Beautiful and talented Charlize Theron is another future Oscar®-winning actress—who like Jessica Lange with *King Kong*—also got her career start in the hands of a great ape in *Mighty Joe Young*.

Made in Paradise

In God's Hands
1998 Sony

DIRECTED BY	**Zalman King**
SCREENPLAY BY	**Zalman King and Matt George**
PRODUCED BY	**Tom Stern**
CAST	**Patrick Shane Dorian (Shane), Matt George (Mickey), Matty Liu (Keoni)**

Three surfer friends search the world for the perfect wave, from Madagascar to Bali, from Mexico to Hawai'i. During their search, one surfer falls in love with a local girl, another gets killed, and the other seeks to ride that ultimate perfect wave. Real-life surfing champions played the characters in the film. A segment was filmed at Jaws Beach on Maui for this movie with magnificent surf cinematography by John Aronson.

Six Days Seven Nights
1998 Touchstone Pictures

DIRECTED BY	**Ivan Reitman**
SCREENPLAY BY	**Michael Browning**
PRODUCED BY	**Ivan Reitman, Roger Birnbaum, Wallis Nicita**
CAST	**Harrison Ford (Quinn Harris), Anne Heche (Robin Monroe), David Schwimmer (Frank Martin), Temuera Morrison (Jager), Cliff Curtis (Kip), Jacqueline Obradors (Angelica)**

Six Days Seven Nights is, at best, a mildly amusing big-budget production with lots of Garden Isle eye candy due to its Kaua'i location shooting, doubling for French Polynesia.

In the movie, Robin works as *Dazzle* magazine's assistant editor, and her boyfriend Frank Martin (David Schwimmer) works as a stockbroker. The two hustling and bustling Manhattanites lead hectic lives that leave little room for romance, so at a Trader Vic's type of South Seas-themed restaurant called the Blue Lagoon, Frank surprises Robin with tickets to a tropical vacation in the Tahitian Islands for—you guessed it—six days and seven nights (although countless caricatures ensue). There, in a resort with bamboo-thatched huts on Makatea, the Wall Streeter plans to propose marriage.

To get from Tahiti to Makatea, the urbanites charter a propeller-driven de Havilland Beaver flown by Quinn (Harrison Ford), an irreverent pilot and beachcomber. His past includes a heartbreak that lead to the successful businessman relocating to the South Pacific to "simplify" his life. The earthy Quinn and sophisticated, citified Robin clash—and then crash, when the driven career woman must leave the resort, unexpectedly,

Harrison Ford and Anne Heche are the stars of the romantic adventure comedy Six Days Seven Nights *filmed on Kaua'i doubling for Tahiti. Kaua'i had doubled for Tahiti previously n 1951 for MGM's* Pagan Love Song.

Robin Monroe (Heche, left) has planned a relaxing holiday in a tropical wonderland. However, her itinerary changes, and she reluctantly becomes a passenger on Quinn Harris's (Ford, center) dilapidated cargo plane.

Made in Paradise

and make an urgent flight back from Makatea to Tahiti for a last-minute photo shoot (Pacific shipwrecks and plane crashes go as far back as Daniel Defoe's 1719 *Robinson Crusoe* and Dorothy Lamour's first movies, 1936's *The Jungle Princess* and 1938's *Her Jungle Love*). There the marooned antagonists return to nature and somehow find time to fall in love—in between fending off murderous pirates.

Ghostbusters' Ivan Reitman directed this completely derivative, cartoonish plane wreck of a movie, with some lovely location shots of Kauaʻi standing in for French Polynesia. Popcorn munchers may find *Six Days Seven Nights* entertaining.

And oh yeah—that snake Quinn snatches from Robin's panties? There are no snakes in the Tahitian Islands. Or Kauaʻi. Or anywhere in Polynesia, for that matter.

Harrison Ford and Anne Heche survive a crash landing on a desert island in *Six Days Seven Nights*.

Harrison Ford goes over a waterfall in *Six Days Seven Nights*.

Beyond Paradise
1998 Pray For Rain Pictures

DIRECTED BY	**David Cunningham**
SCREENPLAY BY	**David Cunningham, David Walker**
PRODUCED BY	**David Cunningham, Anthony Bozanich**
CAST	**Roy Newton (Mark), Priscilla Basque (Lehua), Darryl Bonilla (Keao), Lorenzo Callendar (Ronnie Roy), Kalani Nakoa (Zulu)**

Once Were Warriors, the powerful, hard-hitting New Zealand 1994 drama about domestic abuse among Maoris, was so successful that it inspired other indigenous and island societies around the world to re-examine their preconceived paradisiacal stereotypes in a cycle of features. These range from the 1997 Jamaica-set *Dancehall Queen* to Andrew Okpeaha MacLean's

David Cunningham (Director, left) and Graham Driscoll (Director of Photography, right) discuss a scene from *Beyond Paradise*, a story of stunning beauty and violent contrasts.

Made in Paradise

After proving himself, Mark (Roy Newton, center) earns the respect and friendship of three local surfers, Keao (Daryl Bonilla, left), Ronnie Boy (Lorenzo Callender, second from left), and Zulu (Kalani, right). Beautiful Lehua (Priscilla Basque, second from right) also befriends Mark and introduces him to a Hawai'i much different from the picture-perfect paradise.

Beautiful Lehua (Priscilla Basque) befriends Mark in *Beyond Paradise*. The newborn friendship, however, is tested by the choices she has made in the past.

2011 Alaska-set *On the Ice* about Inupiaqs (the film's credits tellingly mention the late Maori moviemaker Merata Mita). Inevitably, this cinematic trend would reach the shores of Hawai'i with 1998's *Beyond Paradise,* which candidly depicts domestic violence, substance abuse, racial problems, and teen pregnancy at the Big Island, where the movie was shot with a local cast and crew.

Director David Cunningham says *Beyond Paradise* "was absolutely influenced by *Warriors*. I felt how that film rocked a nation. It's definitely an inspiration." Cunningham was born in Switzerland, but moved to the Big Island at age four after his missionary parents established a campus of the University of the Nations at Kona. Not surprisingly, *Beyond Paradise's* lead character reflects the coming-of-age experiences of Cunningham, who shares writing credits with David Walker. The movie has the age-old South Seas Cinema theme of the Westerner encountering an "exotic" culture and, of course, a sexy wahine.

Made in Paradise

Godzilla
1998 TriStar

DIRECTED BY **Roland Emmerich**
SCREENPLAY BY **Dean Devlin and Roland Emmerich**
PRODUCED BY **Dean Devlin and Roland Emmerich**
CAST **Matthew Broderick (Dr. Niko Tatopoulos), Jean Reno (Philippe Roaché), Hank Azaria (Victor 'Animal' Palotti), Michael Lerner (Mayor Ebert), Harry Shearer (Charles Caiman), Nancy Cartwright (Caiman's Secretary), Bodhi Elfman (Freddie), Maria Pitillo, and Godzilla (creature vocals by Gary Hecker and Frank Welker)**

Just as 1995's *Waterworld* serves as a cautionary tale about climate change, *Godzilla* ominously warns against nuclear weapons. Japan's Toho Studios produced the first of these modern day dinosaur-like creature films directed by Ishirô Honda (who went on to helm 1956's *Rodan*, various *Godzilla* sequels and other monster movies) in 1954, and to date the 1998 version is the most explicitly anti-nuke picture in the franchise.

Onlookers flock to the site of a demolished ship to witness the terrifying results of Godzilla's wrath.

Godzilla takes place sometime after 1986 as the Chernobyl nuclear power plant meltdown in the Ukraine figures into its plot. The Nuclear Regulatory Commission reassigns Dr. Niko Tatopoulos (Matthew Broderick), who is studying the DNA of irradiated earthworms at Chernobyl. As an expert researching what he calls "mutated aberration hybrids created by fallout from nuclear tests," Dr. Tatopoulos investigates a strange phenomenon that has emerged in the wake of the aforementioned N-blast at Moruroa, which has been making its way across the Pacific Ocean to Panama and Jamaica.

The scene where Godzilla's gigantic footprints are discovered were actually shot not in Central America or the Caribbean, but at Oʻahu's Kaʻaʻawa Valley. The oversized gecko's paw mark can still be seen on tours at Kualoa Ranch, "Hawaiʻi-wood's" backlot.

Godzilla's huge footprints trace an ominous path as he journeys undeterred across the globe in the TriStar Pictures presentation, *Godzilla*. The footprints can still be seen on a tour at Kualoa Ranch.

Made in Paradise 77

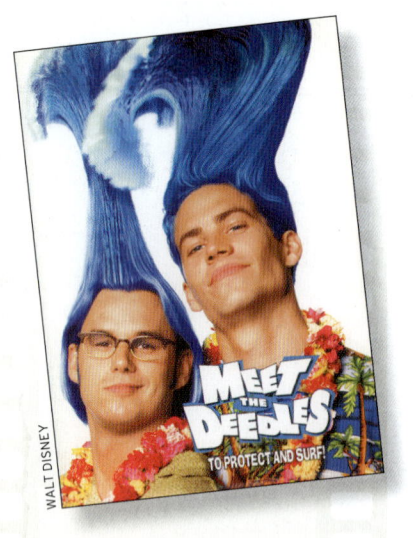

Meet the Deedles
1998 Walt Disney

DIRECTED BY	**Steve Boyum**
SCREENPLAY BY	**Jim Herzfeld**
PRODUCED BY	**Dale Pollock, Aaron Meyerson**
CAST	**Steve Van Wormer (Steve Deedle), Paul Walker (Phil Deedle), A.J. Langer (Jesse Ryan), John Ashton (Capt. Douglas Pine), Dennis Hopper (Frank Slater), Eric Braeden (Elton Deedle)**

In this action comedy, spoiled rich teenaged surfer brothers from Hawaiʻi have to leave the Islands and go to the mainland. They find themselves in Yellowstone National Park, Wyoming, and must circumvent the plans of a deranged park ranger bent on revenge to save the Old Faithful geyser. In most films, the protagonists are usually trying to get to Hawaiʻi. But this one moves in reverse, starting off in paradise, and most of the story takes place on the mainland.

Deedles had four days of location shooting in Oʻahu, including one day at the Paul Mitchell estate and three days of stunt work at Waikīkī harbor.

Krippendorf's Tribe
1998 Touchstone

DIRECTED BY	**Todd Holland**
SCREENPLAY BY	**Charlie Peters based on the novel by Frank Parkin**
PRODUCED BY	**Larry Brezner**
CAST	**Richard Dreyfuss (James Krippendorf), Jenna Elfman (Veronica Micelli), Lily Tomlin (Ruth Allen)**

Krippendorf's Tribe is the story of James Krippendorf, an anthropologist who, for the last two years, has been living off of a grant to study an "undiscovered" tribe in Papua New Guinea. With no tribe in evidence and all of the money spent on raising his dysfunctional children, James is shocked to learn that the grant requires filmed proof of the tribe's existence. Out of desperation, he uses the only "primitive" group he knows—his family! With the help of his opportunistic colleague Veronica Micelli (Elfman), James sets out to pull off the anthropological scam of the century. *Krippendorf's Tribe* is a mildly amusing comedy that has its moments, although its story premise is very farfetched and unbelievable as it spoofs those ethno-reels previously referred to.

The movie was primarily filmed at Kualoa Ranch on Oʻahu.

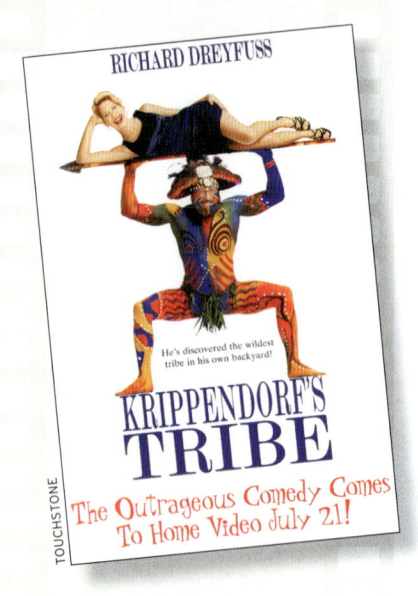

Made in Paradise

Lani Loa
1998 Chrome Dragon Films

DIRECTED BY **Sherwood Hu**
SCREENPLAY BY **John Marsh**
PRODUCED BY **Francis Ford Coppola, Wayne Wang, Sherwood Hu**
CAST **Ray Bumatai (Hawaiian Kenny), Angus Macfadyen (Turner), Leo Akana (Auntie Wana), Chris Tashima (Bong), Carlotta Chang (Jenny), Kamaka Mahoe (Joe), Shawn Kui Lee Ibarra (Sonny), Zachary Kapule (Sonny's Dad), Ponchoman Kuanoni (Big Hawaiian), Sherwood Hu (Waiter)**

Despite the fact that *Lani Loa* had some heavy hitters behind it, sadly this Hilo and Asia shot feature didn't take off; perhaps its subject matter was too esoteric. In any case, *Lani Loa* is an especially interesting movie, because it's an exceedingly rare fiction film that has a Hawaiian Sovereignty subtext. The cast includes Kanaka Maolis, in particular the late great Ray Bumatai as Hawaiian Kenny and actress and composer Leo Akana as Auntie Wana (Akana is noted for portraying Queen Liliʻuokalani in productions such as 2009's *Princess Kaʻiulani*).

Lani Loa's native rights theme is mixed with crime, supernatural, and Asian elements. Turner (Angus Macfadyen) is a local haole policeman whose wedding day is ruined when, en route to the ceremony, he foils a bank robbery in process. Turner chases the criminals, who are led by Bong (Chris Tashima). They lead Turner to the farm where the nuptials were supposed to take place. The robbers almost rape his fiancée Jenny (Carlotta Chang), who is murdered in the ensuing shootout that also slaughters the wedding guests. After the ordeal, police captain Hawaiian Kenny (Bumatai) advises Turner to take a vacation; instead, he investigates and pursues the killers of Jenny. Her ghost appears to wreak vengeance on the villains in this movie made on location at the Big Island and China.

Francis Ford Coppola served as the executive producer and was also the director of the 1970s' classics *The Godfather* and the Vietnam-set, Philippines-shot *Apocalypse Now*. Among others, Hong Kong-born producer Wayne Wang directed the 1982 cult-hit *Chan Is Missing*, 1993's *The Joy Luck Club,* and 1997's *Chinese Box* with Jeremy Irons Li Gong and Maggie Cheung, based on a Paul Theroux story. According to Wikipedia, *Lani Loa* "was the first film from Coppola's and Wayne Wang's Chrome Dragon Films, a short-lived film company that was to specialize in utilizing Asian talent on American-financed projects." Unfortunately, it was not to be. *Lani Loa* appears to be the company's sole project to be made. Although probably never theatrically released in the U.S.A., the movie was screened at Spain's San Sebastian Film Festival and the Hawaiʻi International Film Festival and released on VCD in Asia.

Wind on Water
1998 NBC

DIRECTED BY **Zalman King (with Matt George)**
PRODUCED BY **Zalman King (with Matt George)**
WRITTEN BY **Zalman King (with Matt George)**
CAST **Bo Derek (Ciel Connolly), William Gregory Lee (Cole Connolly), Brian Gross (Kelly Connolly), Lee Horsley (Gardner Poole)**

This short-lived Hawai'i-set drama series emphasizing extreme sports lasted only four episodes. In *Wind On Water*, Cole (William Gregory Lee) and Kelly Connolly (Brian Gross), world-class surfers and skiers, help run the family's struggling cattle ranch on the Big Island while hitting the extreme sports circuit to raise money. Val Poole (Shawn Christian) is their rival in surf competitions. Val's father, Gardner Poole (Lee Horsley), is the Connolly's wealthiest neighbor and determined to seize their ranch for a planned development. Gardner has two adversaries to his plan, strong-willed Ciel Connolly (Bo Derek, who'd co-starred in 1979's *Ten*, wherein Hawai'i doubled for Mexico), who is Cole and Kelly's mother, and Katie Jacinda Barrett, Gardner's defiant young daughter.

Zalman King created and produced the show and produced and directed an acclaimed surfing film, *In God's Hands* (1998), earlier that year. *Wind On Water* was filmed almost entirely in the northwest part of the Big Island, except for some surfing scenes shot on O'ahu's North Shore.

The cast of *Wind on Water*. *Left:* Lee Horsely is Gardner Poole. *Right:* The beautiful Bo Derek is Ciel Connolly. Derek played the beautiful girl who drove Dudley Moore crazy in 1979's *Ten*, where in selected scenes Hawai'i stood in for Mexico.

Made in Paradise

Fantasy Island
1998–1999 ABC

EXEC. PRODUCERS **Barry Sonnefeld, Andrew Schneider**

CAST **Malcolm McDowell (Mr. Roarke), Fyvush Finkel (Fisher), Louis Lombardi (Cal)**

A darker, more sinister, and twisted remake of the original (1977-1984) ABC series *Fantasy Island* (the original starred the elegant Ricardo Montalban as the mysterious but charming Mr. Roarke and Hervé Villachaize as his diminutive assistant Tattoo). In this remake, the lead from Stanley Kubrick's 1971 *A Clockwork Orange,* Malcolm McDowell, portrays Mr. Roarke, who has the power (via special effects) to make the *Fantasy Island* guests' wishes come true—but in ways they might not have expected. For this updated version, nothing short of a real-island setting would do, and Maui and Kualoa Ranch on Oʻahu became the central locations for the short-lived series.

The original *Fantasy Island* series used second-unit footage of Kauaʻi's Wailua Falls and Nā Pali Coast. Exterior shots and two episodes were filmed on Kauaʻi. Numerous stock shots, backgrounds, and inserts of Hawaiʻi were used in most episodes through the life of the series. The series was primarily filmed at the Los Angeles County Arboretum and the Burbank studios.

Malcolm McDowell (who starred in Stanley Kubrick's feature film *A Clockwork Orange*) is Mr. Roarke who awaits his *Fantasy Island* guest in this updated version of the classic television series *Fantasy Island.* Roarke is aided by Edward Hibbert (left) and Louie Lombardo (center).

Ricardo Montalban as Mr. Roarke and Herve Villechaize as Tatoo in the original *Fantasy Island* series.

Made in Paradise 81

Moloka'i:
The Story of Father Damien
1999 In Motion

DIRECTED BY	**Paul Cox**
SCREENPLAY BY	**John Briley**
PRODUCED BY	**Tharsi Vanhuysse, Grietje Lammertyn**
CAST	**David Wenham (Father Damien), Peter O'Toole (William Williamson), Kris Kristofferson (Rudolph Meyer), Sam Neill (Walter Murray Gibson), Derek Jacobi (Father Leonor Fousnel), Leo McKern (Bishop Maigret), Michael W. Perry (Royal Physician George Philippe Trousseau)**

David Wenham as Father Damien comforts a patient stricken with Hansen's disease.

The saga of Father Damien, the legendary nineteenth-century Belgian priest who sacrificed himself to minister to the "Leper Colony" on Moloka'i, has been turned into a courageous and beautiful biopic that elevates the human spirit with its unflinching portrayal of love and human suffering.

To tell this extraordinary story, Dutch-Australian director Paul Cox assembled a distinguished international cast featuring Kris Kristofferson, Sam Neill, Derek Jacobi, Leo McKern, and Peter O'Toole. The English-language production stars Australian actor David Wenham in the title role, who believably performs as Father Damien, conveying vision, zeal, and human frailty. John Briley developed the screenplay, as his literary specialty is depicting actual historical personages of people of conscience and consciousness. Briley earned an Academy Award® for writing 1982's *Ghandi* (for which Ben Kingsley won a Best Actor Oscar®) and also wrote the script for 1987's *Cry Freedom*, co-starring Denzel Washington as the anti-apartheid activist Steve Biko.

The film begins in 1872 when Hawai'i is still a Kingdom. Prime Minister Gibson (Neill), who governs the Kingdom, is more concerned with business and religious interests than the humane control of the disease. Church officials send Father Damien, a young Belgian priest who volunteers to establish a church presence and help the lepers, to Moloka'i. The Bishop (McKern) tells Father Damien to minister to the people, but naively warns him not to touch anyone, a clear physical impossibility. A young doctor accompanies Damien, but is so appalled by the conditions at the leper colony that he immediately leaves.

Damien asserts himself with the local authorities, a German rancher named Mayer (Kristofferson). In establishing a church, he asks for medical and building supplies and food. Damien respects the Native Hawaiian beliefs and at one point persuades then-Princess Lili'uokalani to visit the leper colony after his pleas for financial help have been ignored.

In one of the most moving scenes in the film, Princess Lili'uokalani, magnificently played by Australia-born Kate Ceberano, visits her people at the colony. Standing at the foot

Made in Paradise

of the makeshift hospital surrounded by the infirm, Her Royal Highness pledges her support and sings "Aloha Oe" to her stricken people. The singing symbolizes a cry from the heart illustrating the decimation of the indigenous people.

Keanu Kapuni Szasz plays Maulani, a beautiful, young island girl with the disease. She tempts the vulnerable Father Damien, but he ultimately rejects her advances. Peter O'Toole plays Williamson, a philosophical Englishman in the advanced stages of the disease, who Damien befriends upon his arrival. Norbert Palea plays the Islander Ute; popular Hawaiian singer Henry Kapono plays Mason; and Randy Fujimori plays the overseer Kahoʻohuli.

Director Paul Cox remarked in a press conference at the Toronto Film Festival, "This is the story of one man of extraordinary faith who goes out and spreads that faith and makes his life an act of love."

For more than a century, Father Damien has been a conscience of the Western World. In an era of mindless screen heroes and senseless violence, *Molokaʻi: The Story of Father Damien* serves as a cinematic testament to a true-life hero of amazing ideals. Pope Benedict XVI canonized Father Damien de Veuster and made him a saint in a ceremony at the Vatican on October 11, 2009.

Molokai: The Story of Father Damien was filmed on location on Molokaʻi where the story took place.

Too Rich: The Secret Life of Doris Duke
1999 CBS

DIRECTED BY	**John Erman**
TELEPLAY BY	**Dennis Turner, Ronni Kern**
PRODUCED BY	**John Erman, Richard Arredondo, Stephanie Germain, Randy Sutter**
CAST	**Lauren Bacall (Doris Duke 1970s to 1990s), Richard Chamberlain (Bernard Lafferty), Brian Stokes Mitchell (Duke Kahanamoku), Lindsay Frost (Doris Duke 1930s to 1950s), Kathleen Quinlan (Nanaline Duke), Brian Dennehy (Louis Bromfield), Mare Winningham (Chandi Heffner), Lindsay Frost (Doris Duke 1950s to 1970s), Michael Nouri (Porfirio Rubirosa), Joe Don Baker (Buck Duke), Lisa Banes (Barbara Hutton), Hayden Panettiere (Young Doris Duke), Ray Bumatai (Hawaiian Chef), Cynthia Yip (Hawaiian maid)**

This two-part, four-hour miniseries is based on biographies and magazine articles about the real-life tobacco heiress. *Too Rich* opens with Lauren Bacall (Humphrey Bogart's widow and a great actress) as the elderly Doris Duke nearing death. Her butler Bernard Lafferty

Made in Paradise

Lauren Bacall as Doris Duke and Richard Chamberlain as Bernard Lafferty in front of Aliʻiōlani Hale during the location filming in Hawaiʻi.

Broadway stage actor and singer Brian Stokes Mitchell plays legendary native Hawaiian Olympic swim champion and father of modern surfing, Duke Kahanamoku in *Too Rich: The Secret Life of Doris Duke*.

(Richard Chamberlain, who starred as TV's *Dr. Kildare* and the part-Hawaiian Dr. Daniel Kulani in the 1989-1990 Hawaiʻi-set television drama *Island Son*) is a scheming, manipulative boozer with possibly bad intentions. The biopic, which was originally broadcast in four parts, flashes back and reviews Doris' colorful, if tumultuous, life with two failed marriages and a number of affairs.

Part of the production was shot at Oʻahu, where Doris built her Arabic-style "Shangri La" mansion on 4.9 acres of primo real estate at Black Point with splendid views of Diamond Head and the Pacific Ocean. According to *Too Rich*, during the 1930s, one of Doris' rumored romances was with the Hawaiian Olympiad Duke Kahanamoku (Brian Stokes Mitchell). Duke reportedly taught Doris (played by Lindsay Frost) to surf; they fall for each other, and in the telepic, Duke impregnates her. In a lovely, picturesque scene with Mokoliʻi (Chinaman's Hat) at Kāneʻohe Bay in the background, Duke strolls down the beach with Doris supposedly carrying his baby. The Olympic champion cites the names of two black men who he says "looked like me" and were recently lynched on the U.S. mainland. "All they did, maybe, was admire a white woman. And now the kind of people who killed them are going to know that I've had sex with the richest white woman in the world," once word of Doris' pregnancy gets out.

Too Rich stirred controversy in Hawaiʻi. Some denied that Duke and Doris had a sexual relationship and that he made her pregnant. Some Hawaiians also disliked that a non-Hawaiian portrayed the iconic swimmer, surfer, and "Ambassador of Aloha." Stokes, who grew up in military bases in Guam and the Philippines, is of mixed ancestry and is reportedly German, Scottish, African, and Native American—but not Hawaiian.

In a March 2, 2007 *Honolulu Advertiser* piece by veteran entertainment reporter Wayne Harada, Stokes is quoted as saying, "'I heard about (the controversy), on my first day of filming, when I was getting out of the shower, hearing my name on the radio,' he recalled. 'People wanted to talk to me; I think it was Brickwood (Galuteria, who was a morning radio jockey), and for me, the problem was with a lack of understanding about what was going on... It was an honor for me to play him, and I wanted to honor his

84   Made in Paradise

spirit. There's much value in people keeping their own folklore in their own image, their own language; they will guard and protect this, and I respect that.'"

According to a Jan. 17, 1999 article in *Variety* by Tim Ryan, *Too Rich* had a scheduled shoot of nine days in Oʻahu. During the miniseries' Hawaiʻi segment, sumptuous shots featured surging surf and banyan, pandanus and palm trees. However, Ryan notes, "The Von Zerneck-Sertner Films production is not shooting at Duke's 5.5-acre, $50 million-plus Diamond Head estate known as Shangri La, but instead at a nearby rented mansion."

Shangri La's Islamic architecture was inspired by Doris Duke's ten-month-long, 1935 honeymoon in North Africa, the Middle East, Central Asia, India, and Indonesia. A partnership between the Honolulu Museum of Art and the Doris Duke Foundation of Islamic Art provides guided tours to Hawaiʻi's version of *Citizen Kane's* Xanadu.

Other locations in *Too Rich*, of which there is a 192-minute version, include Los Angeles (Duke's Falcon's Lair estate—once owned by silent-film star Rudolph Valentino—in Beverly Hills), Montreal, and Bora Bora, French Polynesia. A cheat shot that is supposed to be Oʻahu shows the twin peaks of Mount Otemanu and Mount Pahia.

Brian Stokes Mitchell as Duke Kahanamoku and Lindsay Frost as the young Doris Duke on the beach at Waikīkī.

Johnny Tsunami
1999 Disney Channel

DIRECTED BY	**Steve Boyum**
TELEPLAY BY	**Ann Knapp, Douglas Snow**
PRODUCED BY	**David Portland, Douglas Sloan, Gerald T. Olsen, Harlan Freeman**
CAST	**Brandon Baker (Johnny Kapahala), Cary-Hiroyuki Tagawa (Johnny Tsunami), Ray Bumatai (Mike)**

A Disney Channel movie starring Brandon Baker as thirteen-year-old Johnny Kapahala, who has two great loves—surfing and his grandfather, surfing legend Johnny Tsunami, played by Cary-Hiroyuki Tagawa. When his father lands a job at a Vermont school, Johnny has to go to the Green Mountain State, where he finds himself out of place. Unhappy there, he sneaks back to Hawaiʻi on a cargo plane. But his grandfather tells Johnny he must go back, face his fears, and learn to adapt to the situation.

Johnny returns to Vermont and enters a snowboarding competition, where his surf skills serve him well.

Filmed on location, this movie gives a rare, modern Disney glimpse at local Hawaiʻi characters. This made-for-TV movie also shows a tender and heartwarming relationship between Johnny and his grandfather.

Made in Paradise

Baywatch Hawaii
1999-2000 Pearson Television

EXEC. PRODUCER **Gregory J. Bonann**

CREATED BY **Gregory J. Bonann**

CAST **David Hasselhoff (Mitch Buchannon), Jason Brooks (Sean Monroe), Brandy Ledford (Dawn Masterton), Michael Bergin (J.D. Darius), Brooke Burns (Jessie Owens), Jason Momoa (Jason Ioane), Simmone Mackinnon (Allie Reese), Stacy Lee Kamano (Kekoa Tanaka)**

Headquartered on Oʻahu's scenic North Shore, the *Baywatch Hawaii* team must be ready to respond to any call that leads them to dramatic rescues throughout the Islands. From Kauaʻi's rugged mountainous terrain to Maui's monstrous waves and the daunting dangers of the Big Island's active volcanoes, the lifeguards must face the biggest obstacles of their careers. As season nine opens, Lt. Mitch Buchannon (David Hasselhoff) dreams of opening an international lifeguard training center, where the best lifeguards from around the world can exchange ideas and techniques. To achieve his goal, he will have to face overwhelming barriers, find the resources to finance it and equipment and manpower to run it and attain the cooperation of Hawaiʻi residents. New cast members include Hawaiʻi actress Stacy Lee Kamano as Kekoa Tanaka, a competitive lifeguard who knows the local terrain and pushes herself to the limit. Honolulu-born Jason Momoa (Khal Drogo in HBO's *Game of Thrones* series) plays the team's prodigy, Jason Ioane, who returns to his birthplace for the first time to deal with his lost heritage and fulfill his destiny as an ocean man.

Baywatch debuted on NBC in 1989. Though it enjoyed good ratings, the network cancelled the series after only one season. Undeterred, Hasselhoff and his partners acquired the rights to the show and—based on Hasselhoff's popularity overseas (due to the previous series *Knight Rider* and a recording career)—they were able to secure financing and revive *Baywatch* in 1991. In its tenth year of production, the show enjoyed continued success with its switch from a Southern California locale to the Aloha State as *Baywatch Hawaii*. During the height of its popularity, over one billion viewers in 140 countries watched *Baywatch* each week.

The cast of Pearson Television's *Baywatch Hawaii* includes *(left to right)*: Stacy Lee Kamano (Kekoa Tanaka), Jason Brooks (Sean Monroe), Brandy Ledford (Dawn Masterton), David Hasselhoff (Lt. Mitch Buchannon), Brooke Burns (Jessica "Jessie" Owens), Michael Bergin (Jack "JD" Darius), Simmone Mackinnon (Allie Reese), Jason Momoa (Jason).

Made in Paradise

Paniolo O Hawai'i—Cowboys of the Far West

2000 Filmworks Pacific

DIRECTED BY	**Edgy Lee**
PRODUCED BY	**Edgy Lee**
SCREENPLAY BY	**Paul Berry, Edgy Lee**
CAST	**Kindy Sproat, Sonny Keakealani, Jiro Yamaguchi, John Lake, Willie Nelson, Will Rogers**

Long before those riders of the purple sage rode the range in continental America's wild, wild West cowboys roped cattle and busted broncos in the Kingdom of Hawai'i. Edgy Lee sets the record straight in *Paniolo O Hawai'i—Cowboys of the Far West*, revealing the hidden history of those indigenous cowboys who were also, in a sense, "Indians." The beautifully shot seventy-nine-minute documentary traces Paniolo heritage, which goes back to the 1790s—when British explorer Captain George Vancouver gave Hawaiian royalty Mexican longhorns—and continues to today. Narrated by Country Western singer Willie Nelson, John Lake and others, with archival footage shot by a Thomas Edison camera crew and of Will Rogers in Hawai'i, plus lots of actuality of and interviews with contemporary Hawaiian cowboys, *Paniolo* has an elegiac tone and won two Chicago International Film Festival Silver Awards. Like *The Descendants*, *Paniolo's* soundtrack includes hauntingly lovely Hawaiian songs; a companion CD, *Na Mele O Paniolo*, was released by Warner Reprise with music by Sonny Lim, Clyde "Kindy" Sproat, Sonny Chillingworth, Leabert Lindsey, Michael Martin Murphy and Ledward Ka'apana. From 2002-2003 *Paniolo* aired on National Geographic Worldwide Channels.

Edgy Lee

After working for years in the entertainment industry in Los Angeles, Edgy Lee returned with her finely honed artistic expertise to O'ahu, where she was born, raised and attended Punahou, and established FilmWorks Pacific. This production company produces Hawai'i-themed and based documentaries. In 1998's *Papakolea—A Story of Hawaiian Land*—produced with Academy Award®-winning cinematographer Haskell Wexler and Emmy® Award-winning documentary writer and producer Saul Landau—director/co-writer Lee examines Honolulu's only community where the federal government set land aside for Native Hawaiians under the 1920 Hawaiian Homes Commission Act. Lee's 2001 *Waikīkī—In the Wake of Dreams* traces the evolution of Hawai'i's most famous tourist destination and has a companion coffee table type book. 2006's *The Hawaiians—Reflecting Spirit* is a moving look at the Aloha State's indigenous inhabitants, focusing on sovereignty and self-determination issues: land, water, culture, political and religion rights. From 2003-2006 FilmWorks Pacific produced two chronicles hosted by investigative reporter Matt Levi about the crystal meth "ice" crisis in the 50th State. FilmWorks Pacific also launched Pacific Network, a Hawai'i and Oceania-themed Internet television network.

Back in the day Lee, who is of half-Chinese ancestry, was cast as "Miss Chun King" and, as a traditionally costumed representative of that prepared canned food company, appeared on NBC-TV's *The Tonight Show,* charming host Johnny Carson and sidekick Ed McMahon. Lee—whose nonfiction films have been broadcast in Hawai'i and screened at prestigious venues such as Washington's Smithsonian Museum of the American Indian and the L.A.-based Autry National Center, a museum dedicated to the American West founded by the silver screen's "singing cowboy," Gene Autry—is arguably Hawai'i's greatest non-indigenous local filmmaker. As of this writing Lee is working on a documentary called *Sandalwood Mountain—A Cautionary Tale*.

In December 2014 KGMB and KHNL broadcast Lee's documentary *Unprescribed—Prescription for Addiction,* which provided a Hawai'i angle on the nationwide epidemic of pharmaceutical drug abuse.

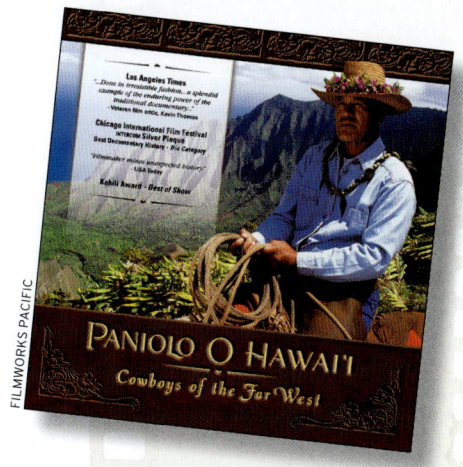

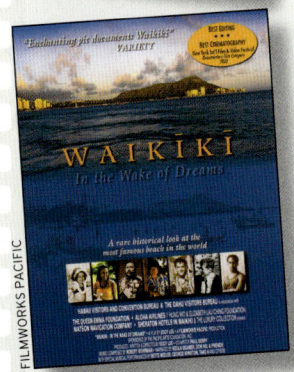

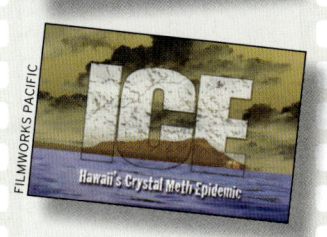

Made in Paradise

Pearl Harbor
2001 Touchstone

DIRECTED BY **Michael Bay**
SCREENPLAY BY **Randall Wallace**
PRODUCED BY **Jerry Bruckheimer**
CAST **Ben Affleck (Rafe McCawley), Josh Hartnett (Danny Walker), Kate Beckinsale (Evelyn Johnson), Jon Voight (Pres. Roosevelt), Alec Baldwin (Lt. Col. Jimmy Doolittle), Cary-Hiroyuki Tagawa (Cmdr. Minoru Genda), Mako (Adm. Isoroku Yamamoto)**

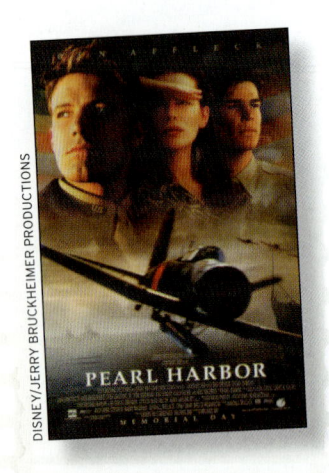

While enemy bombs rain down and destroy the U.S. Pacific fleet, daring young pilots Rafe McCawley (Affleck) and Danny Walker (Harnett) scramble to get airborne amidst the destruction of the attack on Pearl Harbor in the epic war drama *Pearl Harbor*.

Michael Bay directed *Pearl Harbor*, a big-budget blockbuster (which probably cost more to produce than Admiral Yamamoto's sneak attack cost to stage) on location in Hawai'i in 2000, with Randall Wallace (*Braveheart*) as his screenwriter. Bay framed the catastrophe with a creaky story about two daring young pilots who fall in love with the same girl. They land at Pearl Harbor just before that fateful day on December 7th, 1941.

The three-hour film contains three acts. The first act establishes the relationship of the two lifelong friends and their love of flying, as well as their mutual love for a nurse. Rafe goes to England to help the British, and Danny and Evelyn are sent to Pearl Harbor. The latter two find love in romantic Hawai'i when they believe Rafe has been killed in action. In this harebrained plot, Rafe surprisingly turns up at Pearl Harbor very much alive and well—complications ensue among the two best friends and their mutual love interest. The film's second act vividly recreates in great detail Imperial Japan's surprise attack on Pearl Harbor. The third act sees Rafe and Danny volunteering for the April 18, 1942 daring Doolittle Raid on Tokyo.

> *Pearl Harbor*'s Christopher Boyes and George Watters II won Oscars® for Best Sound Editing. The overblown epic was also nominated in three other Academy Award® categories: Best Visual Effects, Best Sound and Best Original Song.

Made in Paradise

Affleck's and Hartnett's characters were modeled in part on Lts. Kenneth Taylor and George Welch, who managed to fly their planes and shoot down Japanese planes during the attack. Cuba Gooding Jr. portrays real-life Dorrie Miller, an African-American sailor who—because of racial discrimination in the Navy at that time—was never allowed to receive weapons training, but valiantly grabs a machine gun and downs an enemy plane. Alec Baldwin plays the foulmouthed (talk about typecasting!) Lt. Col. Doolittle, who plans and then leads the retaliatory air raid on Japan.

Spectacularly staged, the attack on Pearl Harbor is very realistic, violent and hard edged in its detailed depiction of Japanese planes bombing and strafing American ships and personnel. The film contains scenes of ships exploding, rising out of the water and turned over on their side as men fall from the ships into water burning with oil. With gut-wrenching intensity, the film portrays nurses handling the burned and wounded armed services personnel being brought into the hospital and objectively presents obligatory shots of the ominous Japanese in the brief scenes leading up to the attack.

The film received mixed reviews. It got praise for its technical achievements, but also criticism for its weak storyline and performances by the young cast.

On Sunday April 2, 2000, in a special ceremony, producer Jerry Bruckheimer, director Michael Bay and the main members of the cast gathered at the USS *Arizona* Memorial to lay wreaths the day before the principal photography was to begin. The producers needed the cooperation of the Navy and Defense Department (DOD) to have access to the Navy's historic Ford Island and other military installations, many relatively unchanged since World War II.

According to *Pearl Harbor's* production notes, "The Oʻahu, Hawaiʻi portion of the massive 85 day shooting schedule took five weeks to complete. 60 local technicians were hired to work on the film alongside 200 crew members from Los Angeles. In addition, over 1,600 military enlistees and dependents were signed on as extras for the filming. Two of the movie's biggest scenes were filmed within the first few days, employing 12 Panavision cameras, 90 extras, and a 43 boat marine department. Special-effects coordinator John Frazier, a 40 year film veteran who worked on *Apocalypse Now* created the biggest explosions of his career. 14 vintage aircraft were used in the production to portray the Japanese Zeros and bombers in the air."

Filming also took place in England, Los Angeles, and Texas. The second act sequence of the sinking of the USS *Arizona* was completed at Fox studios, Rosarito, Mexico, in an exterior water tank also used for the filming of *Titanic*.

The world premiere of *Pearl Harbor* took place in Pearl Harbor on May 21, 2001, at an outdoor screening aboard the deck of the nuclear aircraft carrier, the USS *John C. Stennis*. Disney promoted the premiere as the largest in the film studio's history with over 2,000 guests, including the film's stars, production staff, media, Pearl Harbor survivors and special invited guests. Along with the actual film production, this gala event brought worldwide media attention and an economic boost to Hawaiʻi. Less than four months later the tragedy of September 11, 2001 unfolded on American soil.

Evelyn (Kate Beckinsale, center) and her fellow Navy Nurses, Barbara (Catherine Kellner, far left) Betty (James King, second from left) Sandra (Jennifer Garner, second from right) and Martha (Sarah Rue) arrive in Hawaiʻi for their assignment at Pearl Harbor.

Dorrie Miller (Cuba Gooding Jr.) was one of the first African-Americans decorated with the Navy Cross. The mess attendant manned one of the USS *West Virginia's* machine guns during the attack, though he had never been trained in their use. During that era, African-Americans due to racism and segregation were restricted in their naval service duties.

Made in Paradise

Planet of the Apes
2001 Twentieth Century Fox

DIRECTED BY	**Tim Burton**
SCREENPLAY BY	**William Broyles Jr., Lawrence Konner, Mark Rosenthal**
PRODUCED BY	**Richard D. Zanuck**
CAST	**Mark Wahlberg (Leo Davidson) Tim Roth (General Thade), Helena Bonham Carter (Ari), Michael Clarke Duncan (Attar), Cary-Hiroyuki Tagawa (Krull), Paul Giamatti (Limbo), David Warner (Sandar), Charlton Heston (Zaius)**

Director Tim Burton and crew filming on the Big Island's black lava field for *Planet of the Apes.*

Planet Of The Apes is based on the 1963 novel *Monkey Planet* by Pierre Boulle and is a remake of the classic 1968 film of the same name, which starred Charlton Heston *(Ben Hur, The Ten Commandments, The Hawaiians)*, one of the most popular actors of his era, and was co-scripted by the acclaimed writer Rod Serling (*The Twilight Zone* TV series) and former Communist Michael Wilson, who put many veiled references to the Hollywood Blacklist into the screenplay. This 2001 remake was one of the highest-grossing films of the year.

Astronaut Leo Davison (Wahlberg) crash lands on a planet inhabited by intelligent apes. The super simians treat the humans as slaves, but with the help of an ape named Ari (Carter), Leo starts a rebellion. The production filmed a sequence of this sci-fi flick at the black lava plains below Mount Kīlauea on the Big Island of Hawai'i.

Final Fantasy: The Spirits Within
2001 Sony

DIRECTED BY	**Hironobu Sakaguchi, Montonori Sakakibara**
SCREENPLAY BY	**Hironobu Sakaguchi, Al Reinert, Jeff Vintar, Jack Fletcher**
PRODUCED BY	**Chris Lee, Jun Aida**
CAST	**Alec Baldwin (Capt. Grey Edwards), Steve Buscemi (Neil), Ming Na Wen (Dr. Aki Ross), Ving Rhames (Ryan), Donald Sutherland (Dr. Sid), James Woods (General Heir)**

In this futuristic flick, Earth is a wasteland where the remnants of the population live in fear. To survive, eight isolated Earth-bound spirits who hold the key to survival of the planet must search for and harness an awesome power.

This movie was based on a popular computer video game, *Final Fantasy: The Spirits Within*. After four years in production, this movie became the first computer-animated motion picture with photographically realistic characters. The cast members provided the voices for the film's characters. The $135 million film grossed only $73 million worldwide and $32 million for the domestic box-office.

Square USA, the film production side of the video games entrepreneur, opened its Honolulu Studio at the Harbor Court in 1997 and also worked out of the Hawai'i Film Studio. According to Tim Ryan in a Jan. 30, 2002 *Honolulu Star-Bulletin* article, during its five-year stay in Honolulu, the Harbor Court Studio spent $1.5 million every month and more than $90 million overall. The failure at the box office of *Final Fantasy: The Spirits Within* forced the closure of Square USA in 2002—and was apparently the final fantasy for that ambitious company.

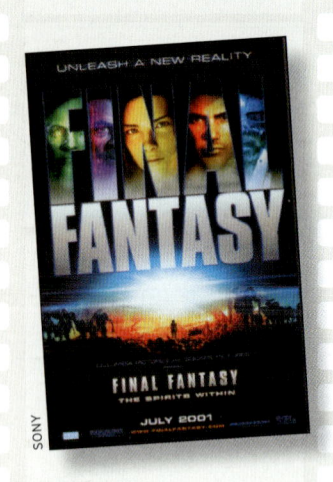

Made in Paradise

Jurassic Park III
2001 Universal

DIRECTED BY	Joe Johnston
SCREENPLAY BY	Peter Buckman, Alexander Payne, Jim Taylor
PRODUCED BY	Larry J. Franco, Kathleen Kennedy
CAST	Sam Neill (Dr. Allen Grant), William H. Macy (Paul Kirby), Tea Leoni (Amanda Kirby)

Renowned paleontologist Dr. Allen Grant (Neill), who swore he would never go back to an island full of dinosaurs, is tricked into accompanying a wealthy adventurer and his wife on an aerial tour of Isla Nublar, the ingenuous breeding ground for prehistoric creatures. But when they crash land and are stranded on the island, Dr. Grant discovers his guests have other intentions.

This non-stop action sequel has dinosaurs devouring humans at every turn. This film is the first in the franchise not adapted from a Michael Crichton novel although the author created the characters and concepts.

Laura Dern, who plays Dr. Ellie Sattler in *Jurassic Park* and *Jurassic Park III*, returned to Hawai'i in one of TV's finest series, the HBO *Enlightened* (2011-   ). As the lost, middle-aged Amy Jellicoe, the first season opens with Dern's character attending the serene, costly Open Air Treatment Center in Hawai'i in order to attain peace of mind. In the second season Amy's estranged husband, the drug-addled Levi Callow (Luke Wilson), likewise signs into Open Air to find tranquility and overcome his addiction at the Hawai'i facility.

Before settling at the Universal Studios backlot in Los Angeles, the company travelled to Hawai'i to film Kaua'i and O'ahu sites, including Dillingham Airfield, the He'eia Kea Ranch, the rainforests in the Mānoa Valley, the Mary Lucas Ranch, the Wailua River, Hanalei Valley, and the Moloka'i Coast.

To End All Wars
2001 Pray For Rain Pictures

DIRECTED BY	David Cunningham
SCREENPLAY BY	Brian Godawa based on the book by Ernest Gordon
PRODUCED BY	David Cunningham, Jack Hafer
CAST	Kiefer Sutherland (Lt. Jim 'Yankee' Reardon), Robert Carlyle (Maj. Ian Campbell), Ciarán McMenamin (Capt. Ernest 'Ernie' Gordon), Daryl Bonilla (Young POW), Ernest Gordon (Himself)

After David Cunningham made *Beyond Paradise* on location in the Big Island, his next feature was shot in Kaua'i. Unlike Beyond, *To End All Wars* was set long ago and far away from Hawai'i in the Burmese jungles during World War II. *To End All Wars* is in the tradition of grimly realistic prisoner-of-war dramas in the Pacific Theater, such as Nagisa Oshima's 1983 *Merry Christmas Mr. Lawrence* (which starred singer David Bowie and was shot in the Cook Islands) and David Lean's 1957 classic *The Bridge on the River Kwai* (which was set in Thailand and made on location in Sri Lanka, starring William Holden and Alec Guinness). Similar to the latter movie, Cunningham's mostly British POWs work as slave laborers coerced by their Imperial Japanese captors to build not a bridge, but a railroad through the sweltering jungle. The film is based on fact, as the author of the source book for the screenplay, Eric

Gordon, served as a captain incarcerated in a Japanese forced labor prison camp. *To End All Wars* is full of graphic brutality, resistance, as well as the themes of forgiveness and redemption, which reflect the director's missionary background. Northern Ireland actor Ciarán McMenamin plays Captain Ernest Gordon, Scottish actor Robert Carlyle (1996's *Trainspotting*, 1997's *The Full Monty*, and the Bond villain Renard in 1999's *The World is Not Enough*) plays Major Ian Campbell, Kiefer Sutherland (Paul Gauguin in 2003's *Paradise Found* and agent Jack Bauer in the 2001-2010 TV series *24*) plays Lt. Jim "Yankee" Reardon and the Japanese actors Yugo Saso (2007's *United Red Army*), Sakae Kimura, Masayuki Yui (who appeared in several Akira Kurosawa features), and Shû Nakajima portray Imperial soldiers.

Waianae actor and comedian Daryl Bonilla, who played Kaeo in *Beyond Paradise,* plays a "Young POW" in a small part. According to Chris Cook's article in the Nov. 15, 2001 issue of *The Garden Island* newspaper, "Over 200 extras cast on Kauaʻi play POWs… Perhaps the most striking Kauaʻi extra visible in the film is beekeeper David Maki of Hanapēpē." Cook adds, "Most of the film was shot at locations in a valley near Kōloa… Two restored sugar cane locomotives play a key role in the Kauaʻi-set scenes. Grove Farm Homestead Museum allowed the film crew to move the locomotives from their warehouse in Puhi to the Kōloa end of the Wilcox Tunnel in mauka Kōloa."

To End All Wars had the misfortune of being released just before the Sept. 11, 2001 terrorist attack, which probably hampered this harsh, uncompromisingly realistic war movie's efforts at the box office.

Lilo & Stitch
2002 Buena Vista

DIRECTED BY	**Chris Sanders and Dean DeBlois**
SCREENPLAY BY	**Chris Sanders and Dean DeBlois, based on an original idea by Chris Sanders**
PRODUCED BY	**Clark Spencer**
CAST	**Daveigh Chase (Lilo), David Michael Sanders (Stitch), Tia Carrere (Nani), David Ogden Stiers (Jumba), Kevin McDonald (Pleakley), Ving Rhames (Cobra Bubbles), Zoe Caldwell (Grand Councilwoman), Jason Scott Lee (David Kawena)**

This full-length cartoon is about a Hawaiian girl who befriends an extraterrestrial. *Lilo & Stitch* is set in Hawaiʻi and utilizes many Aloha State elements, but was produced at the Walt Disney Feature Animation Florida $70 million facility. The production notes says, "There is trouble and plenty of laughter in paradise when a lonely Hawaiian girl named Lilo wishes upon a falling star for someone to be her friend and the galaxy's most mischeivious alien answers her call in Walt Disney Pictures' delightful animated comedy *Lilo & Stitch*. Combining unforgettable characters, an imaginative, offbeat story and colorful artistry, the film follows Lilo's close encounter with Stitch, an out of control

Lilo & Stitch was nominated for an Academy Award® for Best Animated Feature.

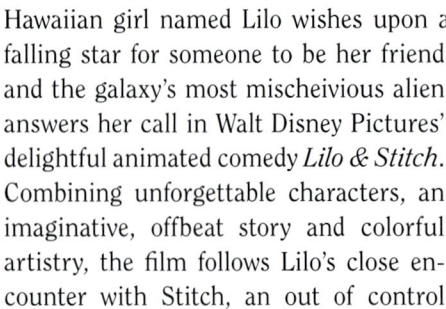

Tia Carrere, voice of Nani.

Made in Paradise

genetic experiment who has escaped from an alien planet and crash landed on earth. Posing as a small strange looking dog, Stitch is adopted by Lilo and leaves a wide path of chaos in his wake. Through her love, faith, and unwavering belief in "'Ohana" (the Hawaiian word and concept for family), Lilo helps unlock Stitch's heart and gives him the one thing he was never designed to have, a family."

Jason Scott Lee, voice of David Kawena.

The animated film's production notes go on to say, "guiding *Lilo & Stitch* from inception through production was the writing directing team of Chris Sanders and Dean DeBlois... Tia Carrere's warm sweet reading for the part of Nani landed her the role of Lilo's older beleaguered sister. Jason Scott Lee (who played Mowgli in Disney's live action adaptation of *The Jungle Book*) also a native of Hawai'i, provided the voice of Nani's former boyfriend and surf companion, David Kawena."

The production notes state, "Set against the magnificent colorful backdrop of Hawai'i, the filmmakers and a group of artistic supervisors captured the natural beauty and incredible tropical settings of this island paradise. They packed their cameras, paintbrushes and sketchbooks and headed to Hawai'i for a two week study session. Most of the trip was spent on the island of Kaua'i and they visited such places as Hanalei, Hanapēpē, the Nāpali Coast, Princeville, and Ke'e Beach."

Chris Saunders and Dean DeBlois in Hawai'i during their two week study session.

Mark Keali'i Ho'omalu recorded several Hawaiian chants for the film. Two chosen chants were combined with a piece of music. Ho'omalu then contacted a children's choir of forty singers at the Kamehameha Schools. Composer and songwriter Alan Silvestri collaborated with Ho'omalu, and two songs were recorded: "He Mele No Lilo" and "Hawaiian Roller Coaster Ride," a completely original song.

"The filmmakers did an excellent job of capturing the imagery of Hawai'i," said Jason Scott Lee at the film's Honolulu premiere. He continued, "Lilo's village looks like a little place in Kaua'i that I know with its plantation homes. They represented Hawai'i well and with a real sensitivity to the culture. The hula scene is also very accurate with its music, movements, and presentation of the children."

Tia Carrere tapped into her Hawaiian heritage for her vocal performance as Lilo's older sister. "It was really cool being from Hawai'i and getting to play a Hawaiian character," remarked the actress in the film's press notes. "I was born and raised in Honolulu, so when they asked me to infuse the character with some Hawaiianism, I put in some Pidgin English like the locals speak. It is an amalgam of the various ethnic backgrounds putting simple English words together in a specific way. There's a different intonation to it that is kind of sing-songy."

Lilo serves as a Native Hawaiian leading animated character and one of the five contemporary Disney non-white animated characters, which have found universal acceptance, including *Pocahontas, Mulan,* Jasmine from *Aladdin,* and Tiana from *The Princess and the Frog.* The movie and its characters became unofficial ambassadors for the Hawai'i Visitors Bureau and introduced children the world over to Hawai'i and its cultural values.

Made in Paradise

The Time Machine
2002 Warner Bros.

DIRECTED BY	**Simon Wells**
SCREENPLAY BY	**John Logan based on *The Time Machine* by H.G. Wells**
PRODUCED BY	**Walter F. Parkes, David Valdes**
CAST	**Guy Pearce (Dr. Alexander Hartdegen), Samantha Mumba (Mara), Mark Addy (David Philby), Jeremy Irons (Über-Morlock), Yancy Arias (Toren)**

The classic 1960 MGM film *The Time Machine* is set in London, starring Australian Rod Taylor in this H.G. Wells 1895 novel-turned film. However, this 2002 loose adaptation is set in 1899 New York City, where Dr. Alexander Hartdegen (Guy Pearce), a Columbia University professor, develops a time-travel machine. His fiancée is murdered, and he uses the machine to go back in time to prevent her death. While time traveling, Hartdegen goes back and forth in time and comes upon an earth in the future that has undergone radical changes, regressing to a primitive state. Sci-fi author H.G. Wells' great-grandson, Simon Wells, directed this remake and also helmed 2011's *Mars Needs Moms*.

Producer David Valdes says, "Upon completion of principal photography in Los Angeles and Albany, New York, a small 'Plate Unit'—plates are establishing shots that are used as backgrounds or an integral part of a sequence through green screen or a computer generated imagery process—was sent to the North Shore of Oʻahu to shoot plates for our visual effects team, as well as some aerial shots that were used for the Eloi environment."

Windtalkers
2002 MGM

DIRECTED BY	**John Woo**
SCREENPLAY BY	**John Rice, Joe Batteer**
PRODUCED BY	**John Woo, Terence Chang, Tracie Graham, Alison Rosenzweig**
CAST	**Adam Beach (Ben Yahzee), Roger Willie (Charlie Whitehorse), Nicolas Cage (Sgt. Joe Enders), Christian Slater (Sgt. Pete Anderson), Frances O'Connor (Rita)**

Director John Woo confers with actor Nicolas Cage on the Kualoa Ranch location of *Windtalkers*.

A thrilling World War II movie, *Windtalkers* features lots of rousing battle scenes and an indigenous twist, helmed by the great action director John Woo. When *Windtalkers* was released, London's *The Guardian* gushed, "John Woo is arguably the most influential director making movies today." Woo's fast-paced, action-packed choreography mixed with stylish slow-motion cam-

Made in Paradise

The Marines land on Saipan led by Sgt. Joe Enders (Nicolas Cage) in *Windtalkers* filmed at Ka'a'awa Valley, which is part of Kualoa Valley on O'ahu.

Adam Beach as Ben Yahzee, a Navajo code talker in *Windtalkers*.

Adam Beach (front left) and Roger Willie (front right) star in Metro-Goldwyn-Mayer Pictures' epic drama *Windtalkers*.

erawork caught the attention of Hollywood. By the 1990s, the director had successfully crossed over from Hong Kong to the American studio system.

This epic culminates with 1944's extremely bloody Battle of Saipan, one of the penultimate and fiercest battles of the Pacific Theater's island-hopping campaign (which was depicted in the 1960 movie *Hell to Eternity* starring Jeffrey Hunter). But what elevates *Windtalkers* from being just another WWII actioner is not only Woo's direction, but also its plot that involves American Indians—the Navajos, to be precise. In the early days of World War II, Ben Yahzee (Adam Beach) and Charlie Whitehorse (Roger Willie) leave the reservation and enlist together to fight for what they insist is *their* country, too. The Navajos have a unique value for the U.S. military, which goes far beyond the legendary aura of the Indian warrior.

To ensure that the Imperial Japanese do not crack the code that the Americans use in radio messages, the high command decides to use the Navajo language. Thus, Yahzee and White-

Made in Paradise

Frances O'Connor as nurse Rita and Nicolas Cage as Joe Enders in Metro-Goldwyn-Mayer Pictures' epic drama *Windtalkers*.

Sgt. Pete Anderson (Christian Slater) shoots at the enemy after his comrade has been killed in *Windtalkers*.

Noah Emmerich (center) and Mark Ruffalo (right) star in Metro-Goldwyn-Mayer Pictures' epic drama *Windtalkers*.

horse join other recruits from the Navajo Nation to be trained to verbally express modern military terms such as coordinates, combat equipment such as airplanes and tanks, and so on in the heat of combat.

These Navajo radiomen, whose voices are carried over the air by modern communications devices, are called "Windtalkers." They prove their invaluable worth to the U.S. war effort, which has been hampered by the enemy's ability to break all previous codes used by the Americans.

Sergeant Joe Enders (Nicolas) is a valiant leatherneck from south Philadelphia (tellingly, he comes from the "City of Brotherly Love"), who is wounded in brutal hand-to-hand combat in the Solomon Islands. He was sent to a military hospital (shot at the Veteran's Administration Hospital on the Westside of Los Angeles) to recover, and a nurse named Rita (Frances O'Connor) cares for him, but Enders itches to return to combat.

The movie follows the developing relationship between Enders and Yahzee and also between Sgt. Pete "Ox" Anderson (Christian Slater) and Private Whitehorse, the radioman Anderson is designated to protect—and possibly assassinate. Anderson is more simpatico with Whitehorse than the gruff Enders is vis-à-vis his charge.

Ultimately, more than anything else, this 134-minute big-screen World War II movie is about "Let's send the Marines!" The Marines ship out from Hawai'i (the base location was actually shot in Southern California at the Naval Air Weapons Station, Point Mugu) as the Americans invade Saipan in the Northern Mariana Islands. The Yankee assault and Japanese defense are visually stunning, with all the cinematic hallmarks of Woo's wizardry. This long segment of *Windtalkers* was shot at O'ahu's Ka'a'awa Valley, with the segment's swooping planes, cannon fire, explosions, flamethrowers, charging Marines and brave radiomen frantically informing naval ships the coordinates of where the enemy's artillery is located.

Made in Paradise

Die Another Day
2002 MGM/UA

DIRECTED BY **Lee Tamahori**
SCREENPLAY BY **Neal Pervis, Robert Wade**
PRODUCED BY **Barbara Broccoli, Michael Wilson**
CAST **Pierce Brosnan (James Bond), Halle Berry (Jinx), Toby Stephens (Gustav Graves), Rick Yune (Zao), Jude Dench (M), John Cleese (Q)**

Even Bond, James Bond has gone Hawaiian. In *Die Another Day*, British billionaire Gustav Graves plans to utilize his powerful solar energy weapon Icarus to break through the Korean Demilitarized Zone to wage war between North and South Korea—and only 007, the spy who is licensed to thrill, can stop him.

Prior to the commencement of principal photography, a small crew shot scenes in Maui, where Laird Hamilton and other professional surfers were hired to perform the pre-title surfing sequence that was filmed Christmas Day 2001 on Peahi Beach. The Valley Isle location was to double for the shores of the Democratic People's Republic of Korea, where Bond surfs into North Korean territory, which triggers an elaborate hovercraft chase. New Zealand Maori Lee Tamahori *(Once We Were Warriors)* directed *Die Another Day*. And yes, this is the flick wherein Halle Berry plays the bikini-clad Bond Girl rising from the sea, reprising Ursula Andress' appearance forty years earlier in *Dr. No*, as well as Sandro Botticelli's 1486 painting *The Birth of Venus*.

Pierce Brosnan as James Bond lands on the North Korean Peninsula after surfing his way into the danger zone.

Dragonfly
2002 Universal

DIRECTED BY **Tom Shaydyac**
SCREENPLAY BY **David Seltzer, Mike Thompson, Branden Camp**
PRODUCED BY **Gary Barber, Roger Birnbaum, Mark Johns**
CAST **Kevin Costner (Joe Darrow), Susana Thompson (Emily), Ron Rifkin (Charlie Dickinson), Joe Morton (Hugh Campbell), Jacob Vargas (Victor)**

Doctor Joe Darrow's (Costner) young wife Emily (Thompson) goes to the Amazon in South America to help a poor Venezuelan village and dies in a tragic bus accident. The devestated Darrow returns to his work treating sick children. Joe believes her spirit has contacted him and goes to the Amazon to find some peace. He follows the clues and symbols that lead him back to the South American village where she died. At the hamlets, he contacts some natives to find out what happened to Emily's remains.

The Venezuelan Amazon sequences were filmed on Kaua'i.

Made in Paradise 97

Blue Crush
2002 Universal

DIRECTED BY **John Stockwell**
SCREENPLAY BY **Susan Orlean, Lizzy Weiss, John Stockwell**
PRODUCED BY **Brian Grazer, Karen Kehela Sherwood**
CAST **Kate Bosworth (Anne Marie), Michelle Rodriguez (Eden), Sanoe Lake (Lani), Matthew Davis (Matt Tolman)**

Marie Chadwick (Kate Bosworth), Eden (Michelle Rodriguez) and Lena (Sanoe Lake) are best friends who surf and work together on Oʻahu in *Blue Crush*.

This mid-budget movie features women in sports girl-power theme and includes pro-surfers such as Keala Kennelly, who plays herself, in a cast with many locals (such as Kimo Kahoano as a lūʻau emcee) and Oʻahu locations. It's North Shore meets NFL in this surf movie about three girlfriends, Anne Marie Chadwick (Kate Bosworth), Eden (Michelle Rodriguez), and Lena (Sanoe Lake). The best friends live as surfers by dawn and maids by day, working at the JW Marriott Ihilani Resort & Spa at Ko Olina. Together, they help raise Anne Marie's fourteen-year-old sister, Penny (Mika Boorem), as their mother has moved to Las Vegas with her boyfriend.

Anne Marie serves as *Blue Crush*'s central character: Once a promising surfer, following a life-threatening wipeout, she's trying to overcome her anxiety, get back in the nautical saddle and ride the wild surf again. At Ko Olina, she meets quarterback Matt Tollman (Matthew Davis), who is staying in the Ihilani and came to Hawaiʻi for the Pro Bowl at Aloha Stadium. The plot revolves around Anne Marie's triumphant return to wave riding at the Pipeline Masters surf competition and her growing romance with Matt. Overcoming anxiety and not allowing fear to hold one back—in the ocean, as well as in love—is the movie's subtext.

Blue Crush has exciting surf sequences with scenes shot at Oʻahu's North Shore, Mākaha, and Waikīkī. While the actresses in the three main parts learned to surf, top female surfers performed in the more dangerous breaks, while the three leads' faces were digitally superimposed onto their surf doubles. Tapping into the local talent used onscreen, the rest of the wave riding was actually performed in the Pacific, not via special effects.

Made in Paradise

Japanese lobby card for *Blue Crush*.

Blue Crush was inspired by a magazine article written by journalist and screenwriter Susan Orlean, who co-wrote the 2002 film *Adaptation* with Meryl Streep, Nicolas Cage, and Chris Cooper. In 2011, an unrelated "sequel," the straight-to-video *Blue Crush 2*, came out with a different set of female surfers at Malibu and South Africa.

Punch-Drunk Love
2002 Columbia

DIRECTED BY	**Paul Thomas Andrews**
SCREENPLAY BY	**Paul Thomas Andrews**
PRODUCED BY	**Paul Thomas Andrews, Daniel Lupi, Joanne Selan**
CAST	**Adam Sandler (Barry Egan), Emily Watson (Lena Leonard), Luis Guzman (Lance), Philip Seymour Hoffman (Dean Trumbell), Mary Lynn Rajskub (Elizabeth)**

In this offbeat, quirky romantic comedy, Barry Egan (Sandler) is a small business owner with seven sisters, whose abusive treatment has kept him home alone and unable to fall in love. When he finds a harmonium (a musical instrument) in the street and a mysterious young woman, Lena (Emily Watson), enters his life, his romantic journey begins. He pursues Lena to Hawaiʻi, where the film's color palette naturally opens up to the sights and sounds of Hawaiʻi. Lena and Barry romantically stroll along Waikīkī Beach and wind up at the Royal Hawaiian Hotel for dinner and drinks as they watch a hula show.

Punch-Drunk Love won the Best Director prize for Paul Thomas Andrews at the 2002 Cannes Film Festival. Andrews served as the celebrated writer and director of *Boogie Nights* (1998) and *Magnolia* (1999).

Made in Paradise

Janet Jackson: All For You, Live In Concert From Hawai'i
2002 HBO

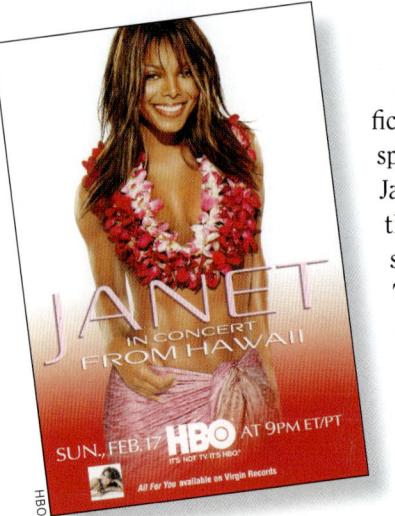

A Live Home Box Office cable TV concert special starring Janet Jackson, the sister of the late Michael Jackson, the King of Pop. The special aired on February 17, 2002, from Aloha Stadium in Hawai'i.

The program was nominated for an Emmy® Award for Outstanding Multi-camera Picture editing for a miniseries, movie or special.

Charlie's Angels: Full Throttle
2003 Columbia

DIRECTED BY	McG
SCREENPLAY BY	John August, Cormac Wibberly, Marianne Wibberly
PRODUCED BY	Leonard Goldberg, Drew Barrymore, Nancy Juvonen
CAST	Cameron Diaz (Natalie Cook), Drew Barrymore (Dylan Sanders), Lucy Liu (Alex Munday), Bernie Mac (Jimmy Bosley), Crispin Glover (Thin Man), Justin Theroux (Seamus O'Grady)

Diaz, Barrymore, and Liu reunite in *Charlie's Angels: Full Throttle*, a sequel to *Charlie's Angels*, the blockbuster comedy hit in 2000. The popular TV series of that same name (1976-1981) inspired *Charlie's Angels*.

In this screen incarnation of the Angels, the female detectives search for encrypted bands listing every person in the federal witness protection program's database. When these federally protected witnesses start turning up dead, the Angels must find out who is committing these heinous acts and stop them.

As for the movie's ties in Hawai'i, the second-unit surfing scenes were shot on the North Shore of O'ahu near the Turtle Bay Resort.

The second season 1977 premiere episode of the *Charlie's Angels* television series titled "Angels In Paradise" was filmed on location in Waikīkī on O'ahu, Hawai'i. The trio traveled to Hawai'i in order to save a kidnapped Charlie.

Left to right: Jaclyn Smith, Cheryl Ladd, and Kate Jackson, the original Angels, in Hawai'i filming an episode of the *Charlie's Angels* television series in the 1970s.

Made in Paradise

The Rundown
2003 Universal

DIRECTED BY **Peter Berg**
SCREENPLAY BY **James Vanderbilt**
PRODUCED BY **Kevin Misher, Karen Glasser, Marc Abraham**
CAST **Dwayne "The Rock" Johnson (Beck), Seann William Scott (Travis), Christopher Walken (Hatcher), Rosario Dawson (Mariana)**

The Rundown shot for five weeks on Oʻahu at Nuʻuanu Valley and Kualoa Ranch under the title of *Helldorado*. The jungle locale figured prominently in the script. Although set in the Brazilian Amazon, the filmmakers preferred the lush verdant beauty of Hawaiʻi's rainforests, complete with towering banyan trees, spectacular waterfalls, and other locales for the film's exotic setting. The producers had wanted to film in Brazil, but an advance location-scouting trip resulted in local bandits assaulting and holding the producers for ransom. The producers were eventually rescued, but that incident persuaded them to shoot the production in secure Los Angeles and Hawaiʻi locations.

Of African-American and Samoan ancestry, Dwayne "The Rock" Johnson is a former wrestler and athlete-turned-actor with Hawaiʻi roots. He grew up on Oʻahu near Daiei (now Don Quijote) on Kaheka Street and on Kapiʻolani Boulevard and attended Washington Intermediate School and McKinley High School.

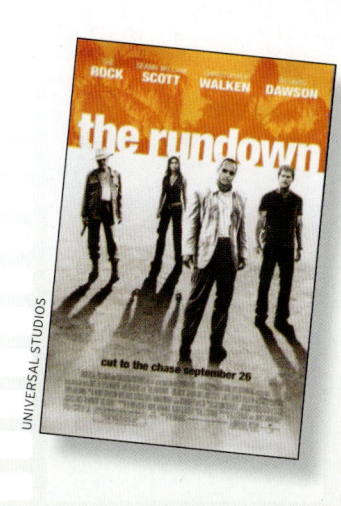

Beck (The Rock), Mariana (Rosario Dawson) and Travis (Seann William Scott) do their best to get along—and survive—in the action-adventure *The Rundown*.

The Rock as Beck in the action-adventure *The Rundown*.

Made in Paradise

Tears of the Sun

2003 Cheyenne Enterprises, Revolution Studios

DIRECTED BY **Antoine Fuqua**
SCREENPLAY BY **Alex Lasker, Patrick Cirillo**
PRODUCED BY **Ian Bryce, Mike Lobell, Arnold Rifkin**
CAST **Bruce Willis (A.K. Waters), Monica Belluci (Dr.Kendricks), Tom Skerritt (Capt. Bill Rhodes)**

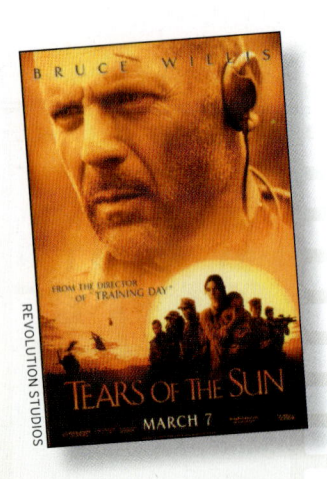

A Navy SEAL team is dropped into central Africa and embark on a hazardous rescue mission in Revolution Studios' action-packed *Tears of the Sun*, a Columbia Pictures release. The film stars *(left to right)* Paul Francis, Johnny Messner, Nick Chinlund, Bruce Willis, Cole Hauser and Eammon Walker.

Paul Francis, Bruce Willis, Monica Bellucci and Cole Hauser star in Revolution Studios' epic action adventure *Tears of the Sun*, a Columbia Pictures release.

Captain Bill Rhodes (Tom Skerritt) orders Lt. A.K. Waters (Bruce Willis, star of the *Die Hard* franchise) to lead a Navy SEAL team into war-torn Nigeria to rescue a damsel in distress. Their orders are to safely extract Dr. Lena Fiore Kendricks (Italian actress Monica Belluci, who starred in 1999's *Mediterranees*, 2000's *Malena*, played Persephone in *Matrix* movies and Mary Magdalene in Mel Gibson's 2004 *The Passion of the Christ*), a U.S. citizen by marriage, from the jungle hospital where she works. As the civil war intensifies, the question becomes should the SEALs go beyond their official orders and also try to rescue unarmed Africans—who are not American citizens—from the raging conflict?

Antoine Fuqua stylishly directs the action-packed *Tears of the Sun* and previously helmed the 2001 Los Angeles Police Department-drama *Training Day*. As in *Mighty Joe Young*, "deepest, darkest" Oʻahu once again doubles for Africa with scenes shot at the Dole Plantation, Kaʻaʻawa Valley, Mānoa Falls, Maunawili Valley, Haleʻiwa, and the Hawaiʻi Film Studio, as well as Los Angeles.

> Since the Rwanda genocide, which claimed almost a million lives in 1994, the question of humanitarian intervention by the United States has been debated in public and policymaker circles. President Bill Clinton later apologized to the Rwandans for America not doing anything, instead of decisively ending the mass slaughter in the central African nation. *Tears of the Sun* features the philosophical backdrop of the Rwanda crisis.

Made in Paradise

The Big Bounce
2004 Warner Bros.

DIRECTED BY	George Armitage
SCREENPLAY BY	Sebastian Gutierrez from an Elmore Leonard novel.
PRODUCED BY	Steve Bing, George Armitage
CAST	Morgan Freeman (Walter Crewes), Owen Wilson (Jack Ryan), Sara Foster (Nancy Hayes), Gary Sinise (Ray Ritchie), Charlie Sheen (Bob Rogers Jr.), Bebe Neuwirth (Alison Ritchie)

This remake is based on the Elmore Leonard novel that inspired the 1969 film of the same title (starring Ryan O'Neal and Leigh Taylor Young). The 2004 production notes describe *The Big Bounce* as, "a comic film noir about an everyman who finds trouble in the form of a beautiful blonde. Jack Ryan (Owen Wilson) is a small time scam artist who is determined to leave that life behind after yet another run in with the law. But when he meets the mistress of his former gang boss, Ray Ritchie (Gary Sinise), all bets are off. Nancy (Sarah Foster) is hot, mischievous, and up to no good, but Jack is too smitten to use his better judgment. It isn't long before he's agreed to help her steal $200,000 from Ray. Along the way he must contend with a series of shady characters, which might not be what they seem."

According to *Honolulu Advertiser* entertainment writer Wayne Harada in a Jan. 30, 2004 article, "Hawai'i is the real star of *The Big Bounce*… And Hawai'i is the real deal—notably, O'ahu's North Shore where the entire movie was filmed in the winter of 2002-2003." The Hale'iwa locations include Kua'aina Sandwich shop, the Waialua Courthouse, Waimea Valley and waterfall, Hale'iwa Joe's Restaurant (the location of a scene between Freeman and Wilson), the Hale'iwa Bridge, Kainoa's Sports Bar and Restaurant on Kamehameha Highway in Hale'iwa, and Mokoli'i islet (Chinaman's Hat). Unfortunately, *The Big Bounce* landed with a big thud at the box office.

Owen Wilson and Sara Foster in Shangri-La Entertainment's *The Big Bounce*, also starring Morgan Freeman, and distributed by Warner Bros. Pictures.

Charlie Sheen, Morgan Freeman and Owen Wilson in Shangri-La Entertainment's *The Big Bounce*, distributed by Warner Bros. Pictures.

Made in Paradise

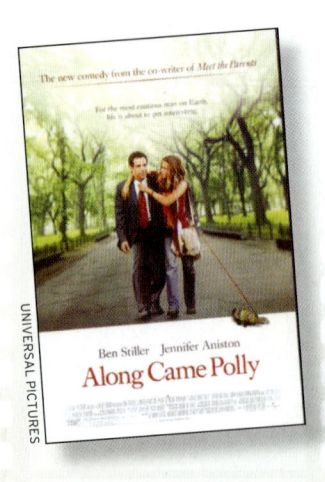

Along Came Polly
2004 Universal Pictures

DIRECTED BY	John Hamburg
SCREENPLAY BY	John Hamburg
PRODUCED BY	Danny DeVito, Michael Shamberg, Stacy Sher
CAST	Ben Stiller (Reuben Feffer), Jennifer Aniston (Polly Prince), Debra Messing (Lisa Kramer), Hank Azaria (Claude), Philip Seymour Hoffman (Sandy Lyle), Bryan Brown (Leland Van Lew), Alec Baldwin (Stan Indursky)

Ben Stiller plays risk-adverse Reuben Feffer. His best-laid plans for life and love zoom wildly offtrack when his wife (Messing) dumps him on their honeymoon for an exotic scuba instructor (Azaria). Stunned, humiliated and in the grip of acute indigestion, Reuben plans to act more cautiously than ever. But a chance encounter with adventure-craving, globetrotting Polly Prince (Aniston, a co-star of the long-running TV comedy *Friends*), a friend from middle school, propels him into a whirlwind of extreme sports, spicy foods, ferrets, salsa dancing, and living in the moment.

The scenes that take place on St. Barts in the Caribbean at the beginning and the end were actually filmed on Oʻahu's Windward side. Mokoliʻi (Chinaman's Hat) can be seen in some shots, as well as Kāohikaipu Island (Turtle Island) on southeast Oʻahu.

50 First Dates
2004 Columbia Pictures

DIRECTED BY	Peter Segal
SCREENPLAY BY	George Wing
PRODUCED BY	Jack Giarraputo, Steve Golin, Nancy Juvonen
CAST	Adam Sandler (Henry Roth), Drew Barrymore (Lucy Whitmore), Rob Schneider (Ulu), Sean Astin (Doug), Blake Clarke (Marlin Whitmore), Amy Hill (Sue), Pomaikaʻi Brown (Nick), Dan Aykroyd (Dr. Keats), Maya Rudolph (Stacy), Kevin James (Factory Worker), Esmond Chung (Sheriff)

50 First Dates, an Oʻahu-set romantic comedy, stars Drew Barrymore as the attractive Lucy Whitmore, who—due to a car accident—suffers from a fictional memory impairment, Goldfield's Syndrome. She meets the womanizing Sea Life Park veterinarian Henry Roth (Adam Sandler) at the Hukilau Café owned by Sue (Amy Hill). The com-

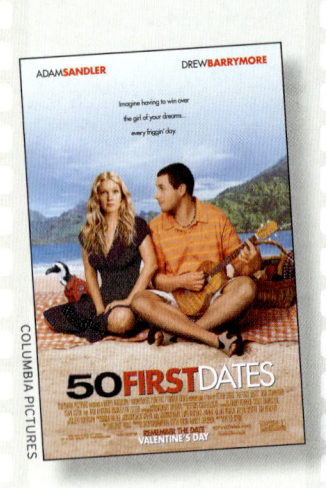

Drew Barrymore and Adam Sandler star in Columbia Pictures' romantic comedy *50 First Dates*.

Made in Paradise

mitment-phobic Henry falls for Lucy, but because of her short-term memory loss, after each get-together, Lucy forgets who Henry is, and Ms. Whitmore loses her wits (get it?). Lucy's traumatic brain trauma necessitates Henry reintroducing himself at each rendezvous with the adorable fair-haired beauty—she is arguably cinema's ditziest blonde since Judy Holliday.

Rob Schneider and Adam Sandler co-star in Columbia Pictures' romantic comedy *50 First Dates*.

A series of comic complications arise out of Lucy's condition. Sean Astin is Lucy's brother, Doug Whitmore, a bodybuilder who takes steroids, since juicing is also fodder for comedy. Blake Clark plays Lucy and Doug's father who has an appropriately fishy name, Marlin Whitmore. San Francisco-born Rob Schneider—who is Caucasian, Jewish, and Filipino—plays the dreadlocked, pakalolo-smoking Hawaiian to da max bruddah named Ula. Dan Aykroyd portrays Dr. Keats, a specialist in brain disorders. Pomaikaʻi Brown, who plays Nick, is a well-known Hawaiian musician and a Kamehameha Schools graduate. Henry has a pet African penguin named Willy.

Originally the story for *50 First Dates* was set in Seattle. However, Adam Sandler suggested moving the story's setting to Hawaiʻi. The movie shot on location for six weeks there and six weeks in Los Angeles. The Oʻahu locations include Marlin's house in Waikane; Henry's boat at Heʻeia Kea Harbor in Kāneʻohe; Kualoa Ranch in Kaʻaʻawa Valley; dirt roads of Wahiawā and Waialua; the Dole Food Company's pineapple fields; the Hawaiʻi Film Studio at Diamond Head; Island Seaplane Airport; the Dillingham Ranch; Makapuʻu Lighthouse; Sandy Beach; Hālona Cove (also known as the *From Here to Eternity* Beach); and Sea Life Park in Waimānalo on Oʻahu's southeast shore. The exterior of the Hukilau Café was built on the Kuaola Ranch. Exteriors were shot at Kāneʻohe Bay, Makapuʻu, Waimānalo, Kaʻaʻawa, and in the plantations near Wahiawā. The walrus tank was reportedly filmed in California's Six Flags Discovery Kingdom while the golf course and some interiors were shot in Los Angeles.

Drew Barrymore and Adam Sandler on the set of Columbia Pictures' romantic comedy *50 First Dates*.

The soundtrack contains notable songs, including Bruddah Iz's "Somewhere Over the Rainbow/What a Wonderful World" medley, the Makaha Sons of Niʻihau's "Aloha Ka Manini," Maile Serenaders' "My Sweet Sweet," plus Leon Redbone and Ringo Starr's rendition of "My Little Grass Shack in Kealakekua, Hawaiʻi."

This film has an extremely dubious premise—Lucy's condition, "Goldfield's Syndrome," is fictitious. *50 First Dates* was the second pairing of Sandler and of the cute, kooky Barrymore, since their 1998 *The Wedding Singer*.

Made in Paradise

Lost
2004-2010 ABC

PRODUCED BY Carlton Cuse and J.J. Abrams
CREATED BY Damon Lindelof and J.J. Abrams
CAST Matthew Fox (Jack Shephard), Josh Holloway (James 'Sawyer' Ford), Evangeline Lilly (Kate Austen), Jorge Garcia (Hugo 'Hurley' Reyes), Naveen Andrews (Sayid Jarrah), Terry O'Quinn (John Locke), Daniel Dae Kim (Jin Kwon), Yunjin Kim (Sun Kwon), Zuleikhaha Robinson (Ilana Verdansky)

Lost is an addictive, enigmatic hit about stranded plane crash survivors on an eerie Pacific Island. These disparate, resilient souls are bedeviled by flashbacks to their pasts, ever-changing group dynamics, otherworldly predators, and hostile island inhabitants, who the survivors call the "Others." (Plot Spoiler Alert:) Six of the survivors of the downed Oceanic Air Flight 815 are eventually rescued and return to the United States—for awhile.

Locations for this mysterious, eerie series include Mokulēʻia Beach on Oʻahu's North Shore for the crash site and the island; Police Beach, also on the North Shore, for

Cast of the filmed-in-Hawaiʻi hit series *Lost* at the banyan trees location at Turtle Bay Resort on Oʻahu.

Cast of the television series *Lost* at the crash landing site of Oceanic Flight 815 on Mokulēʻia Beach on Oʻahu with the airplane fuselage in the background.

106 Made in Paradise

the survivors' encampment site; Kualoa Ranch for the jungle and mountain scenes; and the Ilikai Hotel for Jin Soo Kwan's home. The Hawai'i Convention Center doubles as an Australian airport; the First Hawaiian Bank's downtown building serves as Sun Kwon's father's business headquarters. O'ahu's Waimea Bay also served as a location, and part of the series was shot at the Hawai'i Film Studio.

Lost had a main cast of 15 actors and employed at least 230 local crewmembers. The popular program kickstarted several of its talents' careers, launching a pre-*Star Trek* J.J. Abrams into the front ranks of Hollywood film directors. After *Lost*, Daniel Dae Kim and Terry O'Quinn—who won the Outstanding Supporting Actor in a Drama Series Primetime Emmy® in 2007 (and was nominated for the same category two additional times) for portraying John Locke in 116 episodes—both found homes on another series shot in the Fiftieth State: *Hawaii Five-0*.

> The long-running *Lost* serves as one of the most honored works in the entire history of Hawai'i productions. In its debut season, *Lost* garnered the most Primetime Emmy® nominations—twelve—of any network show, winning in six categories, including for Outstanding Drama Series and Outstanding Directing for a Drama Series. Over the course of the complex program's airing, *Lost* was nominated for more than fifty Primetime Emmys®, winning ten Emmy® Awards. Other accolades this critically acclaimed, groundbreaking television show won include a Golden Globe® and ten Saturn Awards presented by the Academy of Science Fiction, Fantasy & Horror Films.

Made in Paradise 107

North Shore
2004 Fox Broadcasting

CAST **Brooke Burns (Nicole Booth), James Remar (Vincent Colville), Jason Momoa (Frankie Seau), Robert Kekaula (Sam), Shannen Doherty (Alexandra Hudson)**

This ensemble drama was set in the Grand Waimea Hotel, a luxury hotel on Oʻahu's North Shore (the fictionalized property was actually shot at the Turtle Bay Resort near Kahuku, Oʻahu). James Remar plays the owner of the fictionalized Grand Waimea, Vincent Colville; Kristoffer Polaha plays general manager Jason Matthews; and Brooke Burns plays Jason's old flame, Nicole Booth. Jason's world is turned upside down when Nicole enters the picture. They had previously been lovers, but her billionaire father made her break off the relationship in this prime-time soap opera with a tropical setting.

Flight 29 Down
2005-2006 Discovery Kids NBC

DIRECTED BY **D.J. MacHale, Steve De Jarnatt**
TELEPLAY BY **D.J. MacHale, Tim O'Donnell**
PRODUCED BY **Stan Rogow, D.J. MacHale**
CAST **Lauren Storm (Taylor), Hallee Hirsh (Daley), Johnny Paar (Jackson), Jeremy Kissner (Eric), Kristy Wu (Melissa), Corbin Bleu (Nathan)**

Sort of a juvenile precursor to *Lost*, *Flight 29 Down* is about ten teenagers stranded on a desert island while en route to an eco-adventure camp. With little hope of rescue, the kids must learn how to navigate the challenges of the island together, using their intellect and instincts.

Flight 29 Down became the first Hawaiʻi-based series produced by a local production company to air on national television. The live-action series was filmed on locations throughout Oʻahu. Hawaiʻi Film Partners and Discovery Kids/NBC produced the filming for thirteen episodes.

The Hawaiʻi Film Partners aims to build a viable local film industry in Hawaiʻi using local services and personnel. The Honolulu-based company also participated in making 2011's feature film *You May Not Kiss the Bride*.

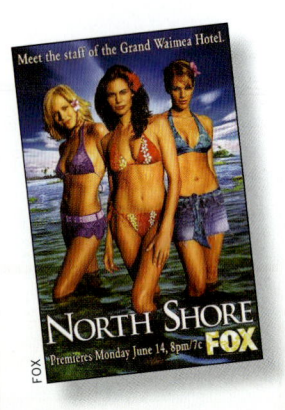

The young cast of *Flight 29 Down*.

Made in Paradise

You, Me and Dupree
2006 Universal

DIRECTED BY	Anthony Russo and Joe Russo
SCREENPLAY BY	Michael LeSieur
PRODUCED BY	Mary Parent, Scott Stuber, Owen Wilson
CAST	Owen Wilson (Randolph Dupree), Seth Rogen (Neil), Kate Hudson (Molly), Matt Dillon (Carl), Michael Douglas (Bob Thompson)

Molly (Kate Hudson) and Carl (Matt Dillon) are preparing for their wedding day in Hawai'i when Carl's troublesome best friend, Randolph Dupree, gets lost. The opening sequences of Carl and Molly's wedding, reception, and honeymoon were shot during the first ten days of principal photography in October 2005 on a pineapple field in Ka'a'awa and at Kualoa Ranch in O'ahu.

You, Me and Dupree filming at Kualoa ranch

Snakes on a Plane
2006 New Line Cinema

DIRECTED BY	David Ellis
SCREENPLAY BY	Josh Friedman
PRODUCED BY	Craig Berenson, Ron Granger, Gary Levinsohn
CAST	Samuel L. Jackson (Neville Flynn), Nathan Phillips (Sean Jones), Sunny Mabrey, Mark Houghton, Julianna Marguilies (Claire Miller), Bobby Cannavale (Hank Harris), Taylor Kitsch (Kyle)

While taking part in motocross in Hawai'i, Sean Jones (Phillips) witnesses the brutal murder of a prosecuting attorney on O'ahu's North Shore. Samuel L. Jackson as FBI-agent Neville Flynn is assigned to takes Jones on a flight from Honolulu to Los Angeles. On the flight, an assassin releases hundreds of deadly snakes on a commercial airliner to eliminate the witness before he can testify against a mob boss. Flynn, along with a rookie pilot, frightened crew, and passengers, must then band together to survive.

This low-budget film takes place almost entirely on the plane. Samuel L. Jackson's profanity-shouting hero battling the airborne snakes provides a wild, fun film ride that is not to be taken seriously. The aerial serpents are a combination of real snakes and computer-gener-

Made in Paradise

ated imagery. Predecessor movies *The High and the Mighty, Airport,* and *Airplane!* influenced *Snakes on a Plane.*

The movie was filmed in Vancouver with a few establishing aerial shots of Hawai'i. At the time of its release, *Snakes on a Plane* was one of the first movies heavily promoted on the Internet and social media sites, which influenced the production of the movie. The movie went viral online and created much anticipation. However, all of this cyberspace publicity did not result in the anticipated big-time payoff at the box office.

Pirates Of The Caribbean: At World's End
2007 Walt Disney

DIRECTED BY	**Gore Verbinski**
SCREENPLAY BY	**Ted Elliott, Terry Rossio**
PRODUCED BY	**Jerry Bruckheimer**
CAST	**Johnny Depp (Capt. Jack Sparrow), Orlando Bloom (Will), Keira Knightly (Elizabeth), Geoffrey Rush (Captain Hector Barbossa)**

Will (Bloom) starts a desperate quest to find and rescue Capt. Jack Sparrow (three-time Best Actor Oscar® nominee Depp), who is trapped in Davy Jones' Locker at the bottom of the sea. In the franchise's previous film, *Dead Man's Chest,* Sparrow sells his soul to the legendary Davy Jones. In the franchise's first film, *Curse of The Black Pearl,* Capt. Barbossa (Rush) steals Sparrow's ship, the *Black Pearl,* and attacks the town of Port Royal. After the success of the original *Pirates of the Caribbean,* the franchise decided to make two films, *Pirates of the Caribbean: Dead Man's Chest* and *At World's End,* at the same time, to justify the enormous production costs of the special effects and period-laden films.

The last two days of principal photography in January 2007 were shot with a reduced crew for scenes with Orlando Bloom and Keira Knightly on Maui and Moloka'i at rugged coastal locations. Sharp, black volcanic rocks dotted the Moloka'i beach location nearly a mile from the nearest road. According to IMDB.com, this installment of the *Pirates* franchise also filmed scenes at the Hanalei Plantation Resort on Kaua'i and O'ahu, as well as at actual Caribbean locations, including the Bahamas and Dominica in the Lesser Antilles.

The Pirates of the Caribbean movie franchise is the first instance where a popular Disney theme park ride inspired a movie. The piracy-themed attraction meanders through a Spanish fortress at the Adventureland portion of the original Disneyland in Anaheim, California, while robotic buccaneers (among them Captain Jack Sparrow) lustily sing, "Yo Ho, Yo Ho (A Pirate's Life for Me)."

Orlando Bloom in the surf.

Made in Paradise

Tropic Thunder
2008 Dreamworks SKG/Paramount

DIRECTED BY **Ben Stiller**
SCREENPLAY BY **Justin Theroux, Ben Stiller**
PRODUCED BY **Stuart Cornfield, Ben Stiller, Eric McLeod**
CAST **Ben Stiller (Tugg Speedman), Jack Black (Jeff Portnoy), Robert Downey Jr. (Kirk Lazarus), Nick Nolte (John Four Leaf Tayback), Brandon T. Jackson (Alpa Chino), Jay Baruchel (Kevin Sandusky)**

In this satirical comedic look at Hollywood and the production of an epic Vietnam War film, the actors unexpectedly find themselves in a real-life combat situation. This handsomely produced, funny movie takes aim at such movies as *Apocalypse Now, Platoon, Rambo,* and *Uncommon Valor* (which had a Kauaʻi-filmed Vietnam set). The movie also comments on the influence of Hollywood on popular culture, as well as on the filmmaking process, from the dealmaking to the actual finished product.

Robert Downey Jr. was nominated for an Academy Award® for Best Performance by an Actor in a Supporting Role.

While filming a Vietnam War epic on location in Southeast Asia, three of Hollywood's biggest stars find themselves in a strange situation. While the trio believe they are filming second-unit scenes for a movie with new hidden-camera techniques, it turns out they are in a real life-and-death war zone in Laos' Golden Triangle, pitted against warlords and drug gangs.

Stiller plays Tugg Speedman, an action hero whose star is dimming. Jack Black plays Jeff Portnoy (coincidentally also the name of a real-life prominent Honolulu attorney), an out-of-control actor with a serious drug problem. Robert Downey Jr. steals the movie (if controversially) with his smart and funny portrayal of the five-time Oscar®-winning white Australian actor Kirk Lazarus, who darkens the pigment of his skin to fully immerse himself in the role of an African-American G.I.

Left to right: Ben Stiller, Robert Downey Jr., Nick Nolte, Jack Black, Brandon T. Jackson, and Jay Baruchel in *Tropic Thunder*.

Made in Paradise

Brandon T. Jackson plays an African-American rap star named Alpa Chino (get it—Al Pacino?), who confronts Lazarus over his casting. Nick Nolte plays a burned-out Vietnam veteran who writes the book on which *Tropic Thunder* is fraudulently based on. Ben Stiller co-authored the script in addition to directing and playing a leading role in the ensemble cast.

Kaua'i's various jungles, rivers, cliffs, waterfalls, and other terrains provided multiple locations to mimic the film's Southeast Asian locales. John Toll's beautiful cinematography captured the lush green locations, which added to a semi-realistic, surreal feeling to the movie.

Toll assembled a crew with Los Angeles and local Hawai'i-based personnel in all departments. Most Kaua'i scenes were filmed in daylight at exterior locations. The logistics of moving the cast, crew, and equipment through the jungle settings and getting to the right places at the right times was a daily challenge.

In Bob Fisher's July 2008 article in *ICG Magazine*, Toll remarked, "One would assume that moving around and finding interesting locations on a beautiful and relatively small island like Kaua'i wouldn't be that difficult. Wrong. Somehow, the locations that seemed most appropriate to the story were also the least accessible and the most difficult to shoot."

Left to right: Brandon T. Jackson, Jay Baruchel, and Robert Downey Jr., in *Tropic Thunder*.

In terms of the total days of filming and manpower, *Tropic Thunder* is the largest production to date ever staged on Kaua'i. Crew members worked on the Garden Island from February to October 2007 for scouting, pre-production, production, wrap, and breakdown. The film's production notes say, "The movie's exterior filming took place at seven locations primarily on Kaua'i's northern and Eastern sides before relocating back to Los Angeles for the Los Angeles locales and various interiors… The movie's two major set pieces, the Hot LZ and the Flaming Dragon Compound, were both shot on Kaua'i."

The Hot LZ (landing zone) was situated on an expansive valley of tropical land, part of the privately owned 40,000-acre Grove Farm Property in Kaua'i's county seat of Līhu'e. A few miles inland across rocky, winding roads, the movie's final action sequence takes place at the Flaming Dragon Compound. The expansive set was built over several months around the remnants of a couple of hydroelectric plants from the 1930s, including a working 100-foot wooden bridge leading to the compound. The Tinseltowners turned the Kaua'i Sands Hotel into a Vietnamese village. Hooray for Hollywood!

Made in Paradise

Forgetting Sarah Marshall
2008 Universal

DIRECTED BY **Nicholas Stoller**
SCREENPLAY BY **Jason Segel**
PRODUCED BY **Judd Apatow, Shauna Robertson**
CAST **Jason Segel (Peter Bretter), Kristin Bell (Sarah Marshall), Mila Kunis (Rachel Jansen), Russell Brand (Aldous Snow), Jonah Hill (Walter), Taylor Wily (Kimo)**

Devastated by a recent break-up with his TV-star girlfriend Sarah Marshall (Kristin Bell), Peter Bretter (Jason Segel) takes a Hawaiian vacation. Little does Peter know that Sarah is vacationing at the same Turtle Bay Resort with her new boyfriend, a rock star (Russell Brand).

Peter's idea was to go to Hawai'i to escape from his problems—or so he thought. At the resort, he meets a beautiful hotel clerk, Rachel (Mila Kunis), whom he finds himself attracted to. While at the resort, situations arise that complicate matters between the two couples. Taylor Wily plays Kimo, a hotel worker who becomes a confidante of Peter. Sarah breaks up with her rock star lover and wants to return to Peter, but he has fallen in love with Rachel.

The film captures spectacular island images and locality that enhance the story setting around the Turtle Bay Resort. Located on 800 acres of prime coastal property, Turtle Bay Resort became a lush backlot for the production. It gave the filmmakers multiple location options from pristine beaches and an open-plan hotel lobby to the nearby helicopter pad.

Sarah's production notes say, "For inspiration, screenwriter Jason Segel tucked himself away in a bungalow on O'ahu's North Shore to write the romantic disaster comedy. When taking a break from scriptwriting, Segel often found himself drinking or dining at the North Shore's only large hotel complex, the Turtle Bay Resort."

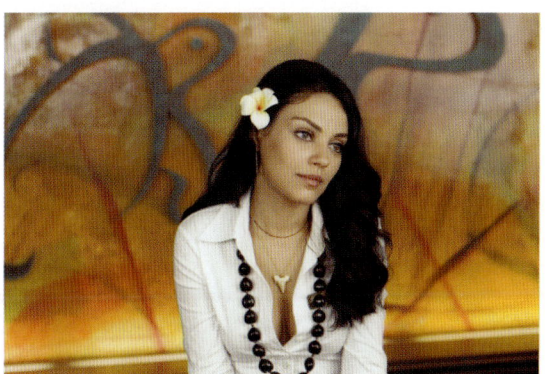

The production did venture outside of Turtle Bay for various O'ahu filming setups, including coastline shots of the dramatic cliffs at Lā'ie Point, Mokulē'ia Beach (which once housed the plane fuselage from ABC's *Lost*), and the pristine turquoise waters and sandy beaches at Keawa'ula Bay. Surf action was staged on the shores of Hale'iwa and photographed by renowned underwater cinematographer Don King.

Jonah Hill is a waiter at the Turtle Bay Resort, and Jason Segel is Peter Bretter in the romantic comedy Forgetting Sarah Marshall.

Mila Kunis co-stars as Rachel Jensen, the girl Peter (Jason Segel) eventually falls in love with in Forgetting Sarah Marshall.

Made in Paradise

Indiana Jones And The Kingdom Of The Crystal Skull
2008 Paramount

DIRECTED BY **Steven Spielberg**
SCREENPLAY BY **David Koepp based on a story by George Lucas**
PRODUCED BY **Frank Marshall**
CAST **Harrison Ford (Indiana Jones), Shia LaBeouf (Mutt Williams), Cate Blanchett (Irina Spalko), Ray Winstone (Mac), Karen Allen (Marion Ravenwood)**

Indiana Jones (Harrison Ford) fights off Russian agents on a dirt jungle road in Peru that was actually filmed at the Shipman Ranch in the Puna district of the Big Island.

Harrison Ford returns to the role of Indiana Jones in his last outing as the iconic, adventurous archaeologist in this popular series (which began with the blockbuster *Raiders of the Lost Ark* and continued through *Indiana Jones and the Temple of Doom* and *Indiana Jones and the Last Crusade*). Ford came to embody the quintessential American hero due to his portrayal of Indiana Jones and Hans Solo in the *Star Wars* franchise.

During the Cold War era of the 1950s, Professor Jones returns to Marshall College. There his recent activities have put him under suspicion, and the government has pressured the college to fire him. On his way out of town, Indiana Jones meets up with a young man, Mutt (LaBeouf), with an intriguing proposition: If Indy will help Mutt with a personal mission, it might lead to one of the biggest finds in archaeological history, the Crystal Skull of Akator.

The Big Island of Hawai'i stands in for the jungles of Peru in this latest adventure. The middle of the movie shows a major car chase between amphibious vehicles and a jeep. This sequence—where Indy outraces and outruns Russian villains in a 1957 jeep through a dirt jungle road—was filmed in the Puna District at the Shipman Ranch. The filmmakers chose the Big Island because of its tropical locations and its proximity to nearby production resources on O'ahu.

Shia LaBeouf co-stars as Mutt Williams in *Indiana Jones and the Kingdom of the Crystal Skull*.

Made in Paradise

Special Delivery
2008 Lifetime Cable Channel Movie

DIRECTED BY **Michael Scott**
TELEPLAY BY **Matt Dearborn**
PRODUCED BY **Francis Conway, Michael D. Jacobs, Fernando Szew**
CAST **Brenda Song (Alice Cantwell), Lisa Edelstein (Maxine Carter)**

Maxine Carter (Lisa Edelstein) is the best bonded courier in the Pacific Rim. She is assigned to take a bratty fifteen-year-old Alice (Hmong Chinese/Thai-American actress Song) from her father in China back to her mother on the continental United States. During the course of the journey, they bicker, fight, and eventually bond. Maxine realizes a trap has been set and that she must protect Alice when her life is threatened. This TV movie was filmed on Oʻahu.

Flirting With Forty
2008 Lifetime Cable Channel Movie

DIRECTED BY **Mikael Salomon**
TELEPLAY BY **Julia Dahl based on the book by June Porter**
PRODUCED BY **Lynn Raynor, Michael D. Jacobs, Frank Von Zerneck, Fernando Szew**
CAST **Heather Locklear (Jackie), Robert Buckly (Kyall), Vanessa Williams (Kristine)**

Jackie (*Dynasty* and *Melrose Place's* Locklear) is a divorced single mother just about to turn forty years old. When her daughter spends the holidays with her ex-husband, Jackie decides to go to Hawaiʻi for a vacation. There she meets an attractive, young surfer. The tagline of this TV movie was "Boy. Oh boy…" with a close-up image of a smiling Locklear in bed with her surfer stud. The movie premiered on the female-oriented Lifetime network and was filmed on the North Shore of Oʻahu.

Tyrannosaurus Azteca
2008 Sci-Fi Channel

DIRECTED BY **Brian Trenchard Smith**
TELEPLAY BY **Richard Manning**
PRODUCED BY **David Kemper**
CAST **Marc Antonio (Gonzalez), Allen Gumapac (Matial), Ian Ziering (Cortes)**

The sixteenth-century Spanish explorer Hernán Cortés and a group of conquistadors come upon an Aztec tribe in Mexico, which worships a T-Rex dinosaur that has somehow survived the Jurassic period. The natives offer human sacrifice to the "Thunder Lizard" at their temple site. *Tyrannosaurus Azteca* (aka *Aztec Rex*) is a low–budget, special-effects cable TV movie shot entirely at Kualoa Ranch and Turtle Bay in Oʻahu standing in for Mexico.

Made in Paradise

Heatstroke
2008 Sci-Fi Channel

DIRECTED BY	**Andrew Prowse**
TELEPLAY BY	**Richard Manning, David Kemper**
PRODUCED BY	**David Kemper**
CAST	**D.B. Sweeney (Capt. Steve O'Bannon), Danica McKellar (Caroline)**

Space alien creatures take over a Pacific Island. A military captain and a bikini-clad model must save the world in this low-budget cable TV movie, in which the extraterrestrials cause global warming. *Heatstroke* was filmed on Oʻahu.

Avatar
2009 Twentieth Century Fox

DIRECTED BY	**James Cameron**
SCREENPLAY BY	**James Cameron**
PRODUCED BY	**James Cameron, Jon Landau**
CAST	**Sigourney Weaver (Grace), Sam Worthington (Jake Sully), Zoe Saldana (Neytiri), Wes Studi (Eytukan), Stephen Lang (Col. Miles Quaritel), Michelle Rodriguez (Trudy Chacon), CCH Pounder (Moat), Laz Alonso (Tsuʻtey)**

James Cameron directed *Avatar* after 1997's *Titanic* (which won eleven Oscars®, including for Best Picture and Best Director and in the special effects categories). In terms of success at the box office and technical razzle-dazzle, sci-fi maestro Cameron's *Avatar* proved to be another stylish crowd-pleasing blockbuster, scoring three Oscars® for visual effects, cinematography, and art direction.

In this futuristic extravaganza, Jake Sully (Sam Worthington), a wounded warrior, takes part in an ex-

> *Avatar* received a total of nine Academy Award® nominations, winning in the visual effects, cinematography and art direction categories. It was also nominated for Best Picture; Best Director; Best Film Editing; Best Sound Editing; Best Sound Mixing; and Best Original Score.

Sam Worthington as Jake Sully (back to camera) and Zoe Saldana as Neytiri in a scene from *Avatar*.

Made in Paradise

Kaua'i rain forest Blue Hole area site where director James Cameron and cast members rehearsed and shot reference footage for *Avatar*.

perimental program overseen by Grace (Sigourney Weaver, who had starred in Cameron's *Alien*). The genetic engineering transfers the inner self, or mind of the paraplegic soldier, from his wheelchair to an *Avatar*. The experiment is done as part of the humans' avaricious scheme to take over the planet of Pandora to exploit this rain-forest type realm's natural resources. However, Pandora's indigenous inhabitants—the Na'vi, blue-skinned, elongated, "primitive" humanoid beings with long tails—oppose the expansion of the mining of the cleverly named "unobtanium" on their land. Jake becomes one of the Na'vi through the Avatar program, eventually falls in love with Neytiri (Actress Zoe Saldana), switches sides and joins the revolution against the invaders.

Avatar includes groundbreaking motion capture, stereoscopic 3D, IMAX, and other special effects that render Pandora so breathtakingly otherworldly and eye-poppingly vivid. The Hawai'i Health Guide.com says, "You may have recognized the Hāpu'u Tree ferns and botanical scenery from Kaua'i's Keahua Arboretum and the nature preserve surrounding the Wailua River when cast and crew visited the rain forests of Hawai'i to rehearse and shoot reference footage for visual effects." Cameron sent his stars to experience a "rain forest 101" or jungle boot camp in Hawai'i. There the actors could get a feel for the tropical environment that Pandora was supposed to have, as they were shooting mostly inside of sound stages and studios using green screen and other special effects technology for the CGI laden film. Zoe Saldana told *Entertainment Weekly*, "We did a sense-memory experiment in Hawai'i. We trekked around the rain forest for three days, building campfires and cooking fish, trying to live tribally… That experience helped us so much. Sigourney, Sam, and I were shooting the movie on a regular cement floor on a sound stage, but we needed to know what it was like to walk in a jungle world, what that felt like." Besides Kaua'i, the production also used the rain forest along the Hāmākua Coast at the Big Island's northeastern coast. Principal photography reportedly took place in both L.A. and Wellington, New Zealand.

Avatar became the bestselling Blu-ray of all time and the first movie in history to earn more than $2 billion. Just about the biggest movie moneymaker ever, according to Box Office Mojo.com, *Avatar* earned $2.782 billion.

Made in Paradise

A Perfect Getaway
2009 Rogue Pictures

DIRECTED BY	**David Twohy**
SCREENPLAY BY	**David Twohy**
PRODUCED BY	**Ryan Kavanaugh, Mark Canton, Tucker Tooley Robbie Brenner**
CAST	**Timothy Olyphant (Nick), Milla Jovovich (Cydney), Kiele Sanchez (Gina), Steve Zahn (Cliff)**

Left to right: Kiele Sanchez, Milla Jovovich and Steve Zahn in *A Perfect Getaway*. The actual Kalalau trail on Kaua'i has red dirt as opposed to the white dirt shown in the film. The trail also does not have the large white rocks and palm trees along the oceanside as in Puerto Rico where it was filmed. Only locals and those who have hiked the trail would be able to tell the differences in locales.

According to *Getaway's* production notes, while vacationing at lush Kaua'i, "Twohy was inspired to plot his latest project, one that happily breaks the conventional rules of three act linear storytelling. As he hiked the switchbacks of Kaua'i's remote trails, Twohy began imagining an intricate thriller of switchback deceptions about two serial killers who track and eliminate their victims."

A Perfect Getaway is an intelligent, well-crafted thriller with an unexpected twist. A newlywed couple has their honeymoon at Kaua'i, where they plan to hike the Kalalau Trail. They find themselves in fear for their lives when they suspect a couple who they meet on the trail are serial killers who have fled Honolulu. Though the film takes place in Kaua'i, only those familiar with the Kalalau Trail will know the difference between the real location and the reel location.

While the movie was set in the Garden Island, only computer-generated-imagery shots of Kaua'i were filmed there, including aerial, background, and cover shots to establish the location. This low-budget film was filmed primarily in the Commonwealth of Puerto Rico because of the favorable financing arrangements and economic tax incentives for the producers. Puerto Rico's El Yungue National Rain Forrest stood in for the verdant Nā Pali Coast State Park. The movie used visual effects to top off Puerto Rico vistas to turn them into Kaua'i.

King Kalākaua (Ocean Kaowili) and his favorite niece Princess Ka'iulani (Q'orianka Kilcher).

Princess Ka'iulani
2009 Island Film Group, Content Media

DIRECTED BY	Marc Forby
SCREENPLAY BY	Marc Forby
PRODUCED BY	Nigel Thomas, Ricardo Galindez, Roy Tjioe, Lauri Apelian, Mark Forby
CAST	Q'orianka Kilcher (Princess Ka'iulani), Barry Pepper (Lorrin A. Thurston), Will Patton (Sanford Dole), Shaun Evans (Clive Davies), Leo Anderson Akana (Queen Lili'uokalani), Ocean Kaowili (King Kalākaua)

After a U.S.-backed coup topples the Hawaiian monarchy, young Princess Ka'iulani returns to her homeland from Europe to help her beleaguered people. Her impatient suitor, Clive (Shaun Evans), who has not received replies to his letters, follows her across the globe to the Islands, where his family also has large plantations. Once the lovers are reunited, Clive gives the princess an ultimatum: return to Britain to marry him or they're through. Ka'iulani's loyalty is to Hawaiians, so she refuses. Of course, the simple solution to this dilemma would be for the Englishman to stay in Hawai'i and run his family's agricultural holdings, but somehow this solution never occurs to him. No Romeo and Juliet are they.

This $9 million indie co-starring Barry Pepper (Thurston) and Will Patton (Sanford B. Dole) premiered to a sold-out crowd at Honolulu's historic Hawai'i Theater. The film also stirred enough controversy that director Marc Forby changed the original title of the film from *Barbarian Princess* (an ironic reference to the U.S. journalists who only realized after meeting her in New York that she was anything but barbaric) to *Princess Ka'iulani*. Some Hawaiians expressed concern that a non-Hawaiian would depict their

Princess Ka'iulani (Q'orianka Kilcher) prepares to address the public upon her arrival in New York.

Princess Ka'iulani (Q'orianka Kilcher) and Clive Davies (Shaun Evans) share an intimate moment.

Made in Paradise   119

Queen Liliʻuokalani (Leo Anderson Akana) mourns the loss of the Hawaiian Monarchy along with Prince Kawanānākoa (Ruapena Sheck), Captain Nowlein (Vince Keala Lucero), Archie Cleghorn (Jimmy Yuill) and Princess Kaʻiulani (Q'orianka Kilcher).

Lorrin Thurston (Barry Pepper) preparing for a scene outside historic ʻIolani Palace.

Princess Kaʻiulani was the first movie permitted to film in the interior of ʻIolani Palace.

beloved royal highness. The actress depicting Kaʻiulani, Q'orianka Kilcher, grew up on Oʻahu and is of Peruvian, Alaskan, Swiss, and other mixed European heritage. Kilcher portrayed Pocahontas in Terrence Malick's 2005 *The New World* and has participated in native and environmental protests at South America. Kilcher obviously intended to honor Kaʻiulani as a courageous female standing up against the enemy.

The film is at its best when it raises awareness about the plight of Hawaiʻi, which suffered an American-backed overthrow and invasion in 1893, leading to U.S. annexation in 1898. Kaʻiulani throws herself into the fray as a champion for native rights and meets with President Grover Cleveland (Peter Banks) in Washington before returning home to support the Hawaiians. The movie features great, rare interior shots of ʻIolani Palace, where cinematography is generally tabu.

Academy Award®-winning composer Stephen Warbeck *(Shakespeare in Love)* composed the original score for *Princess Kaʻiulani,* and the Honolulu Symphony Orchestra performed it.

120   Made in Paradise

Honoka'a Boy
2009 Robot Communications, Twin Planet Films

DIRECTED BY	**Atushi Sanada**
SCREENPLAY BY	**Takuma Takasaki**
PRODUCED BY	**Gary Bassin**
CAST	**Chieko Baisho (Bee), Keiko Matsuzaka (Edeli), Masaki Okada (Leo), Jun Hasegawa (Mariah), Tom Suzuki (James), Chaz Mann (Buzz)**

Honokaa Boy is an adaptation of Leo Yoshida's novel of the same name. Based on Yoshida's experience, this Japanese-language movie depicts a visiting Japanese student who became a projectionist at the Honoka'a People's Theatre and befriended Beatrice Okamoto, an endearing elderly Honoka'a seamstress. The film draws on the history of Japanese immigration to Hawai'i in the last century.

This celebrated Japanese production filmed for thirty days at the actual location of the story in the tiny town of Honoka'a on the Big Island's east side. The production employed seventy-six people locally, including twenty crew members from the Big Island, and spent about $1.3 million there.

Hereafter
2010 Warner Bros.

DIRECTED BY	**Clint Eastwood**
SCREENPLAY BY	**Peter Morgan**
PRODUCED BY	**Kathleen Kennedy and Robert Lorentz**
CAST	**Matt Damon (George Loneger), Cecile de France (Marie), Frankie and George McLaren (Marcus/Jason)**

A sensitive supernatural tale, *Hereafter* centers on three people: a blue-collar American, the French journalist Marie, and a London schoolboy, who are touched by death in different ways. *Hereafter* makes a fine companion piece to the partially filmed-in-Hawai'i supernatural tale *Dragonfly*. When a tsunami strikes a resort where she is vacationing, Marie (de France) narrowly escapes death. The Indian Ocean tidal wave ravages a coastal town, leaving its streets filled with corpses and wreckage.

Hereafter involved location shooting in the town of Lahaina on Maui. The first few minutes of the film show an imaginary tsunami flooding the Sheraton on Kā'anapali Beach followed by Front Street in Lahaina. Steven Spielberg executive produced this special effects-laden extravaganza.

Hereafter was an Academy Award® Nominee for Achievement in Visual Effects by Michael Owens, Bayon Grill, Stephan Trojansky and Joe Farrell.

Cecile de France as Marie Lelay, Jessica Griffiths as Island Girl and Lisa Griffiths as Stall Owner become aware that a tsunami is about to strike. Filmed on Front Street in Lahaina, Maui, by Oscar®-winning director Clint Eastwood.

Made in Paradise

The Tempest
2010 Miramax

DIRECTED BY	**Julie Taymor**
SCREENPLAY BY	**Julie Taymor**
PRODUCED BY	**Robert Chartoff, Jason K. Lau, Julie Taymor, Lynn Hendee**
CAST	**Helen Mirren (Prospera), Russell Brand (Trinculo), Alfred Molina (Stephano), Felicity Jones (Miranda), David Strathairn (King Alonso), Chris Cooper (Antonio), Alan Cumming (Sebastian), Djimon Hounsou (Caliban)**

This modern retelling of Shakespeare's final masterpiece presents a visionary magical fantasy. The sorceress Prospera (Mirren) (who is usually portrayed as a male Prospero) is exiled to a mystical island. The kahuna-like Prospera conjures up a storm that shipwrecks her enemies and then unleashes her power for revenge. Director Julie Taymor is best known for her Broadway production of the Tony Award-winning musical *The Lion King*, and her feature-film credits include *Across the Universe* and the Oscar®-winning biopic *Frida* (starring Salma Hayek as the Mexican painter Frida Kahlo).

A local company, TalkStory Productions, teamed up with Chartoff Productions and Artemis Films to produce this movie on Lānaʻi and The Big Island and shot at locations such as Kekaha Kai State Park, Isaac Hale Beach Park, Mackenzie State Park, and Hawaiʻi Volcanoes National Park. The production also spent three weeks on Lānaʻi.

> **HOLLYWOOD**
> Sandy Powell received an Academy Award® nomination for Best Costume Design for *The Tempest*.

Crew sets up a shot of actress Helen Mirren on location on the island of Lānaʻi filming *The Tempest*.

122   Made in Paradise

Predators
2010 Twentieth Century Fox

DIRECTED BY **Nimrod Antal**
SCREENPLAY BY **Alex Litvak, Michael Fine**
PRODUCED BY **Robert Rodriguez, Elizabeth Avellan, John Davis**
CAST **Adrien Brody (Royce), Topher Grace (Edwin), Laurence Fisburne (Noland), Alice Braga (Isabelle), Oleg Taktarov (Nikolai), Danny Trejo (Cuchillo)**

This is the fifth film in the successful *Predator* film franchise that began in 1987, with *Predator* starring Arnold Schwarzenegger, whose commando team is stalked by an alien hunter through the jungles of Central America. In *Predators*, a group of coldblooded human killers, mercenaries, criminals, and Yakuza, all reluctantly led by Royce (Brody), discover that the Predators have selected them to hunt for sport on an alien planet.

Jungle exteriors were filmed over eighteen days at the Shipman Ranch, a 16,000-acre ranch on the Big Island of Hawai'i.

Royce (Adrien Brody) and Isabelle (Alice Braga) take aim during their desperate battle against the alien Predators.

Edwin (Topher Grace) is a doctor who finds himself trapped on an alien planet with a group of tough-as-nails mercenaries, including Isabelle (Alice Braga)—all of them being hunted by Predators.

The principal cast of *Predators* filming on location on the Big Island of Hawai'i.

Made in Paradise

Promotional out-of-character photo of the principal cast of *Hawaii Five-0* Reboot. *Left to right:* Grace Park, Scott Caan, Alex O'Louglin and Daniel Dae Kim.

Scott Caan as Danno, Daniel Dae Kim as Chin Ho Kelly and Alex O'Loughlin as Steve McGarrett in a hot water craft pursuit of the bad guys.

Hawaii Five-O
2010-( ) CBS Television

PRODUCED BY **Peter Lenkov, Roberto Orci, Alex Kurtzman
Based on the series *Hawaii Five-O*, created by Leonard Freeman**

CAST **Alex O'Loughlin (Steve McGarrett), Scott Caan (Danny Williams), Daniel Dae Kim (Chin Ho Kelly), Grace Park (Kono Kalākaua), Masi Oka (Dr. Mark Bergman), Mark Dacascos (Wo Fat)**

During the second season, actor Terry O'Quinn, the Emmy® Award-winning actor from *Lost*, was featured in a recurring role as Lt. Cmdr. Joe White, the Navy SEAL who acts as a father figure to Steve McGarrett. Tom Sizemore (a veteran of war movies, including Steven Spielberg's 1998 D-Day drama *Saving Private Ryan*, 2001's *Pearl Harbor* and *Black Hawk Down*) was also featured in a multi-episode arc in which he played Captain Vincent Foyer, who heads the Honolulu Police Department's Internal Affairs Division, which investigates many of Steve McGarrett's *Hawaii Five-0* tactical decisions. Richard T. Jones plays Lt. Gov. Sam Denning, who assumes the governorship when Gov. Jameson is murdered at the end of season one. (The fact that Gov. Jameson is a woman may be inspired by the fact that Hawai'i actually did elect a female, Linda Lingle, to be governor. And Denning being Black may be a reference to Barack Obama, who was born in O'ahu, while the character's name is suggestive of Richard Denning, who played Gov. Paul—not Pat!— Jameson from 1968-1980 on *Five-O*.) Jeff Cadiente is the stunt coordinator for the series and has directed as well. Cadiente is the son of the late stuntman and actor David Cadiente, who appeared in such Hawai'i based films as *Rampage* and *Donovan's Reef* among many others.

Made in Paradise

ALEX O'LOUGHLIN (Steve McGarrett)

O'Loughlin was born Alexander O'Lachlan on August 24, 1976, in Canberra, Australia and grew up in Sydney, Australia. He began his acting career as a teenager appearing in short films and theatre productions. After attending several acting classes, he was accepted to the prestigious Australian theatre school, the National Institute of Dramatic Art, at the age of 22. He graduated in three years in 2002, with a bachelor's degree in Dramatic Art.

After graduation, Alex had several guest-starring roles on Australian television including *White Collar Blue*, the *Mary Bryant* miniseries, and the *BlackJack: Sweet Science* made-for-TV movie. In 2006 he appeared in the Australian miniseries, *The Incredible*, as William Bryant. His performance earned him two nominations as lead actor, one for an AFI (Australian Film Institute) Award, Australia's most prestigious motion picture accolade, and the other for a Silver Logie.

Alex's film career started in 2004 with the Australian romantic comedy, *Oyster Farmer*, in which he had the lead role of Jack Flange. Alex made his feature film debut in the states with the sci-fi horror film *Man-Thing*, based on a Marvel comic book. While discussing a documentary about the underground world of feeders and gainers, Alex and a friend came up with their own idea for a screenplay. Directed by Brett Leonard, *Feed* was Alex's screenwriting and producing debut. He also starred as serial killer Michael Carter in the controversial film, which was introduced in limited release in the U.S. in 2009.

In 2005 Alex packed up his belongings and moved from Australia to Los Angeles to follow his dreams. In 2006, after auditioning for the lead role in *The Holiday*, starring Cameron Diaz and Kate Winslet, he was given the small part of "half of a kissing couple" and can be seen in the first 15 seconds of the movie. In 2007 he landed the role of Marcus Bohem in the sci-fi film *The Invisible*. Switching back to the small screen in 2007, Alex had a recurring role as Detective Kevin Hiatt for seven episodes during the sixth season of the critically acclaimed FX series, *The Shield*, with Michael Chicklis.

Alex's big break came when he landed the role of Mick St. John, a private investigator/vampire with a big heart, on the CBS cross-genre show *Moonlight*. The show ended in 2008 after 16 episodes, but it earned Alex an avid fan following. Impressed with Alex, CBS Television offered him a one-year holding deal after the cancellation of *Moonlight*. After a one-year absence from television, Alex had a guest starring role on the CBS crime drama, *Criminal Minds*, as serial killer Vincent Rowlings.

In 2009, Alex landed the lead role of Dr. Andy Yablonski on a short-lived TV series called *Three Rivers*, which was cancelled after only eight episodes. In 2009 Alex also appeared in the film *Whiteout* opposite Kate Beckinsale. As part of his contract with CBS, Alex landed the starring role of Stan opposite Jennifer Lopez in the 2010 romantic comedy *The Back-up Plan*, which failed at the box office. However, CBS offered him the lead role of Steve McGarrett on the new *Hawaii Five-0* without asking him to audition.

Made in Paradise

DANIEL DAE KIM (Chin Ho Kelly)

According to the CBS *Hawaii Five-0* website and Daniel Dae Kim's website, onstage and onscreen Korean-American Daniel Dae Kim has brought a wide variety of roles to life, playing a Thai monarch, a Shakespearean character, a social worker for the urban underprivileged and a covert agent. Prior to *Hawaii Five-0*, Kim was best known to audiences for his portrayal of Jin-Soon Kwon, on the long running Hawai'i-shot ABC-TV series *Lost*.

Born in Busan, South Korea, Kim grew up in New York and Pennsylvania and discovered acting while he was a student at Haverford College, near Philadelphia. After briefly considering a career as an attorney, he decided to follow his true passion and moved to New York City, where he began his work on stage. However, despite his early success, he decided to deepen his dedication to the craft by studying at New York University's graduate acting program, where he earned a master's degree in fine arts.

Upon graduation, Kim's film career began in earnest with roles in *The Jackal, For Love of the Game, The Hulk, Spiderman 2, The Cave,* and the Academy Award®-winning *Crash*. More recently he co-starred with Matt Damon in *The Adjustment Bureau* and in *Death Games* with Samuel L. Jackson.

On television, Kim has guest starred on numerous shows, including *CSI* on CBS, *ER,* and two seasons on *24* as Counter Terrorist Unit expert agent Tom Blake. In 2008, he also starred in the Emmy®-nominated miniseries *The Andromeda Strain*. In addition, Kim has lent his voice talents to videogames, creating characters in *Saints Row 1* and *2, Scarface: The World is Yours, Tenchu,* and *24,* as well as the animated television series *Justice League Unlimited* and *Avatar*.

SCOTT CAAN (Danny Williams, aka "Danno")

Like James MacArthur, the actor who portrayed Danno before him, Scott Caan also comes from a prestigious show biz family. His father is the legendary actor James Caan, who memorably played Sonny—Don Corleone's son, who gets rubbed out at a tollbooth—in the 1972 classic *The Godfather*. Although their best-known characters are on the opposite sides of the law, perhaps crime dramas run in the Caans' DNA? In any case, James went on to appear in other movies, such as *Thief, The Gambler,* and *Mercy,* and in 2013 joined the cast of the gangster-oriented Starz cable TV network series *Magic City*.

Made in Paradise

Actor, writer, and director Scott Caan has starred in numerous feature films and has written, directed, and starred in several theatrical productions. Caan attended acting classes at West Los Angeles Playhouse. Caan's feature film credits include the *Ocean's 11* franchise as Turk Malloy, *American Outlaws, Into the Blue, Friends with Money, Boiler Room, Ready to Rumble, Gone in 60 Seconds,* and *Varsity Blues,* playing a hell-raising wide receiver in the latter. In 1998 he landed a part in the late Tony Scott's thriller *Enemy of the State,* opposite Will Smith.

On television, Caan received a Golden Globe® nomination for playing Danno on *Hawaii Five-0* and prior to that praise for his role as Scott Lavin on the HBO cable series *Entourage.* Scott was the original choice for Danny Williams but was initially unavailable; however, as the pilot show was to begin production, Scott became available and was immediately hired without auditioning. He arrived in Hawai'i a few days before the start of production for a table reading of the script, where he first met O'Loughlin and the rest of the cast. The producer's instincts were spot on, and the chemistry and charisma between Caan and O'Loughlin was evident in the reading.

James Caan made a guest appearance on *Hawaii Five-0* as retired NYPD Detective Tony Archer, who is no relation to Danno. *The New Yorker* makes fun of Danno, calling him "hairdo" and "muscles" and refers to Steve McGarrett as McGoo or McGruff. Caan was previously in Hawai'i for his role as Tommy Noonan in the feature film *Honeymoon in Vegas.*

Far left photo, left to right: James Caan and his son Scott share a light moment during a break in filming on the set of *Hawaii-Five-O* reboot.

James Caan was previously in Hawai'i for his role as gangster Tommy Korman in *Honeymoon in Vegas* (1992) opposite Sarah Jessica Parker.

GRACE PARK (Kono Kalākaua)

Grace Park is best known to television audiences for her starring role on the critically acclaimed series *Battlestar Galactica* in which she played not one but two lead roles, as Sharon Valeri and Shannon Agathon. Born in Los Angeles and raised in Canada, Park received a degree in psychology from the University of British Columbia before turning her attention to film and television, where she was almost immediately cast in the Jet Li film, *Romeo Must Die*. More recently she starred in the independent film *West 32nd*.

Park's other television credits include memorable appearances in *Stargate SG-1, The Dead Zone, The Outer Limits*, and *Edgemont*. She also starred in the Canadian television series *The Border*, for which she received a Gemini Award (Canadian Emmy®) for best female performance in a series. She starred opposite Benjamin Bratt in the short-lived, critically acclaimed cable series *The Cleaner*.

Made in Paradise 127

MASI OKA (Dr. Max Bergman)

Masi Oka (Massayori "Masi" Oka) is a Japanese-American actor and digital effects artist. Masi's Max provides much of this often tense, action-packed cop drama's comic relief as *Hawaii Five-0's* quirky, geeky forensic lab specialist. Prior to *Five-0,* Masi was best known for his role as Hiro Nakamura on the hit NBC-TV science fiction series *Heroes* (2006-2010). In 2006, his heroic work on *Heroes* earned Masi a Golden Globe® nomination for Best Supporting Actor on a TV series and an Emmy® nomination for Best Supporting Actor in a drama series.

Born in Tokyo, Japan, and raised in Los Angeles, Oka studied theatre arts and computer science in college. Oka started his career as a computer programmer for George Lucas's Industrial Light and Magic, where he worked on such films as *A Perfect Storm* and the first *Star Wars* prequel. He started his acting career in 2000, when he obtained a Screen Actors Guild card after having appeared in an industrial film. He moved to L.A. and landed small roles before securing a recurring role as Franklyn on the ABC comedy *Scrubs*.

MARK DACASCOS (Wo Fat)

Mark, who plays *Five-0's* criminal mastermind and McGarrett's evil adversary Wo Fat, is a Honolulu-born actor and martial artist of mixed Filipino, Spanish, Chinese, Irish, and Japanese ancestry. His film credits include *The Island of Dr. Moreau* with Marlon Brando and Val Kilmer, *Cradle 2 the Grave* with Jet Li, and *Brotherhood of the Wolf*. On television he starred in the syndicated series *The Crow* and guest starred on such episodic series as *CSI* and *General Hospital*. He appeared as a celebrity contestant on *Dancing with the Stars* and was known as The Chairman, an M.C. on the *Iron Chef America* series on cable TV's the Food Network.

TAYLOR WILY (Kamekona)

Wily plays Kamekona, a recurring Hawaiian character who has a criminal past and is now pursuing the straight and narrow, acting as an informant for Five-0 by providing specific information on underground criminal activities in the Islands. In between helping to solve crimes, the reformed ex-con-turned-entrepreneur runs his own businesses, which include a shaved ice shop, a shrimp truck and in the third season, a helicopter tour operation. Along with Dr. Max, Kamekona brings humor to the crime program that helps to break the mood so *Five-0,* with its frequent violence and gripping plots, doesn't become overly serious. (The wisecracks Danno and Steve hurl at one another also serve to lighten the ambiance.) The roles for both Kamekona and Max have been beefed up since

Made in Paradise

the first season, enhancing the local atmosphere with a sorely needed Hawaiian, as well as Japanese-American sidekicks.

The bolohead, oversized Wily was born and raised in Hawai'i and is a former amateur sumo wrestler. His film credits include a role as Kemo, the hotel worker who befriended Jason Siegel's character in *Forgetting Sarah Marshall*, and a role on the short-lived Hawai'i-set TV series *North Shore*.

PETER M. LENKOV (Executive Producer)

The Canadian-born Lenkov grew up in a small town outside of Montreal. He studied political science at McGill and later at Concordia. A screenwriting course at UCLA spawned his career as a screenwriter, which led to Lenkov writing the story and screenplay for the theatrical feature *Demolition Man* in 1993 starring Sylvester Stallone and Wesley Snipes. His television credits include *CSI: NY, 24, CSI: Miami,* and the USA Network's *La Femme Nikita*.

ROBERTO ORCI and ALEX KURTZMAN (Executive Producers)

As executive producers, Orci and Kurtzman oversee the CBS reboot of the classic TV series *Hawaii Five-O*. Along with J.J. Abrams, they recently released the theatrical feature film sequel to their 2009 *Star Trek, Star Trek: Into Darkness*. Orci and Kurtzman got their start as writers on the cult-favorite TV show *Hercules: The Legendary Journeys*. They received their big-screen break when DreamWorks hired them to rewrite *The Island* for director Michael Bay, which led to them writing the hit *Transformers* and *Transformers 2*, also for Michael Bay. They were producers on *Cowboys and Aliens*. The team wrote a small indie film *Welcome to People*, in which Alex Kurtzman made his directorial debut.

Papa Mau: The Way Finder
2010 Palikū Documentary Films

DIRECTED BY	Nā'ālehu Anthony
SCREENPLAY BY	Leah Kihara, Elisa Yadao
PRODUCED BY	Nā'ālehu Anthony
CAST	Mau Piailug, Nainoa Thompson

Hawaiian director Nā'ālehu Anthony's *Papa Mau: The Way Finder* literally traverses two of the three Pacific Islands regions that compose Oceania. Anthony's own camerawork and archival footage carry us aboard the *Hōkūle'a*, an ancient-style Polynesian voyaging canoe, from Hawai'i to Tahiti and eventually to Satawal atoll in the Caroline Islands, now part of the Federated States of Micronesia.

Rather remarkably, starting in 1976, *Hōkūle'a* (which can be translated as "the Glad Star") made these seafaring odysseys of Homeric proportions minus the use of modern technology: compasses, radio transmissions, GPS, engines, even maps per se, etc. *Hōkūle'a* relied solely on the age-old Polynesian sailing techniques, navigating by following the stars, winds, ocean swells, birds and the like, using dead reckoning and more. Nainoa Thompson of the Polynesian Voyaging Society has explained that he strived to debunk the myth that the pre-contact Islanders were not intelligent enough to chart their courses across the vast stretches of the Pacific Ocean. Thompson argued that rather than separating the isles, the Pacific served as a great highway that linked the scattered islands, and that ancient Islanders had the wisdom and knowledge to be able to cross the seas. This theory sharply contrasted the notion advanced by

Made in Paradise

Thor Heyerdahl, whose Kon Tiki raft was helplessly blown and floated across the Pacific from Peru until it crash landed on the reef of an atoll in French Polynesia in 1947.

Thompson, artist Herb Kane (who rendered superb images of ancient Hawaiian vessels), and their PVS comrades faced the challenge of finding out how to put theory into practice. By the 1970s, their ancestors' traditional technique of way finding had been lost. Even if, using Kane's designs, they were able to recreate a seaworthy canoe, how would they be able to cross the seas in it? The Hawaiians turned to Micronesian Mau Piailug, a way finder who steeped in the Carolinian traditions at far-flung Satawal, which was less Westernized than Hawai'i.

Canoeman Mau came to Hawai'i and became *Hōkūle'a* navigator. Although the Micronesian was completely unfamiliar with the waters between Hawai'i and Tahiti, he successfully charted the canoe's course. After a month or so, he successfully sailed the approximately 2,100 miles between the two Polynesian Islands, following the stars, powered by the winds, breeze, and a deep desire to preserve and spread important cultural practices. *Hōkūle'a's* success helped spur a cultural revival of ethnic pride.

This Palikū production was presented in 2012 at the Los Angeles Asian Pacific Film Festival.

Anthony graduated from Kamehameha Schools in 1993 and received a BA in Hawaiian Studies from the University of Hawai'i at Mānoa as well as an MBA from the University of Hawai'i Shidler College of Business.

Among other things, this documentary reveals why the sweetest thing in life is to chart your own course and to paddle your own canoe.

Rise of the Planet of the Apes
2011 Twentieth Century Fox

DIRECTED BY	**Rupert Wyatt**
SCREENPLAY BY	**Rick Jaffa, Amanda Silver suggested by the novel by Pierre Boulle**
PRODUCED BY	**Peter Chernin, Dylan Clark, Rick Jaffa, Amanda Silver**
CAST	**James Franco (Will Rodman), Freida Pinto (Aranha), John Lithgow (Charles Rodman), Andy Serkis (Caesar)**

Rise, the latest outgrowth of Pierre Boulle's 1963 *Monkey Planet* novel, has spawned a succession of big- and little-screen renditions of the 1968 Charlton Heston version.

The film received an Academy Award® nomination for Best Visual Effects.

In *Rise*, Will Rodman (Franco) creates a genetically engineered chimp in a San Francisco laboratory called Gen-Sys (get it—"genesis"?) to find a cure for his father's Alzheimer's disease. Using his powerful intellect, the chimp's super-simian baby (Caesar, played by Serkis) leads an ape rebellion against humans.

The opening scene of the wild apes being rounded up in the jungle was filmed on O'ahu.

Made in Paradise

The Descendants
2011 Fox Searchlight Pictures

DIRECTED BY	**Alexander Payne**
SCREENPLAY BY	**Alexander Payne, Nat Faxon, Jim Rash, based on the novel by Kaui Hart Hemmings**
PRODUCED BY	**Alexander Payne, Jim Burke, Jim Taylor**
CAST	**George Clooney (Matt King), Beau Bridges (Cousin Hugh), Robert Forster (Scott Thorson), Laird Hamilton (Troy Cook), Judy Greer (Julie Speer), Shailene Woodley (Alexandra King), Amara Miller (Scottie King), Patricia Hastie (Elizabeth King), Nick Krause (Sid), Barbara L. Southern (Alice Thorson), Matthew Lillard (Brian Speer), Kaui Hart Hemmings (Matt's Secretary Noe)**

A unique undertaking in the South Seas Cinema genre, *The Descendants* explicitly debunks the notion that Hawai'i is a problem-free, exotic utopia, which is common in non-crime themed productions. Indeed, according to a January 2012 NPR report, slack key guitarist Keola Beamer, whose music is part of the film's lovely soundtrack, initially hesitated in participating in the project: "Hawai'i has really been poorly portrayed in the past. It's been portrayed very stereotypically—a lot of surface stuff. You know, sunlight and pretty girls in bikinis—comedy-lite kind of stuff. I think this is one of the best movies to come out of Hawai'i, if not the best. I felt proud, you know, as a Hawaiian human being, and that doesn't happen often with Hawaiians in Hollywood."

> George Clooney arguably plays his finest role in this film; he received a well-deserved Oscar® nomination and won a Golden Globe® for his sensitive portrayal. *The Descendants* was also nominated for Best Director (Alexander Payne), Film Editing (Kevin Tent) and Adapted Screenplay (Payne, Nat Faxon and Jim Rash).

This motion picture's paradise definitely has realism and trouble. The film opens with a brief boating accident scene, followed by a montage of images of contemporary O'ahu's social ills. George Clooney's voiceover narration as Matt King muses: "My friends on the mainland think just because I live in Hawai'i, I live in paradise. Like a permanent vacation. We're all just out here sipping Mai Tais, shaking our hips, and catching waves. Are they insane?" Matt goes

George Clooney as Matt King, Shailene Woodley as Alexandra King and Amara Miller as Scottie King stand gazing at one of the last remaining unspoiled piece of paradise in *The Descendants*.

Made in Paradise

Matt King (Clooney) and his two daughters stand gazing at the breathtaking view of Kipu Kai as he contemplates selling the pristine oceanfront land that has been in his family for generations. Kipu Kai on the south east coast of Kaua'i is the setting for the King trust's land holdings.

FOX SEARCHLIGHT

on to declare, "Paradise can go fuck itself." He strives to set the record straight, demystifying the realities of a twenty-first century Hawai'i with crime, homelessness, and many other social problems in a high-cost, low-wage society. Most Hawaiians are landless—except for a handful, such as the Kings, a part-Hawaiian extended 'ohana, whose members are land rich (even if many of the cousins have blown their legacies and are now cash poor).

Unlike, say, scruffy Cousin Hugh (Beau Bridges), Matt has not squandered his inheritance or flaunted his wealth. Instead, he lives off of the income that he earns as a Honolulu attorney and does not spoil his daughters, Alexandra (Shailene Woodley) and Scottie (Amara Miller). Preoccupied with his private law practice (author Kaui Hart Hemmings has a cameo role as his secretary, Noe), Matt has been "the backup parent, the understudy" as he refers to himself until his wife Elizabeth (Patricia Hastie, who spends most of the film in a coma) has the aforementioned nautical disaster that opens *The Descendants*. At the Outrigger Canoe Club, Matt and Scottie bump into a repentant Troy Cook (in a clever piece of casting portrayed

132   Made in Paradise

George Clooney as Matt King and Shailene Woodley as his daughter Alexandra discover the true identity of Brian Speer while driving through a neighborhood and spot his picture and phone number on a real estate sign.

by pro-surfer Laird Hamilton), who was piloting the boat when Elizabeth had her accident, and they fight. As it becomes increasingly likely that Elizabeth will never recover from her injuries, the previously distant dad must step up and become seventeen-year-old Alexandra and ten-year-old Scottie's primary—and solo—parent.

Matt and Scottie make a surprise visit to fetch Alexandra at a Big Island boarding school, only to discover the mischievous teenager misbehaving. Upon returning to the family home in the Upper Nuʻuanu area of Oʻahu near the Pali, Alexandra refuses to go to Queen's Hospital to see her dying mother and finally confesses why to her angered father: Alexandra discovered Elizabeth with another man whom she had been having an affair with. This completely upends Matt, taking him totally by surprise. In one of *The Descendants*' funniest scenes, a frantic, sandal-wearing Matt runs through Nuʻuanu's streets to the home of the Kings' close friends, Kai (Mary Birdsong) and Mark Mitchell (Rob Huebel). The married couple reluctantly admits to knowing of the secret liaison. As the guys stick together, Mark reveals to an insistent Matt the name of his wife's lover: Brian Speer (Matthew Lillard).

During the ensuing death watch, matters become more complicated as Alexandra adamantly insists that her friend, Sid (Nick Krause), be allowed to stay with the family during the vigil, telling her dad, "I'll be a lot more civil with him around." After Sid hugs Matt when they meet and calls him "bro,'" Matt tells him, "Don't ever do that to me again." It doesn't seem very plausible that a grieving father would allow his seventeen-year-old daughter to have a male companion remain at such close quarters—especially as Sid tends to say the wrong things at the wrong time. In fact, Sid's loose lips lead to an altercation with Elizabeth's cantankerous father, Scott Thorson (Robert Forster, who starred in Haskell Wexler's great 1969 *Medium Cool* and Quentin Tarantino's 1997 *Jackie Brown*), with Alexandra's grandfather punching the hapless Sid in his face. The petulant Scott also blames Matt for his daughter's condition. Meanwhile, his wife, Alice Thorson (Barbara L. Southern), Elizabeth's mother, has Alzheimer's and in her dementia, doesn't comprehend what's happening.

As if all this upheaval isn't enough, while these vexing events unfold, under the rule against perpetuities, Matt must also contend with the impending, legally mandated dissolution of the King family's land trust. Their vast land holdings are centered on 25,000 acres at Kauaʻi, which was derived from the nineteenth-century marriage of the Kings' ancestor, a haole banker, with a Hawaiian princess. The modern day Kings' acreage, along a stunning stretch of Garden Isle coastline, has been kept pristine for more than a century, but which

Made in Paradise

developers—and greedy cousins—are itching to develop as the trust's expiration date nears. As a trustee of the estate, Matt has the deciding vote, but is undecided as to what the proper course of action is. Scottie, like her older sister, has behavior issues. After she became embroiled in a dispute with a fellow student, Matt must visit the classmate's home, where her local mother complains about the Kings selling their unspoiled Kauaʻi property to developers.

According to Elizabeth's living will, she must be removed from life support, and Matt announces her imminent death not only to his children, but also to a gathering of friends and family. This legal stipulation cleverly reflects the rule against perpetuities that requires termination of the Kings' land trust. While driving around Oʻahu, Alexandra notices a poster listing the name and phone number of a realtor and recognizes the man in the picture as her mother's clandestine lover. Matt tracks Brian Speer down and takes his daughters plus Sid to Kauaʻi, where Speer, his wife Julie (Judy Greer), and their two sons are vacationing. Matt plans on informing Brian of Elizabeth's approaching demise, so he can go to Queen's Hospital and bid "aloha ʻoe" to the comatose Elizabeth before it's too late. Matt also wants to look the man who has cuckolded him in the eye.

While at the Garden Island, Matt, his daughters, and Sid visit the very-local-kanikapila-style-to-da-max Tahiti Nui restaurant in Hanalei, where the Kanak Attack trio plays lovely Hawaiian music, including yodeling. There, Matt runs into his cousin Hugh (Beau Bridges), who acts friendly, but subtly pressures the attorney to vote in favor of dissolving the trust by selling it to Kauaʻi developer Don Holitzer. Matt reassures the down-on-his-luck, longhaired Hugh, who seems to sense Matt's reluctance. Acting very warmly towards his cousin, Hugh expresses regret that he didn't know Matt was coming to Kauaʻi to visit as he would have offered Matt, his daughters, and Sid his beach house to stay at. While staying at the hotel, Matt and Sid share a special late-night moment, wherein the teenager defends himself, insisting he's not stupid because he was captain of the chess team at Punahou, an elite private school in Honolulu. Matt and Sid make peace with each other.

Matt accidentally encounters Brian while jogging on the beach, trails him and spots the cottage where the Speers are holidaying. Matt later stalks Julie and her sons at the beach while her boys are swimming and chats the unwitting, innocent Julie up. As it turns out, the plot thickens: the beach cottage where the Speers stay belongs to Hugh, who—probably without knowing about the affair between Elizabeth and Brian—tells Matt that Brian is Holitzer's brother-in-law. If the land trust sells the property to Holitzer, Brian—a real estate agent—will

Left to right: Alexandra (Shailene Woodley), Matt King (George Clooney), Scottie (Amana Miller), and Sid (Nick Krause) at Hanalei Bay on Kauaʻi looking for Bryan Speer's beachfront rental cottage.

Made in Paradise

earn a lot of money from commissions. Matt begins to suspect the realtor romanced his wife—who may have been planning to divorce Matt, believing that her love for Brian was reciprocated—to influence the outcome of the impending land transaction in his favor.

Matt shows up at the cottage where the Speers are vacationing. While the unsuspecting Julie shows Alexandra around and talks story with her, Matt corners Brian and confronts him over the affair with his wife. Brian begs Matt to not tell on him, which would destroy his marriage. In the end, a smoldering Matt doesn't disclose Brian's extramarital activities to Julie, perhaps out of deference to the couple's marriage and their children. Instead, Matt tells Brian about Elizabeth's terminal prognosis and advises him to see her while there's still time to say farewell. But as he leaves the cottage, Matt impetuously kisses Julie full on the lips; perhaps trying to get back at the man who slept with his wife.

In one of the movie's most moving moments, the Kings look at the family's exquisite beachfront property at Kaua'i. Back at O'ahu, Matt prepares for his relatives' vote on how to dissolve the land trust by driving out to an old 'ohana ranch-style home, where the descendant gazes at photos of his departed Hawaiian ancestors and ponders what to do. When the cousins gather at the old family home to vote, Matt finally acts.

He vetoes their decision to dissolve the trust and sell out to Holitzer for development, boldly proclaiming, "Even though we're haole as shit and go to private schools and clubs and can't even speak pidgin, let alone Hawaiian, we still carry Hawaiian blood, and we're still tied to this land. And our children are tied to this land…" Matt realizes that according to the law, the land trust still has seven years left before it will be legally forced to dissolve. As an attorney, he is determined to find another way whereby the virgin 'āina won't become overdeveloped by run amok construction of malls, resorts, and the like.

In the process, he has also thwarted Brian Speer. As it turns out, he didn't have deep feelings for Elizabeth and doesn't bother to visit her at Queen's Hospital, although Julie does in another poignant scene. Her husband has told all to Julie, who, instead of bidding Elizabeth farewell, forgives the adulteress interloper for nearly destroying her family.

Matt has also spoiled the get-rich-quick scheme of some of his cousins, notably of down-at-the-heels Hugh. With barely concealed viciousness and greed in his eyes, Hugh turns threatens to come after Matt.

Following Elizabeth's death and the scattering of her ashes out at sea in a beach-boy style ceremony, Matt has bonded with his daughters and even earned a measure of respect from his disputatious father-in-law.

The son of show biz royalty—Clooney's Aunt Rosemary was a very popular singer and actress who appeared in movies such as 1954's *White Christmas*—the prematurely grey-haired George has been known for his preternaturally good looks, charm, and wit, and from his roles on TV series, notably the *ER* medical drama, to his big-screen star turns in 1998's *Out of Sight* and the *Oceans* franchise. Clooney has emerged as the archetypal leading man and has often been likened to Cary Grant, so his depiction of Matt King is all the more impressive, as he is playing against type. Not only does this actor who often plays the romantic lead not get the girl in *The Descendants*, but he loses her, twice—as his wife cheats on him, then dies. In the course of this entire tragicomedy, Clooney doesn't find another romantic interest. Aside from smooching Julie, Matt has zero love life; perhaps he sublimates his passion into a paternal love for his daughters, with whom he eats ice cream on the living room couch while

A makeshift tracking shot using a steadi-cam and a sand vehicle to capture scenes of George Clooney running on the beach in Hanalei for a scene in *The Descendants*.

Made in Paradise

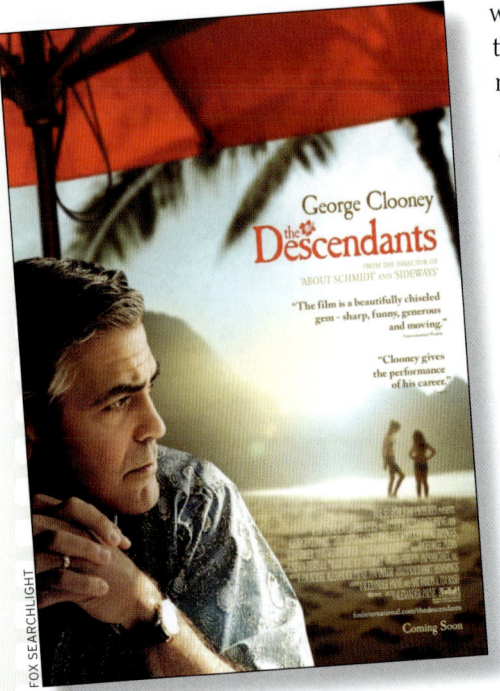

watching that ode to monogamy and the nuclear family, the documentary *March of the Penguins,* on TV in the movie's final scene.

One of the many great things about *The Descendants* is the soundtrack, which consists solely of Hawaiian music, from the 1930s through today, by notable performing and recording such as Keola Beamer, Sonny Chillingworth, Rev. Dennis Kamakahi, Kanak Attack, Ray Kane, Lena Machado, the "Father of Modern Slack Key Guitar" Gabby Pahinui, and Jeff Peterson. *The Descendants'* oldest song dates back to a 1930 arrangement of "Ka Mele Oku'u Pu'uwai" performed by slide steel guitar pioneer Sol Hoopi'i and his Novelty Trio. As Payne related to the *Los Angeles Times,* "For such a small area, there's an intimidating amount to learn about their tremendous musical heritage." According to a Feb. 9, 2012 *San Francisco Chronicle* article by Jeanne Cooper, *The Descendants* is "said to be the first Hollywood movie scored exclusively with Hawaiian music [and] has introduced millions of moviegoers to the giants of slack key guitar and the masters who have come after them."

According to a Jan. 8, 2012 NPR report by Heidi Chang: "Payne didn't know much about the music when he started the project. Then he discovered one of the giants of Hawaiian music, Gabby Pahinui. 'And when I started listening to Gabby, I just fell in love,' Payne says. 'So much so that I considered for a while trying to score the whole film with his music. And I wound up not doing that because there are so many other Hawaiian artists to show and discover. But his remains the anchoring voice in the film.'" In Steve Hochman's Nov. 29, 2011 *Los Angeles Times* story, Payne "cites Simon & Garfunkel's music in [Mike Nichols' 1967] *The Graduate* as a model for how he wanted to use songs by Pahinui—illuminating not just the emotions but the locales."

How realistic is the whole land issue that forms the social backdrop for *The Descendants?* Quite so, according to a Nov. 26, 2011 article in the *Wall Street Journal* by Julia Flynn Siler: "Perhaps the strongest echo of a situation facing the Clooney character was faced in real life a few years back by the trustees of Hawai'i's Campbell Estate. Under the terms of the trust, the 107-year-old Campbell Estate was required to dissolve in January of 2007, twenty years after the death of the last direct descendants who had been alive at the time of the trust's creation."

The *WSJ* article cites authors of books on Hawai'i, Gavan Daws and Randall Roth, who are acknowledged in screen credits at the end of *The Descendants,* and adds, "Professor Roth says there have been perhaps a half dozen family trusts in Hawai'i in recent years that have faced this same situation." Some of these land trusts are derived from Hawai'i's early missionary and so-called Big Five families. The Damons are descended from missionary Samuel Chenery Damon who arrived in Honolulu in 1842, where his son Samuel Mills Damon was born in 1845. The latter became a banker who was influential in Hawai'i's political circles and close to Princess Bernice Pauahi Bishop. Although they did not wed, she bequeathed him land and the Damons, who went on to own a tremendous amount of land on the Big Island. The 20 or so heirs of the Damon estate were, like screendom's King family, legally required to dissolve their land trust during the 1990s and supposedly made millions per each heir in doing so.

Made in Paradise

Moke Action
2011 University of Hawai'i's Academy for Creative Media, Shanghai University's School of Film and Television

DIRECTED BY **Kamakanioka Aina Paikai**
SCREENPLAY BY **John Rice, Joe Batteer**
PRODUCED BY **Chadwick Shimomura**
CAST **Blake "Brutus" La Benz, Brahma "Bull" Furtado, Leona "Aunty Lee" Arruda**

Only five minutes long, *Moke Action* has more cultural authenticity than entire feature length movies, such as *Six Days Seven Nights*. This exceptional, slyly humorous, inventive film takes place at a mom-and-pop shop in Nānākuli, Yuen's Grocery and Liquor Store. An accident involving two young local males triggers an incident that leads to an argument between the pair of so-called "mokes." (Note: According to Peppo's *Pidgin To Da Max* book, a moke is a "Local boy whose idea of a good time is to broke some body's face. Male counterpart of TITA.")

During their vocal pyrotechnics, the pidgin English—a creole of Hawaiian, English, and the other tongues in Hawai'i—flies fast and furious. And here's where *Moke Action's* charm and humor comes in: the subtitles translating the pidgin.

The inspired cinematography by Evan Loney includes a shot inside of a cooler filled with ice cubes and close ups of island delicacies in the general store. The characters' self-reflexive commentary adds to the sheer hilarity.

The following is a statement by director Kamakanioka Aina Paikai at 'Ōiwi TV's website:

> I've always hated films where the Hawai'i based characters speak terrible Pidgin English. A majority of the time, the language sounds forced and inaccurate. This film was dedicated to making a film in Pidgin the right way, from a local perspective. Too often Pidgin gets attacked as a 'dummy' language, but I wanted to showcase its usefulness and at the same time, poke a little fun at those on the opposite end, who speak extremely proper English. I feel Pidgin is Hawai'i's own unique dialect, and as a native speaker, I find it comforting.

The film has been screened at the 2010 Shanghai International Film Festival, won the Audience Award for the Academy for Creative Media Award Ceremony and had multiple showings at the 2010 Hawai'i International Film Festival. *Moke Action* was also screened in 2012 at the Los Angeles Asian Pacific Film Festival on a double bill with *Papa Mau: The Way Finder*.

Maybe this wonderfully witty movie was shot in the "Pidgin to da IMAX" process. Who knows what's next for the imaginative Paikai? Perhaps a sequel entitled *Tita Action?* In any case, let's hope the director continues to bring his quirky, singular vision to the screen. If you want the smile of the day, watch *Moke Action*. Hana hou!

Pirates of the Caribbean: On Stranger Tides
2011 Walt Disney

DIRECTED BY	**Rob Marshall**
SCREENPLAY BY	**Terry Rossio, Ted Elliott**
PRODUCED BY	**Jerry Bruckheimer**
CAST	**Johnny Depp (Captain Jack Sparrow), Penélope Cruz (Angelina Teach), Geoffrey Rush (Captain Hector Barbossa), Ian McShane (Blackbeard), Kevin McNally (Joshamee Gibbs)**

Helmed by Oscar®-winning director Robb Marshall *(Dream Girls)*, the movie is the fourth installment in the *Pirates of the Caribbean* film franchise.

Kauaʻi provided numerous landscapes for the film, as well as a considerable number of background players, in excess of 700. The first day of shooting took place at Honopū Beach on the north shore of Kauaʻi. For the next thirty days, the film shot around Kauaʻi at the National Botanical Gardens in Lāwaʻi, Kipu Ranch, Grove Farm, and Valley House Ranch. The film's production notes said these locations "provided rich landscapes for thick jungle growth, rivers, chasms, and cliffs, much of it ruggedly challenging for the cast and crew to access and film, especially with the two-camera 3D rigs." The production also filmed at Waipake on Kauaʻi's north shore, commonly known as the "Blue Room Cave" to tourists, and the cave grotto serves as an entrance to the caverns to the Fountain of Youth.

The final location in Kauaʻi was in the vicinity of the shuttered remains of the legendary Coco Palms Resort near Kapaʻa, one of the primary locations for Elvis Presley's *Blue Hawaii*. Marshall and his crew shot in the vast coconut grove for which the hotel was named; 773 palms were harvested before filming to prevent the heavy nuts from falling on the cast and crew.

Much of the filming in Oʻahu was out at sea with Blackbeard's pirate ship, the *Queen Anne's Revenge*, at either Barbers Point or the Heʻeia Kea Boat Dock in Kāneʻohe. Every night,

Johnny Depp as Captain Jack Sparrow and Penelope Cruz as Angelina Teach make their way through dense tropical underbrush.

138 Made in Paradise

hundreds of locals and tourists would come out and watch the actors ride on the little boats to the ship. The production notes say, "The crowds were awed by the sight of the *Queen Anne's Revenge*, off in the distance." During the filming of the mutiny against Blackbeard led by Jack Sparrow, movie fog and smoke shrouded the pirate ship, which was surrounded by camera and support craft from marine coordinators.

The mermaid attack on Captain Jack and Blackbeard's pirates takes place in Oʻahu's legendary *From Here to Eternity* Beach, also known as Hālona Cove Beach. The production crew built atmospheric mermaid pools at the North Shore's Turtle Bay Resort. The tourists and hotel guests at the resort had no idea of the nightly shoots taking place.

Soul Surfer
2011 Sony Pictures

DIRECTED BY	**Sean McNamara**
SCREENPLAY BY	**Sean McNamara**
PRODUCED BY	**Anthony Romano, Michael Shane, Ray Hofstetter, Seth Goldberg, David Brookwell**
CAST	**AnnaSophia Robb (Bethany Hamilton), Dennis Quaid (Tom Hamilton), Helen Hunt (Cheri Hamilton), Carrie Underwood (Sarah Hill), Kevin Sorbo (Holt Blanchard), Lorraine Nicholson (Alana Blanchard), Craig T. Nelson (Dr. David Rovinsky), Branscombe Richmond (Ben Aipa)**

Soul Surfer is based on the true story of Bethany Hamilton, a promising young surfer from Kauaʻi who discovers the purpose of life as she overcomes the loss of her arm. On Oct. 13, 2003, Kauaʻi resident Hamilton—who was thirteen years old at the time—was surfing off of Tunnels Beach on the Garden Island's North Shore when a fourteen-foot tiger shark attacked her. The attack took her left arm and seemed to end her career as a professional surfer. After losing more than 60 percent of her blood, and making it through several surgeries without infection, just one month after the attack, Hamilton miraculously returned to the water to continue pursuing her goal to become a professional surfer.

Since the loss of her arm, hundreds of media outlets around the world have told Hamilton's story. She shared her life story in her au-

Dennis Quaid as Tom Hamilton, AnnaSophia Robb as Bethany Hamilton and Helen Hunt as her mother Cheri in *Soul Surfer*. Note the green covering on her right arm that will allow CGI to remove her arm in post production that will look on screen as if her arm is missing.

AnnaSophia Robb and Lorraine Nicholson on the set of the movie *Soul Surfer*.

tobiography, *Soul Surfer*, which receives a writing credit for the movie of the same name. Hamilton also inspired Becky Baumgartner's 2007 documentary *Heart of a Soul Surfer*.

The production crew filmed *Soul Surfer* on a thirty-day shooting schedule set largely around the North Shore of Oʻahu, with AnnaSophia Robb cast as Hamilton. Dennis Quaid played her father Tom, and Helen Hunt played her mother Cheri. Country singer Carrie Underwood makes her acting debut in the film as Sarah Hill.

The Turtle Bay Resort, where the movie company made its headquarters, also stood in for Thailand. After the devastating 2004 tsunami, which killed more than 200,000 people, Hamilton went to Thailand to contribute to the humanitarian relief efforts. Production designer Rusty Smith strewed debris and broken trees in the area around the resort to make it look like the devastated beach town of Phuket. The filmmakers brought in hundreds of extras, as well as a few animals native to Thailand—such as the water buffalo—to recreate the area struck by the tidal wave.

In addition to Oʻahu, some establishing shots were done on Kauaʻi, shooting three North Shore locations: Tunnels Beach, the beginning of the Kalalau Trail (to Hanakapiʻai Beach), and the Hanalei Pier.

An uplifting inspirational story, *Soul Surfer* resonates especially with young children, teenage girls, and people with disabilities. Filmed in a direct, unassuming, spare style, this film demonstrates strong control of its story's intent and content with a very robust cast and firm direction by Sean McNamara.

Made in Paradise

Hop
2011 Universal

DIRECTED BY	**Tony Hill**
SCREENPLAY BY	**Ken Daurro, Brian Lynch, Cinco Paul**
PRODUCED BY	**Chris Meledandri, Michelle Imperato Stabile**
CAST	**Russell Brand (E.B.), Hugh Laurie (E.B.'s Dad), James Marsden (Fred O'Hare), Hank Azarria (Carlos & Phil), Elizabeth Perkins (Bonnie O'Hare), Chelsea Handler (Mrs. Beck), David Hasselhoff (Self)**

Hop is an Easter-themed animated and live-action comedy. Kaua'i's North Shore doubles as Easter Island in the opening scenes of the movie.

You May Not Kiss The Bride
2011 Hawai'i Film Partners

DIRECTED BY	**Rob Hedden**
SCREENPLAY BY	**Rob Hedden**
PRODUCED BY	**Rann Watumull, Gina Watumull, David Jackson, Shauna Shapiro Jackson**
CAST	**Rob Schneider (Ernesto), Kathy Bates (Bryan's Mother), Mena Suvari (Tonya), Ken Davitian (Vadik Nikitin), Katharine McPhee (Masha Nikitin), Vinnie Jones (Brick), Tia Carrere (Lani), Al Harrington (Resort Bartender), Willie K. (Tahitian Village Mayor)**

In *You May Not Kiss The Bride*, Hawai'i doubles for Tahiti and Chicago of all places. In the film, a Croation mobster tries to arrange for his daughter to obtain U.S. citizenship by setting her up with a Chicago pet photographer. The production was filmed over five weeks on O'ahu. *You May Not Kiss the Bride* is Hawai'i Film Partners' first feature, and the film company previously produced two seasons of the national TV show *Flight 29 Down*.

Some popular island talents play small roles in this romantic comedy film. Tia Carrere, who played important parts in major Tinseltown productions, such as 1992's *Wayne's World* and 1994's *True Lies*, plays Lani in *You May Not Kiss the Bride*. Hawaiian singer Willie K. plays the mayor of a Tahitian village.

Left to right: Dave Annable, Tia Carrere *(front)*, Mena Suvari and Rob Schneider *(back)* on an O'ahu Beach doubling for Tahiti. Honolulu also provided convincing Chicago locations.

Made in Paradise

Just Go With It
2011 Columbia

DIRECTED BY **Dennis Dugan**
SCREENPLAY BY **Timothy Dowling, Alan Loeb**
PRODUCED BY **Heather Parry, Adam Sandler, Jack Giarraputo**
CAST **Adam Sandler (Danny Maccabee), Jennifer Aniston (Katherine Murphy), Nicole Kidman (Devlin Adams), Brooklyn Decker (Palmer)**

Adam Sandler has become closely identified with romantic comedies made in Hawai'i. Sandler's previous cinematic excursions to Hawai'i prior to *Just Go with It* include *Punch Drunk Love* and *50 First Dates*.

Adam Sandler as Danny and Brooklyn Decker as Palmer in *Just Go with It*.

In this predictable, modern, romantic comedy, Danny Maccabee (Adam Sandler) is a middle-aged Beverly Hills plastic surgeon who meets and falls for a girl half his age named Palmer (Brooklyn Decker). He recruits his nurse Katherine (Jennifer Aniston) to pretend to be his soon-to-be ex-wife to cover up a careless lie. When more lies result out of a meeting to clear up any misunderstandings, Danny enlists the aide of her two children as well. To win their cooperation in the scheme, Danny promises her young son a dream trip to Hawai'i to swim with the dolphins. The boy mentions the trip to Hawai'i to Palmer, who wants Danny to be a good father and make his son's wish come true. Danny, Katherine, Palmer, the kids, and Danny's best friend go to Hawai'i. There, Danny realizes through a series of ridiculous situations that he really loves Katherine, not Palmer, and proposes to her.

Just Go With It began filming in Los Angeles before moving to Maui and Kaua'i. "Maui is our vacation spot," explained production designer Perry Andelin Blake in the film's production notes. "About three months before we started filming director Dennis Dugan and I went on a scout throughout the islands. We started in O'ahu and went to a couple of hotels there—we were looking for a crazy big beautiful resort hotel, but they just didn't have what we were looking for. We next

142 Made in Paradise

went to Kona—I've been to some of the hotels there, and there were some pretty cool ones. Finally we came to Maui and to the Grand Wailea and we were just blown away. It was the perfect hotel."

Dugan says the hotel had desirable attributes for the film: "It may be the largest of all the hotels; it has a lot of scope. It's got a gigantic set of swimming pools—it's kid friendly, with slides and waterfalls, but also romantic. There are many, many different looks within the hotel. The lobby is magnificent, the front is great, the rooms are beautiful, the lū'au was amazing, and the unit has a whole beautiful beach. The hotel worked beautifully as a movie set."

A set person carries a fake boulder into position at Kīlauea Falls on the North end of the island of Kaua'i in Kīlauea on the set of Adam Sandler's *Just Go with It*.

The production designer added, "After four weeks in Maui, the production moved to Kaua'i. The Kaua'i location was chosen because of its waterfall. Though the waterfall was perfect, the set would still require some design and decoration. Despite the location's jungle vibe, it wasn't really lush and beautiful, so we brought in plants and flowers. You don't find everything you are looking for in any location, so we made the jungle more jungle-ly, but that's the way you do it in the movies."

In addition, the script called for all of the characters to approach the pool of water at the bottom of the falls and dive in. "But the water was much too shallow," said Blake. "The solution was to bring in fake rocks to dress a deeper part of the pool. Brooklyn Decker's character lounges around on foam rocks after her dive. The screenplay also requires the characters to cross a rope bridge, the filmmakers didn't find what they were looking for and so a bridge was built that was aged and covered with plants so as to look rickety and dilapidated but was completely safe." And there we have it: Kaua'i and Maui movie magic.

The River
2011 ABC

SCREENPLAY BY **Oren Peli, Michael R. Perry**

CAST **Bruce Greenwood (Dr. Emmet Cole), Joe Anderson (Lincoln Cole), Leslie Hope (Tess Cole), Eloise Mumford (Lena Landry), Daniel Zacapa (Emilio Valenzuela)**

In this short-lived adventure/horror series, Bruce Greenwood stars as Dr. Emmet Cole, who travels the world to film a popular nature television show. After he goes missing in the Amazon, his family, friends, and crew search for him. The shocking truth about his disappearance is waiting to be discovered. *The River's* executive producers are Michael Green, Oren Peli, Zack Estrin, Jason Blum, and Steven Schneider.

Battleship
2012 Universal Pictures

DIRECTED BY **Peter Berg**
SCREENPLAY BY **Jon Hoeber, Erich Hoeber**
PRODUCED BY **Peter Berg, Sarah Aubrey, Brian Goldner, Duncan Henderson, Bennett Schneir, Scott Stuber**
CAST **Taylor Kitsch (Lieutenant Alex Hopper), Alexander Skarsgard (Commander Stone Hopper), Rihanna (Petty Officer Cora 'Weps' Raikes), Liam Neson (Admiral Shane), Brooklyn Decker (Sam)**

Battleship special effects action sequence.

Rihanna in *Battleship*.

This rip-roaring sci-fi adventure yarn pits the U.S. Navy's guided missile destroyer, the USS *John Paul Jones*, against invaders from outer space, who also wreak havoc on Hong Kong. Bad boy Lt. Alex Hopper (Taylor Kitsch) leads the good guys against the aliens with their futuristic weapons that, along with endless explosions, are rendered via CGI and other movie magic in this special-effects galore.

Of course, in that great American tradition, Lt. Hopper is trying to impress a woman and wages war against the technologically advanced extraterrestrials from Planet-G, who are aiming for world domination. The woman in question is Samantha (Brooklyn Decker), a physical therapist whose father is the by-the-book Admiral Shane (Liam Neeson). A hothead and rule breaker who wants to ask the admiral for permission to marry his daughter, Lt. Hopper distinctly underwhelms Shane.

Battleship was shot on Oʻahu with several Pearl Harbor locations, on the USS *Missouri* battleship as well as Punchbowl and Kualoa Ranch.

Made in Paradise

Journey 2: The Mysterious Island
2012 New Line Cinema

DIRECTED BY **Brad Peyton**
SCREENPLAY BY **Brian Gunn, Mark Gunn, Richard Outten, Jules Verne**
PRODUCED BY **Beau Flynn, Charlotte Huggins, Tripp Vinson, Dwayne Johnson**
CAST **Dwayne Johnson (Hank), Michael Caine (Alexander), Luis Guzman (Gabato), Branscombe Richmond (Tour Guide), Josh Hutcherson (Sean), Vanessa Hudgens (Kailani), Kristin Davis (Liz)**

There have been at least half a dozen screen versions of Jules Verne's *Mysterious Island*—including two silent and one Soviet adaptation—and the latest incarnation is a fun escapist flick with 3D IMAX special effects. *Journey 2: The Mysterious Island* plays fast and loose with authors Jonathan Swift, Robert Louis Stevenson, and especially Verne. Verne's novels have been adapted for the screen at least as far back as 1902, when Georges Melies shot Verne's *A Trip to the Moon*.

In this sequel of the 2008 adaptation of Verne's *Journey to the Center of the Earth*, Dwayne Johnson, also known as "The Rock," portrays Hank, who has married Sean's mother played by Kristin Davis. Hank wants to be a good stepfather to the alienated Sean, and this desire leads to their joint adventure in quest of Sean's long-lost Indiana Jones-type grandfather.

Their odyssey takes them to the Pacific Islands. For some mysterious reason, the titular isle is located near Palau, although in Verne's novel, it is situated 1,600 miles east of Aotearoa/New Zealand. Interestingly enough, the film never refers to Dwayne Johnson's Polynesian ancestry, specifically Samoan. However, in a scene, he is singing and strumming the 'ukulele. The movie reprises the song during the final credits, which proves that not only does the

Left to right: Luis Guzman, Vanessa Hudgens, Josh Hutcherson, Dwayne Johnson, and Michael Caine looking up at the creature in *Journey 2*.

Made in Paradise

ex-wrestler have a decent voice and musical ability, but also that he has a "co-producer" credit. As an actor, Dwayne has a light comedic touch and a telegenic, charismatic presence.

Director Brad Peyton's 3D IMAX whiz-bang wizardry is good, especially in the scene where the characters ride gigantic bees, as if they're "paniolos" atop galloping broncos. But some of the island backdrops look kind of cheesy and painted, and flowers and other flora likewise look unrealistic. The secret to attaining Samuel Coleridge's "willing suspension of disbelief" is to provide enough realism for the beholder to buy into it. The 1961 *Mysterious* version with special effects by the immortal Ray Harryhausen was actually more spectacular. Who can ever forget the scene where the characters discover the "beach" they're walking on is really the shell of a giant crab?! And the new adaptation replaces the original Civil War-era hot air balloon with a helicopter.

A giant creature in *Journey 2*.

Off The Map
2012 ABC

CAST **Martin Henderson (Dr. Ben Keeton), Caroline Dhavernas (Dr. Lily Brenner), Enrique Murciano, Mamie Gummer (Dr. Mina Minard), Jason George (Dr. Otis Cole), Valerie Cruz (Dr. Zita Alvarez), Jose Julian**

In this short-lived ensemble drama, five doctors who have lost their way will go to the ends of the earth to try to remember the reasons why they wanted to become doctors in the first place. Executive producers Shonda Rhimes *(Scandal)*, Betsy Beers *(Grey's Anatomy, Private Practice)*, and creator Jenna Bans *(Grey's Anatomy)* created an uplifting medical drama that explores how far one has to go to truly heal. The series filmed in O'ahu, but was set somewhere in South America. *Off the Map* seemed to be inspired by *Northern Exposure*, but was much less successful than that TV series about a doctor transplanted to Alaska, which ran from 1990 to 1995.

The cast and crew at the blessing of the main exterior hospital set at the start of principal photography of the short-lived series *Off The Map,* filmed at Kualoa Ranch doubling for South America.

146 Made in Paradise

Last Resort
2012 ABC

CAST **Andre Braugher (Capt. Marcus Chaplin), Scott Speedman (Sam Kendall)**

With topical references to the Navy SEALs and more, in this short-lived military-themed sci-fi series, a crippled American atomic submarine arrives at an exotic island where its crew encounters new enemies. Five hundred feet beneath the ocean's surface, the crew of the USS *Colorado*, a fictional ballistic missile submarine, receives their orders over a radio channel, which is to be used only if the U.S. homeland has been wiped out. The crew receives the order to fire nuclear missiles at Pakistan. Capt. Marcus Chaplin demands confirmation of the orders, only to be unceremoniously relieved of duty by the White House. Sam Kendall suddenly finds himself in charge of the submarine and facing the same difficult decision. When he refuses to fire without confirmation of orders, the USS *Colorado* is targeted, fired upon and hit. The submarine and crew find themselves crippled on the ocean floor and declared rogue enemies of their own country.

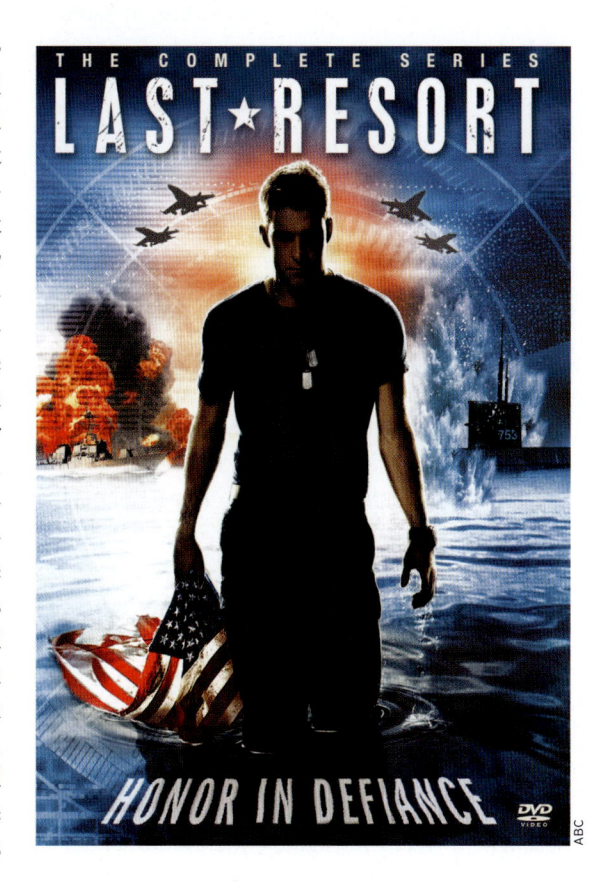

Now with nowhere left to turn, Chaplin and Kendall flee with the submarine and bring the men and women of the USS *Colorado* to a remote island. There they find refuge, romance, and a chance at a new life, as they try to clear their names and get home. *Last Resort* contemplates establishing a new society in the modern world, and character becomes everything when unthinkable decisions must be made.

The pilot and the series were shot entirely in Oʻahu, and Hawaiʻi-based veteran director of photography Don King handled the ocean cinematography on the pilot episode. In addition to serving as an island asylum and the location for the massive submarine set, Oʻahu also stood in for Washington, D.C. locations. Shawn Ryan and Karl Gajdusek serve as *Last Resort's* executive producers and writers.

An actual incident may have inspired the premise of *Last Resort*. According to Oliver Stone's *The Untold History of the United States*, during the Cuban Missile Crisis, the carrier USS *Randolph* damaged a nuclear-armed Soviet B-59 submarine in the Caribbean on Oct. 27, 1962. Unable to reach the Soviet general staff, believing that Moscow and Washington may have already gone to war, the Russian commander of the incommunicado, damaged submarine ordered the preparation of the nuclear torpedo. However, political officer Vasili Arkhipov refused to launch. In doing so, Arkhipov may have prevented World War III from taking place. U.S. President Kennedy's special assistant, historian Arthur Schlesinger, called this "not only the most dangerous moment of the Cold War. It was the most dangerous moment in human history."

Blue Lagoon: The Awakening
2012 Lifetime Movie Network

DIRECTED BY	Jake Newsome, Mikael Salomon
SCREENPLAY BY	Matt Heller, Heather Rutman, Henry De Vere Stacpoole
PRODUCED BY	Kyle Clark, Nellie Nugiel
CAST	Indiana Evans (Emmaline 'Emma' Robinson), Brenton Thwaites (Dean McMullen), Christopher Atkins (Mr. Christiansen), Denise Richards (Barbara Robinson)

The original *The Blue Lagoon* (1949) starring Jean Simmons and Donald Houston.

This made-for-TV movie is at least the sixth production inspired by the 1908 novel *The Blue Lagoon*. Irish author Henry De Vere Stacpoole, formerly a ship's doctor, wrote this novel, the first in a trilogy. Unlike the 1949, 1980, and 1991 versions, *Blue Lagoon: The Awakening* was not shot on location in Fiji, nor set in the South Seas. Indeed, California students Emmaline Robinson (Australian Indiana Evans) and Dean McCullen (Aussie actor Brenton Thwaites) go to Trinidad, which is in the Caribbean, not the South Pacific. However, the tropical island scenes were shot in Maui. (Emmaline Robinson's last name probably refers to the literary castaways Robinson Crusoe and Swiss Family Robinson; in Stacpoole's novel, she is called Emmeline Lestrange.)

The plot and coming-of-age theme of *Blue Lagoon* are similar to those of the previous renditions, although updated. *Blue Lagoon*, a decently made-for-TV movie, aired on a Lifetime channel. The production stays true to the original essence of the prior pictures about young love, although why the setting was relocated from the South Pacific to the Caribbean is not clear.

According to longtime assistant director Matt Locey, the Maui locations for *Blue Lagoon* include Mākena Beach Park, Twin Falls (near Hāna Highway), and Kapalua Bay. Long-time Polynesian performer Branscombe Richmond served as the made-for-TV movie's stunt coordinator.

The Master
2012 Annapurna Pictures

DIRECTED BY	Paul Thomas Anderson
SCREENPLAY BY	Paul Thomas Anderson
PRODUCED BY	The Weinstein Company
CAST	Joaquin Phoenix (Freddie Quell), Philip Seymour Hoffman (Lancaster Dodd), Amy Adams (Peggy Dodd)

The Master is a powerful, well-acted adult drama about a cult for which Joaquin Phoenix was nominated for the Best Actor Oscar, while both Philip Seymour Hoffman and Amy Adams received Best Supporting Actor/Actress Academy Award nominations. It is also notable as one of the last films Hoffman appeared in prior to his untimely death in 2014 at the age of 46 due to a narcotics overdose. Hoffman's Oscar nomination for his portrayal of *The Master*'s charismatic cult leader Lancaster Dodd was the gifted thespian's third Best Supporting Actor Academy Award nomination; in 2006 Hoffman struck Oscar gold for Best Actor for his depiction of author Truman Capote in 2005's *Capote*.

Made in Paradise

In *The Master* three-time Oscar nominee Joaquin Phoenix's character Freddie Quell becomes an acolyte of Dodd and his sect called "The Cause." Although mostly shot and set at the continental U.S., the R-rated *The Master* opens during World War II, while Quell is serving in the Navy in the Pacific Theater. Along with other male sailors Quell appears on a beach at a tropical island where he performs lewd acts, including with a female sand sculpture. This scene was shot at Oʻahu's North Shore, near Haleiwa.

Hawaiian: The Legend of Eddie Aikau
2013 ESPN, TAUBLIEB Films

DIRECTED BY	**Sam George**
PRODUCED BY	**Paul Taublieb, Stacy Peralta**
EXEC. PRODUCER	**Josh Brolin**
NARRATED BY	**Josh Brolin**

Edward Ryon Makuahanai "Eddie" Aikau was a legendary big-wave surf rider who was born in Maui but grew up on Oʻahu. He was famous for not only his incredible surfing skills, but also his dedication to saving lives as a lifeguard on Oʻahu's North Shore. Aikau came into prominence in the late 1960s and 70s, winning numerous competitions as a big-wave surfer.

The thirty-one-year-old Aikau was lost at sea on March 17, 1978. A doubled-hulled voyaging canoe, the *Hōkūleʻa*, of which he was a crew member, capsized at sea at the start of a 2,500 mile journey of Hawaiian cultural rediscovery between Hawaiʻi and Tahiti. In a desperate and valiant attempt to save his fellow crew members, Eddie paddled on his surfboard in rough waters to reach the nearby island of Lānaʻi for help. He was never seen again.

In an interview at the Maui Film Festival, Director Sam George remarked, "Our film is not just about Eddie; it places him in the context of contemporary Hawaiian culture. Aikau was very contemporary, but he also reflected a traditional Hawaiian culture that in modern times has been seriously marginalized." George, who grew up in Hawaiʻi, served as a former editor of *Surfer* and *Surfing* magazines, as well as the co-writer of the surf documentary *Riding Giants*. In another interview with XGames.com, he further explained, "Eddie has earned an interesting place in surf mythology; his achievements were largely undocumented and underappreciated. He became a legend, but few people knew why."

Hawaiian: The Legend of Eddie Aikau is a ninety-minute documentary that uses family photos, historical footage, reenactments, and personal accounts from family members and friends to reveal an intimate portrait of the man behind the legend. The film had its world premiere at the prestigious 2013 Tribeca Film Festival in New York City and was also the opening-night film at the Maui Film Festival. The documentary was broadcast on cable television as part of the second season of ESPN's *30 for 30* series in the fall of 2013.

Edward Ryon Makuahanai "Eddie" Aikau (1946-1978).

The Hunger Games: Catching Fire
2013 Lionsgate

DIRECTED BY **Francis Lawrence**
SCREENPLAY BY **Simon Bearfoy**
PRODUCED BY **Suzanne Collins, Nina Jacobson, Jon Kilik**
CAST **Jennifer Lawrence (Katniss Everdeen), Josh Hutcherson (Peeta Mellark), Liam Hemsworth (Gabe Hawthorn), Lenny Kravitz (Cinna), Elizabeth Banks (Effie Trinket), Woody Harrelson (Haymitch)**

The Hunger Games is part of the hugely popular trilogy of novels by Suzanne Collins. The first *Hunger Games* movie, a massive box-office hit, grossed $685 million worldwide. Set in a futuristic totalitarian society, the lead characters must compete for survival in a gladiatorial contest in a different Hunger Games arena each year. In this sequel to the 2012 dystopian flick, the match takes place at the Quarter Quell, an island rain forest surrounding a beach. Now Katniss and Peeta must fight for their lives, as well as save themselves from the Capitol, the ruling government of Panem, which is out for Katniss' blood.

The movie was shot on the North Shore of Oʻahu and at Mānoa during five weeks of filming from November to December of 2012. Locations included Turtle Bay Resort's lagoon, Kawela Bay, Mānoa Falls, Heʻeia State Park, and Keʻehi Lagoon Beach Park. Jennifer Lawrence won the 2012 Best Actress Oscar® for her performance in *Silver Linings Playbook* at the age of twenty-two.

Crew sets up a shot of Oscar®-winning Best Actress Jennifer Lawrence on the Oʻahu, Hawaiʻi location for *The Hunger Games: Catching Fire*, the sequel to the worldwide blockbuster box office hit film *The Hunger Games*.

Made in Paradise

Godzilla
2014 Warner Bros. / Legendary Pictures / Toho

DIRECTED BY	Gareth Edwards
SCREENPLAY BY	Max Borenstein, Frank Darabont, Dave Callahan
PRODUCED BY	Thomas Tull, Jon Jashni, Mary Parent, Brian Rogers
EXEC. PRODUCERS	Alex Garcia, Patricia Whitcher, Yoshimitsu Banno, Kenji Okuhira
CAST	Aaron Taylor-Johnson (Ford Brody), Ken Watanabe (Dr. Serizawa), Elizabeth Olsen (Elle Brody), Juliette Binoche (Sandra Brody), David Strathairn (Admiral Stenz), Bryan Cranston (Joe Brody)

"Victims" of the tsunami generated by Godzilla while he emerged on the shore of Waikīkī.

According to a press release given at a Honolulu press conference, "An epic rebirth to Toho's iconic Godzilla, this spectacular adventure pits the world's most famous monster against a malevolent creatures MUTO (Massive Unidentified Terrestrial Organism) who, bolstered by humanity's scientific arrogance, threaten our very existence."

Portions of the movie were filmed on Oʻahu over the first two weeks of July in 2013. Locations included the USS *Missouri* standing in for the USS *Saratoga* that tracks Godzilla across the Pacific, Hickam Air Force Base, Kapaʻa Quarry (doubling for a mine entrance), Secret Beach at Kualoa Ranch on the windward side, Waikīkī Beach at Hilton Hawaiian Village Lagoon, and downtown Honolulu. Godzilla comes ashore and wreaks havoc and destruction at Waikīkī. For a scene in front of the Hilton Hawaiian Village, foam blocks made to look like broken concrete walls were strewn about the beach as well as a broken helicopter and boats. Two-hundred and twenty-five local extras were used in that sequence including off duty members of the Honolulu Fire Department and Hawaiʻi National Guardsmen. Another scene involved a beach bar full of people socializing. Bar patrons are seen running from a Godzilla-caused tidal wave which was staged at a resort area, Waikīkī Beach Walk, on Lewers Street between Kalākaua Ave and Kalia Road. State of the art computer generated imagery and special visual effects brings Godzilla to life in a more realistic form than ever before. *Godzilla* was a worldwide Box-office hit, and sequels are being planned as a possible trilogy.

Big Eyes
2014 Weinstein Co.

DIRECTED BY	Tim Burton
SCREENPLAY BY	Scott Alexander and Larry Karaszewski
PRODUCED BY	Lynette Howell, Scott Alexander, Larry Karaszewski and Tim Burton
CAST	Amy Adams (Margaret Keane), Cristoph Waltz (Walter Keane), Danny Huston (Dick Nolan), Jon Polito (Enrico Banducci), James Saito (Judge), Pomaikaʻi Brown (Disk Jockey Big Lolo) Ran Wei (Asian Lady 1), Traci Toguchi (Asian Lady 2) Terence Stamp (Canady), Madeleine Arthur (older Jane)

Made in Paradise

Madeleine Arthur as her daughter, Jane, and Amy Adams as Margaret Keane at the Aliʻiōlani Hale in a scene from *Big Eyes*.

Big Eyes centers on Margaret Keane's evolution as an artist and as a woman in 1950s, 1960s America, the phenomenal success of her Big Eyes paintings of children, and her tumultuous relationship with her husband, Walter Keane, who took credit for her paintings.

One week of location filming in Honolulu included The Royal Hawaiian Hotel in Waikīkī, a historic home in Mānoa which doubled for Keane's Hawaiian home, and the exterior of the Queen street side of the Aliʻiōlani Hale downtown, which was the site of the Federal Court house where the real life events took place in 1985.

James Saito, whose credits include *The Life of Pi*, portrays the Honolulu Federal Court Judge. Pomaikaʻi Brown plays Big Lolo, a local Hawaiian disk Jockey at a radio station where Margaret Keane reveals in an interview that she is the true painter of the Big Eyes kids, not her husband. Brown is a local entertainer and musician who began his film career with a role as the chef in *50 First Dates*. Traci Toguchi, a Hawaiian born actress whose credits include *The Karate Kid II* and *Picture Bride* and Ran Wei, a Chinese-American actress, play Jehovah Witnesses who come to Keane's Hawaiian home. Hawaiian talent in bit parts include actor L.G. Michael Brown and Dan Cooke of KGMB-TV Hawaiʻi New Now as reporters at the courthouse, and Mia Adams as the girl who asks Margaret to autograph her book. Production services on *Big Eyes* for the Hawaiʻi unit were provided by Leroy Jenkins of Production Partners. Jim Triplett was the local location manager. Katie Doyle was the local Hawaiʻi casting director on the film.

For her depiction of Keane, Amy Adams won the Golden Globe for Best Performance by an Actress in a Motion Picture-comedy or Musical in 2015. Adams won the same award in 2014 for *American Hustle*, and previously received four Golden Globe nominations.

Jurassic World
2015 Universal

DIRECTED BY	**Colin Trevorrow**
SCREENPLAY BY	**Derek Connolly**
PRODUCED BY	**Frank Marshall, Patrick Crowley**
CAST	**Chris Pratt (Owen), Bryce Dallas Howard (Claire), Jake Johnson (Lowery), Nick Robinson (Zach), Ty Simpkins (Grey), Vincent D'Onofrio (Morton), Irrfan Khan (Masrani)**

Jurassic World is a Science Fiction terror adventure that takes place 22 years after the events in Jurassic Park.

Steven Spielberg executive produces the fourth installment of the "Jurassic" Franchise for which he directed the first two, and returns to the Hawaiian locations that created Isla Nublar on Kauaʻi and Oʻahu. Locations for Jurassic World include Kualoa Ranch, Makai Pier at Heʻeia Kea Valley Park, the Honolulu Zoo, and the Honolulu Convention Center. Among the Kauaʻi locations are Blue Hole, Lāwai, Olokele Valley, Hanapēpē Valley and Manawaiopuna Falls.

Made in Paradise

CHAPTER 4

Locations! Locations! Locations!

Besides accessible rainforests, waterfalls, rugged green mountains and miles of palm-lined beaches, Hawai'i also offers everything from urban to prehistoric landscapes. O'ahu serves as the production center of the Islands, hosting about seventy percent of the productions in Hawai'i. The varied tropical terrains have been cast as the jungles of Africa, South America, South East Asia and Oceania.

Randy and his sister, Stephanie Spangler's pioneering achievements in location scouting and management are well known, and the industry recognizes them as the originators of most of the primary locations used in Hawai'i to this day.

This page, top photo: AMC cable channels award-winning 1960s-era series *Mad Men* filmed its sixth-season premiere episode on location in O'ahu at the Royal Hawaiian Hotel in Waikīkī. STEPHANIE SPANGLER; *Left photo:* Director Alexander Payne on location at Kipu Kai on Kaua'i for a scene in The Descendants FOX SEARCHLIGHT

Stephanie G. Spangler

Randy Spangler

"We initially called ourselves the 'location liaison' (go-between of the production and the community at large). The job title of location manager didn't even exist at one time. We were the first of the 'road warriors' even before that expression was created. We turned our cars into offices, spending most of our working days on the road, scouting and managing locations.

"Today's location departments sometimes employ up to seven or more assistants. Older shows, such as *Blood and Orchids,* which had a total of thirty-five different locations and a three-to-five week shooting schedule, was managed single-handedly by me.

"Directional maps to locations along with site plans were done by hand. We learned a form of cartography to manage this skill. Randy is famous for creating some of the only cartographical site plans for many of our heavily used island locations, and they are still in use today.

"We were the first location managers to get a fax machine in Hawai'i and pushed to allow for signed permits to be legal via fax, saving time and money by not having to go in person for sign offs on each permit.

"With the advent of cell phones, the work day became practically 24/7. Now with the Internet and the Google search engine and all of the prolific growth of information and maps that became available, a whole new world has opened up. Starting out with a pencil and paper, and Selectric typewriter and then being on the ground floor of the inventions of information technology is awesome. In the beginning of location filming in Hawai'i, film offices, government permits, and insurance were relatively rare. As location managers in Hawai'i, we established trustworthy relationships with private owners and the various government agencies. We would go into the government office and "talk story" with the head of the department, map out the request, discuss how it was to be achieved, etc. and get a verbal approval. Phone calls for changes were all that was needed after that. After the filming, follow-up and clean-up were the most important part of the entire process. Care for the "āina" (land) and the people enabled filming in Hawai'i to continue."

– Stephanie G. Spangler

Locations! Locations! Locations!

Island Of O‘ahu
KUALOA RANCH/ HAWAI‘I'S OWN BACK-LOT

Kualoa Ranch is one of Hawai‘i's most popular sites for Hollywood productions. The ranch is a sprawling 4,000-acre landscape on the windward (eastern) side of O‘ahu and a one-stop shop for movie and television for location managers because of its diverse terrain-verdant forests; lush, extending valleys; soaring, jagged mountain peaks; and sparkling white-sand beaches. Just twenty-five miles from Waikīkī (where most traveling Hollywood productions house their personnel), this working cattle ranch (and popular tourist site) has hosted such projects over the years as *Jurassic Park* and *Jurassic World,* ABC-TV's *Lost*, the current CBS-TV hit *Hawaii Five-0, Pearl Harbor,* and *Godzilla* (1998). Kualoa Ranch's terrain has represented Africa, Asia, Ireland, the Amazon, North Korea, Mexico, and the lost city of Atlantis. Along with movies and television shows, the ranch is also used as a location for commercials, still, and fashion photography shoots.

The hallowed site, once the province of Island royalty and one of the most sacred places on

The crew on site for *Mister Roberts* in 1955, the first movie to utilize Kualoa Ranch property for location filming.

Locations! Locations! Locations!

Ginger Petersen served as location manager for John Woo's *Windtalkers*, a Pacific-set World War II film story of the Navajo code talkers which shot primarily on Oʻahu's Kualoa Ranch. Petersen remarked, "It was a difficult movie to make because of the rain at that time of year. There was a foot to a half foot of mud every day. But it gave the film a gritty realistic look." More than 1,400 extras were used in the first two weeks during the five major battle scenes, and the use of such huge pyrotechnic required permits that were facilitated by the State Film office. Fifty percent of the film crew was hired locally."

Ralph Macchio and Oscar® nominee Pat Morita during a break in filming of *Karate Kid II* at Kualoa Ranch where a Japanese Okinawan seaside village set was constructed at Kahaluʻu.

Bruce Willis and his Navy Seals team on location at Kualoa for *Tears of the Sun*. Though it seemed they trekked across Africa in the movie, it was actually Kualoa ranch and Oʻahu's back country areas.

Adam Sandler on location at Kualoa Ranch for *50 First Dates*.

Oʻahu, has been hosting Hollywood royalty for the last sixty years. The first film to use the ranch as a location was *Mister Roberts* in 1955 with Henry Fonda, followed a decade later by Otto Preminger's 1965 *In Harm's Way*, starring John Wayne and Kirk Douglas. More recently, Nicholas Cage, Adam Sandler, Drew Barrymore, Bruce Willis and Dwayne "The Rock" Johnson have worked on various films at Kualoa Ranch.

The ranch also operates a variety of daily tours of the facility for the paying public. The *Movie Sites and Ranch Tour* allows the visitor to visit the famed Kaʻaʻawa Valley's *Jurassic Park* site, Godzilla's foot prints, *Windtalkers*' battleground and locations for *50 First Dates*, *Pearl Harbor* as well as the TV series *Lost* and the new *Hawaii Five-0*. The old World War II-era bunker houses a movie museum with posters and photos of movies and TV shows filmed at the ranch and exhibits illustrating the ranch's rich history. The ranch provides recreational activities including ATV tours, horseback rides, ocean voyaging and tours of its 800-year-old fishpond, gardens and hidden beach.

Locations! Locations! Locations!

The History:

In 1850, King Kamehameha III sold approximately 622 acres of land in Kualoa and its offshore fishing rights to Dr. Gerrit P. Judd, his personal advisor and missionary doctor. Dr. Judd's son later purchased additional acreage in Hakipu'u and Ka'a'awa, increasing the size of the estate to its current 4,000 acres. The estate operated as Kualoa Ranch since 1927, and today the Morgan Family, descendants of Dr. Judd, owns and operates it. Kualoa means "long back" in Hawaiian, an apt description of the land full of beautiful valleys and mountains.

Visitors at the Movie Museum at Kualoa Ranch, housed in a World War II era bunker.

MOVIE SITES AND RANCH TOUR AT KUALOA RANCH: The ranch located on O'ahu's northeastern shore at 49-960 Kamehameha Highway, Kāne'ohe, HI 96730. The visitors center is open daily 7:00 AM-6:00 PM for tours and information. Tours start at the visitors center and are conducted in English and Japanese. For reservations, call (808) 237-7321.

Alex O'Loughlin as McGarrett on location at Kualoa Ranch's Ka'a'awa Valley filming *Hawaii Five-O*.

Locations! Locations! Locations! 157

HANAUMA BAY

FILMS **Big Jim McLain** and **Blue Hawaii**

Hanauma Bay is an incredible natural pool formed in a volcanic crater on the southern end of Oʻahu. A volcanic burst of activity on the islands created the crater tens of thousands of years ago. The name Hanauma came from two Hawaiian words: "Hana," which means bay, and "uma," which means curved. The development of the Hanauma Bay area began at the turn of the twentieth century with a few dirt roads. Paved roads arrived in 1931 along with modest bathroom facilities and a guide rail for the steep passageway down to the base of the crater wall. Hanauma Bay quickly became a hot tourist spot and suffered from overuse throughout the next few decades. In the 1990s, the City and County of Honolulu started preserving the area and reducing the impact of visitors on the environment. Hanauma Bay limits attendees and educates visitors on the area's natural eco-system. Location filming is no longer permitted.

HANAUMA BAY NATURE PRESERVE is about ten miles east of Waikīkī just off the main coastal road at Kalanianaʻole Highway, Route 72.

Producer Hal Wallis *(Casablanca, Blue Hawaii)* and Elvis Presley confer on the beach during a break in filming of *Blue Hawaii*.

Nancy Olson and John Wayne share a romantic moment at Hanauma Bay for *Big Jim Mclain*.

Elvis (center) and his Beach Boys (left to right) Jose De Vega, Frank Hanalei, Frank Atienza, and Alani Kai break into song and dance at Hanauma Bay in *Blue Hawaii*.

Locations! Locations! Locations!

HĀLONA COVE AT HĀLONA LOOKOUT (*FROM HERE TO ETERNITY* BEACH)

This beach is the site of the famous love scene between Burt Lancaster and Deborah Kerr kissing amidst the crash of ocean waves in the 1953 award-winning classic film *From Here to Eternity*. In addition, the mermaid attack in *Pirates of The Caribbean: On Stranger Tides* was shot here.

HĀLONA COVE: From Waikīkī, take the H-1 Freeway east. The freeway ends and becomes Kalaniana'ole Highway. Travel on Kalaniana'ole Highway until you see the sign for the Hālona Lookout on the right side. The cove is on the west side of the lookout.

Cast and crew on location at O'ahu's Hālona Cove filming that now iconic film moment. In an *LA Times* obituary of 10/19/2007, Kerr was quoted as saying in a 1982 *The Times* interview, of being drenched with water and sand: "The scene turned out to be deeply affecting on film, but, God, it was no fun to shoot."

Locations! Locations! Locations!

ROYAL HAWAIIAN HOTEL

FILMS *The Black Camel, Big Jim McLain, Pearl Harbor, Punch-Drunk Love, Big Eyes*

TV *Blood and Orchids* TV miniseries, *Pearl* TV miniseries, and *Mad Men*

In a scene from *The Black Camel* (1931), Bela Lugosi as Tarneverro is questioned by Warner Oland as Charlie Chan in the lobby of the Royal Hawaiian Hotel.

The Royal Hawaiian Hotel opened on February 1, 1927, ushering in a new era of resort travel to Hawai'i. The hotel was built with a price tag of $4 million and was completed in just eighteen months. The six-story, 400-room structure was fashioned in a Spanish-Moorish pink-color style, popular during the period, and was set on ten acres of prime Waikīkī beachfront. Ed Tenney, who headed the Big Five firm of Castle and Cooke and Matson Navigation, and Matson manager William Roth came up with the idea for the resort. They conceived it as a luxurious resort for Matson luxury liner passengers. Before the advent of air travel across the Pacific, the only means of reaching Hawai'i from the mainland was a five-day sea voyage. Travelers arriving to the islands would stay for a long time, bringing numerous steamer trunks, servants and even their automobiles. The Royal Hawaiian hosted numerous celebrities, financiers and heads of state until World War II. In January 1942, the hotel was exclusively leased to the U.S. Navy as a rest and recreation center. The Royal reopened to the public in February 1947 after a nearly $2 million renovation.

Following statehood in 1959, Waikīkī developed, and now high-rise hotels surround the Royal Hawaiian Hotel. However, the "Pink Palace" still has the romance of the old days.

THE ROYAL HAWAIIAN HOTEL: 2259 Kealakekua Ave., Honolulu, HI 96815. Phone: (808) 923-7311

John Wayne as Jim McLain and Veda Ann Borg as Madge in the lobby of the Royal Hawaiian Hotel in a scene from *Big Jim McLain* (1951).

Locations! Locations! Locations!

HILTON HAWAIIAN VILLAGE WAIKĪKĪ BEACH RESORT

TV *Hawaiian Eye, Hawaii Five-0, Beverly Hills 90210, Pacific Blue, Baywatch Hawaii*

Far left: Hilton Hawaiian Village circa 1960.

The Hilton Hawaiian Village today

In 1954, entrepreneur Henry J. Kaiser and partner Fritz Burns purchased eight oceanfront acres of the John 'Ena Estate in Waikīkī to build a resort. Requiring additional property for an ambitious undertaking, the partners purchased the adjacent site of the Niumalu Hotel and several contiguous.

The *Hawaiian Eye (1959-1963)* detective agency owned by Tom Lopaka (Robert Conrad) was located poolside at the Hilton Hawaiian Village as well was the Shell Bar nightspot where Cricket Blake (Connie Stevens) sang. Only exterior stock shots were filmed on site, and the interiors were sets constructed at Warner Bros. studios in Burbank, California.

In 2010, the hotel entered into an agreement with CBS for the new *Hawaii Five-0* series. Throughout the series, the Hilton Hawaiian Village is featured during beauty and set shots. Its Rainbow Tower offers sweeping ocean views and interiors. In several episodes, the *Five-0* team gathers together at the Hiltons' poolside Tropics Bar and Grill.

HILTON HAWAIIAN VILLAGE WAIKĪKĪ BEACH RESORT: 2005 Kalia Road, Honolulu, HI 96815. Phone: (808) 949-4321

Left to right: Brandon (Jason Priestley) and Steve (Ian Ziering) try to convince Donna (Tori Spelling) that she is doing a great job amidst all the chaos she encounters during the fashion photo shoot on the beach in Hawai'i on the *Beverly Hills, 90210* two-hour season premiere, "Aloha Beverly Hills" on FOX.

Robert Conrad dances the hula at the Hilton Hawaiian Village, circa 1959.

Locations! Locations! Locations!

'IOLANI PALACE

FILMS **The Hawaiians, Princess Ka'iulani**

TV **Hawaii Five-O**

Constructed in 1882, 'Iolani Palace is the only royal palace on U.S. soil, in which King Kalākaua and his sister Queen Lili'uokalani lived in before the monarchy was overthrown in 1893.

In the original *Hawaii Five-O*, the palace serves as *Five-O's* headquarters, and Steve McGarrett's office is in the corner facing the street on the second floor. In reality, the second-floor office space was far too small to house the fictional *Five-0* offices. The much larger McGarrett's office and adjoining space was a permanent practical standing set at the studio. Exteriors of the palace and stairway were used extensively throughout the series.

'IOLANI PALACE: 343 South King St., Honolulu, HI 96813. Phone: (808) 522-0832. Monday-Saturday 9:00 AM- 4:00 PM

ALI'IŌLANI HALE

FILM **Tears of the Sun, Big Eyes**

TV **Hawaii Five-O, Blood & Orchids, Pearl**

The Hawai'i State Judiciary Building is one of the most photographed buildings in Hawai'i thanks to its location behind the famous gold King Kamehameha statue. The building was originally intended to be a royal palace, but instead it housed the government offices of the Hawaiian Kingdom. Today the building houses the Hawai'i State Supreme Court. A judiciary history center inside is free and open to the public.

ALI'IŌLANI HALE: 417 South King Street in downtown Honolulu between Mililani Street and Punchbowl Street. Phone: (808) 539-4999.

Locations! Locations! Locations!

SCHOFIELD BARRACKS

FILMS **From Here to Eternity, Pearl Harbor**

Author James Jones was stationed here during World War II and set his novel *From Here To Eternity* here. The quadrangles of the three-story stucco barracks built surrounding enormous squares of manicured grass that looks as much as they did in the movie. The site serves as an active military base (a valid ID is required).

SCHOFIELD BARRACKS: The Tropic Lightning Museum, located in Building 361 on Waianae Ave., is open Tuesday through Saturday 10:00 AM-4:00 PM

From Waikīkī, take the H-1 Freeway heading west and exit onto the H-2 (the Wahiawā exit). Take the H-2 until it ends and turns into the Kamehameha Highway. Proceed down Kamehameha Highway; Schofield Barracks will be on the left.

The three male stars of Fred Zinnemann's *From Here to Eternity* pose for a picture during a break in filming at Schofield Barracks on location in Oʻahu. Montgomery Clift, Burt Lancaster, and Frank Sinatra.

A "class" picture in every sense of the word. Sinatra, Lancaster, and Clift pose with the men of the Hawaiʻi Infantry Training Center who worked as extras at Schofield Barracks for the filming of the Academy Award®-winning film *From Here to Eternity*.

THE ANDERSON ESTATE

TV **Magnum P.I., Hawaii Five-O, Charlie's Angels, Vega$, and Murder She Wrote**

The Anderson Estate was the location of Robin's Nest, or the Robin Masters Estate, on the TV series *Magnum P.I.* The estate sits on only 3 acres, not the 200 acres described on the series. The actual estate was built in the early 1930s and has a large Spanish Colonial Revival-style main house, a boathouse, a gatehouse (with five bedrooms, two baths, and a two-car garage), a storage wing, a private tennis court, and a beach and tidal pool. All of the rooms seen in the show were interior sets constructed and filmed on a soundstage at the Diamond Head studio.

The Anderson Estate is located between Waimānalo Beach and Sea Life Park. A private residence, the estate is not open to the public.

Locations! Locations! Locations!

NATIONAL MEMORIAL CEMETERY OF THE PACIFIC (PUNCHBOWL CEMETERY)

FILM **Battleship**

TV **Hawaii Five-O, Magnum P.I., and Hawaii Five-O Reboot**

Built in 1948, this cemetery, located in the Pūowaina Crater (Punchbowl), now serves as a memorial to the sacrifices by the men and women in the U.S. armed services, especially those who fought and died in the Pacific Theater during World War II, Korea and Vietnam. This impressive memorial sits high on the wall of the crater overlooking the graves of the cemetery, and the most striking element is a monumental staircase leading from the crater floor. In ancient times, the crater was known as the "hill of sacrifice."

Jack Lord as Steve McGarrett at Punchbowl Cemetery. The statue of Lady Columbia behind him stands guard representing mothers of fallen servicemen.

BYODO-IN TEMPLE

FILMS **Pearl Harbor, Karate Kid II**

TV **Hawaii Five-O, Magnum P.I., Fantasy Island remake, and Lost**

Byodo-In Temple sits at the foot of the Koʻolau Mountains in Valley Of The Temples Memorial Park. The non-practicing Buddhist Temple was built in 1968 to commemorate the 100-year anniversary of the first Japanese immigrants to Hawaiʻi. The temple serves as a smaller-scale replica of a temple of the same name near Kyoto, Japan. The TV series *Hawaii Five-0* and *Magnum P.I.* featured several episodes with the temple. In an episode of the first season of the series Lost, "House of the Rising Sun," the temple serves as the home of Sun's father.

VALLEY OF THE TEMPLES MEMORIAL PARK: Open to the public with admission charge. Thirty-minute drive north of Honolulu, 47-200 Kahekili Highway, Kāneʻohe, HI 96744.

Filming of episode 4 of *Fantasy Island*. Director of Photography Roy Wagner on platform. Producer John Flynn and Erik Henry (Visual Efx, Encore Video)—Valley of the Temples on Oʻahu.

164 Locations! Locations! Locations!

TURTLE BAY RESORT

FILMS **Forgetting Sarah Marshall, Soul Surfer, Along Came Polly, Pirates of the Caribbean: On Stranger Tides, Don Juan DeMarco**

TV **Lost, North Shore**

On Oʻahu's North Shore with almost five miles of beachfront, Turtle Bay is the perfect place to take in the azure beauty of Kawela Bay. The luxury beach resort also features two lushly landscaped pools, championship golf courses, tennis courts, horseback riding, and 443 villas, cottages, guest rooms and suites.

TURTLE BAY RESORT: 57-091 Kamehameha Highway, Kahuku, HI 96731. Phone: (808) 293-6000

Far left: Jonah Hill is a waiter at the Turtle Bay Resort, and Jason Segel is Peter Bretter in the romantic comedy *Forgetting Sarah Marshall*.

Mila Kunis co-stars as Rachel Jensen, the girl Peter (Jason Segel) eventually falls in love with in *Forgetting Sarah Marshall*.

Locations! Locations! Locations!

BATTLESHIP USS *MISSOURI*

FILMS   *Battleship, Pearl Harbor, Under Siege, MacArthur*
TV   *Hawaii Five-O* Reboot

The "Mighty Mo," a 45,000-ton ship, made her onscreen debut in international newsreels as General Douglas MacArthur signed the Japanese instrument of surrender that ended World War II in 1945. The 1976 biographical film *MacArthur*, starring Gregory Peck, recreated the surrender on the USS *Missouri*'s deck. The Iowa-class battleship, which sailed during World War II, the Korean War and Desert Storm, has nine legendary sixteen-inch guns and serves as a floating museum. Through Universal's film production of Battleship, the USS *Missouri* once again took to the open seas in January 2010. She was towed outside of Pearl Harbor far enough to allow filming without having land appear in the shots. This was the first time in more than a decade that the ship went out to the open sea. Moviegoers can attend a movie tour of the filming areas from the movie.

BATTLESHIP MISSOURI MEMORIAL AT HISTORIC FORD ISLAND, PEARL HARBOR: 63 Cowpens St., Honolulu, HI. Phone 1-877-644-4896.

The USS Missouri is docked at Historic Ford Island, located very close to the USS Arizona Memorial. The USS Missouri is accessed through the Pearl Harbor visitors center.

The USS Missouri in a scene from Battleship.

The Missouri's triple 16-inch gun turret No. 1. Each gun can fire two rounds per minute.

Locations! Locations! Locations!

WAIMEA FALLS

TV *Lost*

Waimea Falls is inside the Waimea Valley Audubon Center (Formerly Waimea Falls Park), located on Oʻahu's North Shore. The 1,800-acre center features walking trails through lush grounds, and visitors can swim to a waterfall. The public is welcome, and the center charges an entrance fee.

WAIMEA FALLS (AND GARDENS): 59-864 Kamehameha Highway, Haleʻiwa, HI 96712. Phone: (808) 638-7766

MOKULEʻIA BEACH ON THE NORTH SHORE

TV *Lost*—Island and the crash-site location of the infamous Flight 815.

Kamehameha Highway (99) to Farrington Highway (930), west of Haleʻiwa and Waialua.

On the set of ABC's *Lost*.

PĀPAʻILOA BEACH

TV *Lost*—The survivors camp site was filmed here after the first season.

Better known as Police Beach (the Honolulu Police Department has a lease on the property), Pāpaʻiloa Beach is on Oʻahu's North Shore near Haleʻiwa just past the Dillingham Air Field.

Locations! Locations! Locations!

Kaua'i

Kaua'i, the oldest and most northerly major island in the Hawaiian chain, has a roughly circular shape. It provides lush, colorful and diverse scenery including incomparable mountain ridges and valleys, tropical jungles, 143 miles of magnificent coastline, year-round streams and waterfalls, and arid dunes and canyons.

KE'E BEACH

FILM *The Castaway Cowboy*
TV   *The Thorn Birds*

Located at the end of the road of Highway 560 in the north shore Of Kaua'i, Ke'e Beach is one of the most visited beaches on the Garden Isle. The famous eleven-mile Kalalau trail begins at the western edge of the beach.

Richard Chamberlain and Rachel Ward embrace at Ke'e Beach in the sweeping romantic mini-series saga *The Thorn Birds* in which Kaua'i locations doubled for Queensland, Australia.

HANALEI BAY, LUMAHAI BEACH, BLACKPOT BEACH, NORTH SHORE

FILMS *Beachhead, Miss Sadie Thompson, South Pacific,* and *The Descendants*

Hanalei Bay is a two-mile-long, half-moon bay with white-sand beaches at the foot of dramatic cliffs. *South Pacific's* Nellie Forbush washed that man right out of her hair on nearby Lumahai beach, and sailors sang "Nothing Like a Dame" at Black Pot beach near the historic Hanalei Pier. Hanalei Beach is a great location for a walk along the beach or a swim, which George Clooney did in *The Descendants*.

Locations! Locations! Locations!

ALLERTON GARDENS (NATIONAL TROPICAL BOTANICAL GARDENS)

FILMS **Donovan's Reef, Jurassic Park, and Pirates of The Caribbean: On Stranger Tides**

In the 1800s, Allerton Gardens served as the summer cottage of Queen Emma, wife of King Kamehameha IV. It includes the beautiful scenery of Lāwaʻi Bay, gardens, waterfall and garden walks.

ALLERTON GARDENS: 4425 Lāwaʻi Road, Poʻipū, HI 96756.

Allerton Beach or Lāwaʻi Kai is on the south shore of Poʻipū at the National Tropical Botanical Garden. The house is part of Hawaiian Queen Emma's summer residence.

Locations! Locations! Locations!

NĀ PALI COAST

FILMS **Pirates of The Caribbean: On Stranger Tides, Journey 2: The Mysterious Island, Six Days Seven Nights, Tropic Thunder, Just Go With It,** and **King Kong (1976)**

The cliffs and the Honopū Valley coastline are perhaps the most awesome natural wonder in the Hawaiian Islands. Steep sea cliffs stand sentinel along the coast, shooting up from the blue Pacific. The cliffs are accessible only by boat, helicopter, or an eleven-mile winding trek through the Kalalau trail.

Locations! Locations! Locations!

WAIMEA CANYON

FILMS **Donovan's Reef and Throw Mama from the Train**

Mark Twain called Waimea Canyon "The Grand Canyon of the Pacific." Carved by thousands of years of floods and rivers flowing down from Mt. Waialeale, Waimea Canyon is the largest canyon in the Pacific at ten miles long, a mile wide, and 3,600 feet deep. Lava beds line the canyon walls, which, with the changing light of day, take on reddish hues of colors.

WAIMEA CANYON: Koke'e Road, Waimea, HI 96752. South on 50 into Waimea and turn right on Waimea Canyon Rd. (550) and right on Kekaha, which turns into Koke'e Road.

Hilary Duff on location at Waimea Canyon for a music video.

Above: John Wayne at Waimea Canyon, Kaua'i.

Left: John Wayne on location at Waimea Canyon for *Donovan's Reef.*

WAILUA RIVER

FILMS **Pagan Love Song, Donovan's Reef, Islands in the Streams, and Outbreak**

The three-and-a-half mile Wailua River transverses several ecosystems from forested river banks and tall cliffs to a lush green rain forest upriver from the world-famous Fern Grotto.

Locations! Locations! Locations!

COCO PALMS HOTEL

FILMS   **Miss Sadie Thompson, Blue Hawaii, and Pirates of the Caribbean: On Stranger Tides**

The now-dilapidated Coco Palms Hotel is set in the ancestral home of Kauaʻi's Aliʻi royalty nearby the Wailua river. The hotel opened in 1953 with a pseudo-Polynesian style and served as the premier place to stay for Hollywood stars filming on the island. In 1961, Elvis Presley's *Blue Hawaii* made Coco Palms famous as the fabulous wedding scene at the end of the film takes place among the hotel's lush coconut grooves and lagoons. Bedecked with flower lei's, wearing a white shirt and pants with a red sash draping down the side, Elvis floats down the waterway on a flower-covered double outrigger canoe with his bride singing a rendition of the "Hawaiian Wedding Song." The site has the largest concentration of coconut palm trees on Kauaʻi. The small white chapel on the grounds seen in the film was originally built for the Rita Hayworth film *Miss Sadie Thompson*.

COURTESY COCO PALMS

Elvis Presley loved Hawaiʻi, especially the Coco Palms Resort, which was used for the wedding scene in Blue Hawaii.

ROBERTS HAWAIʻI MOVIE TOURS-KAUAʻI: The fun-filled six-hour narrated guided tour is aboard an air-conditioned mini-bus that will stop at Kauaʻi's iconic movie locations while also showing film clips of some of Hollywood's most notable movies filmed on the island. This tour has the only authorized access to the ruins of the dilapidated and now-shuttered Coco Palms Hotel, which was severely damaged by Hurricane Iniki in 1992. Monday-Saturday. Phone: 1-800-831-5541

HANAPĒPĒ TOWN

FILM   **Flight of the Intruder, Jurassic World**

TV   **The Thorn Birds miniseries**

Native Hawaiians were the first inhabitants of Hanapēpē and the Hanapēpē Valley, which they cultivated. Chinese rice farmers founded this small, rustic nineteenth-century town in the late 1800s. Hanapēpē Town is now home to a host of artists and art galleries and the Hanapēpē Swinging Bridge. The town is located at the south Kauaʻi shore and Hanapēpē River seventeen miles south of Līhuʻe airport off of Highway 150.

ANGELA TILLSON

Locations! Locations! Locations!

ANGELA TILLSON

Angela Tillson is the go-to person on Kaua'i for location scouting and site management. Among her credits are *The Descendants, Just Go With It,* and *Jurassic Park.*

Here is Tillson on an ATV at the Kīlauea Falls location for *Just Go With It.*

Maui

FILMS ***Hereafter, Twilight of the Gods,* and *Devil at Four 'o Clock***

TV ***Fantasy Island* Remake**

Perched on the western edge of Maui, Lahaina serves as the gateway to the pristine beach resorts of Kapalua and Kā'anapali located just to the north. The first Polynesians settlers arrived in Lahaina more than a thousand years ago, attracted by the area's abundant freshwater streams, lush valleys, pleasing climate and bountiful sea. From 1820 to 1845, Lahaina served as the capitol of the Hawaiian Kingdom during King Kame-

Frank Sinatra, Bernie Hamilton and Gregoire Asian at Lahaina, Maui location for *Devil at Four O'Clock.*

Mākena Beach.

Locations! Locations! Locations! 173

"Paniolo" episode of *Hawaii Five-0* aired during the third season in 1970 and starred Jack Lord as McGarrett who due to an unfortunate series of events, must hunt down Frank Silvera as Paniolo Frank Kuakua who resists change and development on his land. Paniolos are the Hawaiian cowboys who are descendants of the Mexican-American vaqueros from California. The episode was filmed on Maui.

hameha III's reign. During much of the nineteenth century, Lahaina served as a bustling whaling port with more than 400 ships a year dropping anchor in Lahaina for supplies and recreation, especially during the peak years of the mid 1890s.

After the whaling industry died out, Lahaina turned to growing sugar as a primary industry. In the 1970s, the town enjoyed a resurgence, this time as a lively tourist destination.

Hālawa Valley, Molokaʻi

Garden of the Gods, or Keahiakawelo, on Lānaʻi. Julie Taymor shot *The Tempest* at this location.

Locations! Locations! Locations!

The Big Island Of Hawai'i

The Big Island is known for its diverse locations including its lava and rainforests. The stark and barren landscape includes fields of cooled black lava and steaming cinder cones, while the tropical side consists of hanging ferns and jungles. The largest island in the Hawaiian chain, the Island of Hawai'i has over 4,000 square miles of locations, containing more land area than all the other Hawaiian islands put together.

MOST POPULAR AREAS TO FILM ON THE BIG ISLAND:
- Old Growth Jungle in the Hilo/Puna area
- Shipman Ranch in Hilo/Puna Area
- Lava fields in Kalapana and off Saddle Road
- Forests above Waipi'o Valley
- Beaches along the West Coast

1) *Rampage* (1963) filmed on the Big Island.
2) Lava fields off Saddle Road.
3) North Kohala waterfall
4) Jungle trail in Onomea
5) Secluded beach in Ka'ū.
6) Coffee farm area near Pāhala.

Locations! Locations! Locations! 175

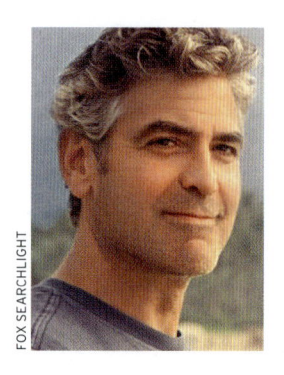

The Descendants Tour

The Descendants has made movie-goers want to visit the locations where it was filmed on Oʻahu and Kauaʻi.

OʻAHU LOCATIONS

Waikīkī Beach

The first scene of the film, with the Honolulu skyline and Diamond Head off shore, contains a beach-boy style ceremonial scattering of ashes and flower leis, after the death of Matt King's wife.

Queen's Medical Center

Also known as Queen's Hospital, this is where Matt King's incapacitated wife is hospitalized. King Kamehameha IV and Queen Emma originally founded the largest private hospital in the islands in 1859.

QUEEN'S MEDICAL CENTER: 1221 Punchbowl St., Honolulu, HI 96813, in downtown Honolulu.

King Family Kamaʻāina Home

In this house, the voting took place, and Matt King told the family that he wasn't signing the documents to transfer the estate from the King family to Don Holitzer.

KIKILA PARTNERS: 55-202 Kamehameha Highway, Lāʻie, HI 96792 (across from Pounders Beach).

Nuʻuanu

Nuʻuanu is a neighborhood just up the Pali Highway, north of downtown. It is where an old Kamaʻāina family like the Kings would live. It is the setting for Matt King's house as well as his friends.

176 Locations! Locations! Locations!

KAUA'I LOCATIONS

Kipu Kai Bay

Kipu Ranch is the setting for the King Trust's land holdings, where King and his two daughters stood and gazed at the breathtaking view of Kipu Kai as he contemplates selling the unspoiled oceanfront land. The Rice family owns Kipu Ranch.

Kipu Ranch Adventures is the only one on the island that has access to the site via a three-hour ATV or vehicle tour.

KIPU RANCH ADVENTURES: 235 Kipu Rd., Līhu'e, HI 96766. Phone: (808) 246-9288.

ANGELA TILLSON

Hanalei Town, North Shore

At Tahiti Nui Restaurant, a real location, Matt King (Clooney) meets with his cousin Hugh, played by Beau Bridges. The actual employees of the Tahiti Nui starred in the film.

TAHITI NUI RESTAURANT: 5-5134 Kūhiō Highway, Hanalei, HI 96754. Phone: (808) 826-6277.

MERIE W. WALLACE

Locations! Locations! Locations! 177

Hanalei Bay

Along the shore of the bay, two rental cottages belonging to the Hanalei Land Co. were used as locations for the vacation rentals where Matt King and his oldest daughter visit and confront his wife's lover, Brian Speer, played by Matthew Lillard.

NALU BEACH COTTAGE & KAUIKEŌLANI ESTATE (PREVIOUSLY KNOWN AS THE WILCOX ESTATE) HANALEI LAND CO.: Turn right on Aku Road off Kūhiō Highway, go one block and turn right on Weke Road (which parallels the bay). Phone: (888) 990-1454.

George Clooney as Matt King goes for a run along the beach in Hanalei Bay on Kaua'i and spots a fellow jogger as the man he is looking for, Brian Speer, in The Descendants.

George Clooney and crew filming a scene on Hanalei Bay for The Descendants *where Matt King seeks to confront Brian Speer at his vacation cottage.*

The beach and cottage where Matt King (Clooney) ran and met up with Brian Speer (Lilliard) in The Descendants.

Locations! Locations! Locations!

St. Regis Princeville Resort

Scenes with Clooney took place in the lobby, in the luxurious Presidential Suite, and at the Princeville Fountain, the focal point of the main entrance to the Princeville area. The luxury resort was a natural choice for select scenes in the movie as the property itself appeared in the original plot of the book. Perched on the cliffs of Kauaʻi's North Shore, the St. Regis Princeville Resort opened in October of 2009 following a multi-million dollar renovation. The resort pays homage to the Garden Island's beautiful land and vibrant culture and offers stunning views of Hanalei Bay and Mt. Makana, luxurious suites, two premiere golf courses, a spectacular infinity pool, Jean-George's Kauaʻi Grill and the Haleleʻa Spa.

ST. REGIS PRINCEVILLE: Thirty-two miles west of Līhuʻe Airport. 5520 Ka Haku Road, Princeville, HI 96722. Phone: (808) 826-9644.

You, too, can stay in the Presidential Suite at the St. Regis Princeville Resort where George Clooney filmed scenes from the movie *The Descendants*.

Locations! Locations! Locations!

CHAPTER 5

Development of the Modern Hawai'i Film Industry

Top left: Director Peter Berg on the set of the action-adventure *The Rundown*. UNIVERSAL STUDIOS
Top right: Kirk Douglas (left) as Commander Paul Eddington and John Wayne (right) as Admiral Rockwell Torrey on location in Kāne'ohe, O'ahu for the filming of Otto Preminger's World War II drama *In Harm's Way* (1965). LUIS REYES ARCHIVES/PARAMOUNT PICTURES
Bottom: Crew setting up in front of the beach at the Hilton Hawaiian Village where an outdoor bar set was constructed for a scene where the bar patrons would react in fear when Godzilla hits the beach. TIM RYAN

Almost one hundred years to the day when theatrical feature film production began in Hawai'i in 1913, the *Hawaii Five-0* Reboot started production of its fourth season at its new location at the state-run Hawai'i Film Studio. Cameras were rolling in Waikīkī on the Japanese sci-fi monster *Godzilla* returning to the big screen in a new mega-budget Warner Bros./Legendary Pictures adventure where the titular creature lays waste to Waikīkī. And actress/director Angelina Jolie was on O'ahu scouting locations for an upcoming Universal film project. This flurry of production activity during the summer of 2013, the centennial celebration year of film production throughout the Hawaiian Islands, signals the coming of age of the modern Hawai'i film industry.

Over a forty-five-year period, Hawai'i has developed a strong work force of film industry professionals and support services that has its roots in the year 1968 with the arrival of the television series *Hawaii Five-O*, which then as now, is a seminal force in the development of a local film industry.

Even though movies have been made in Hawai'i since before the turn of the twentieth century, it was technically difficult in 1968 to film a television series in Hawai'i because no permanent production facilities or infrastructure existed.

From 1951 to 1965, Hollywood feature film productions, such as *Big Jim McLain*, Fred Zinnemann's Oscar®-winning *From Here to Eternity*, Joshua Logan's *South Pacific*, Taurog's *Blue Hawaii*, Otto Preminger's *In Harm's Way*

Frank Atienza as Ito (center) and Ralph Hanalei (left) display their native dancing skills to Elvis in a scene shot at Hanauma Bay on Oʻahu for *Blue Hawaii*. Hawaiian-born Atienza worked with Elvis again in *Girls, Girls, Girls* and *Fun in Acapulco*. The actors' TV credits include *Hawaii Five-O* and *Magnum P.I.* and most of the Hawaiʻi-based series. He later moved into behind the camera technical work. Atienza costarred in an episode of the classic World War II series *The Gallant Men* (1963) called *One Puka Puka* ("puka" means "hole" in Hawaiian) suggested from a story by Doug Mossman. George Takei, Poncie Ponce, Mako, and David Cadiente also co-starred in the episode that revolved around the 100th Battalion made up of members of the Hawaiʻi National Guard that fought in Italy and became part of the Nisei Japanese American 442nd Infantry division.

Numerous people have been pioneers or instrumental in the development of the Hawaiʻi film industry.

Alan Brady began as a stagehand, and in 1961 he worked on *Blue Hawaii* where he learned to trim a Carbon arc light, grip a crab dolly that weighed 600 lbs., and took ten people to push 200 yards down to the beach.

Carey Anderson, son of Hawaiian prop man and set dresser Kenneth "Andy" Anderson, recalls being on the Coco Palms set location of *Blue Hawaii* as a four year old: "I was at the water's edge looking at the fish when I fell into the Lagoon during a take and disrupted the filming. Elvis Presley pulled me out of the water and said, 'Whose kid is this?' my father claimed me and said, 'Don't worry, it won't happen again.' Everyone had a good laugh and continued filming."

and George Roy Hill's *Hawaii*, virtually moved into Hawaiʻi, bringing crew, actors, cameras, equipment and building temporary soundstages and sets on the islands. When production ended, everything was struck and returned to Hollywood.

In the late 1960s, respected Hollywood actor Richard Boone began promoting the idea of a Hawaiʻi film industry located in Hawaiʻi. In response to Boones' and others efforts to create a local industry, veteran producer Hal Wallis *(Blue Hawaii)* pointed out one key problem, however, the necessity of bringing together the corps of technicians needed for both movie and TV production.

Most TV series at that time were made on Hollywood's studio back lots and relied heavily on stock or second unit footage to create the illusion of exotic locations as was the case with the first Hawaiʻi-set TV series, Warner Bros' *Hawaiian Eye* (1959-1963).

Hawaii Five-O changed that and took full advantage of the Islands' locations and by filming in color. Writer/producer Leonard Freeman, through his series creation, pioneered on location TV series production in Hawaiʻi and legitimized it as a business enterprise that acts as a viable on-going economic contributor to the state.

Bernie Oseransky, unit production manager for ten of the show's twelve seasons, recalled in an interview with the author, "There was a nucleus of IA that worked on films or series as they came in for short periods of time but *Five-0* gave them an ongoing on-the-job training and experience that resulted in today's army of trained Hawaiian film professionals. After 12 years on *Hawaii Five-0*, many went on to work on the other Hawaiʻi signature series *Magnum P.I.* in 1980. Their kids entered the business."

Long-term series television, such as *Hawaii Five-0* (twelve years), *Magnum P.I.* (eight

A "gag" photo of supposedly primitive working conditions in Hawaiʻi during first pioneering season of *Hawaii Five-O* in 1968. Jack Lord at Pearl City "Mongoose Manor" converted warehouse production facilities.

Development of the Modern Hawaiʻi Film Industry

years), and *Lost* (six years), helped to build a strong crew and creative talent base. Not only local crew people but also many local actors and entertainers gained experience and Screen Actors Guild cards by working on *Hawaii Five-0* in small roles and bit parts due in large part to producer Leonard Freeman, casting director Ted Thorpe and Jack Lord, who wanted the island feel and atmosphere to the show. "*Hawaii Five-0* opened up a whole new area for Screen Actors Guild and showcased a lot of members from Hawai'i, making it possible for local actors and entertainers to attain active careers in films and television and reap the benefits of a unionized show business." remarked Brenda Ching, executive director of SAG-AFTRA Hawai'i branch.

"Filming entirely on location presented problems at first but gave the show an edge, but the reality of producing a series in paradise involved twelve-to-sixteen-hour days, six days a week with Sunday off to learn your lines and prepare for the coming week," is how Oseransky remembers.

Peter M. Lenkov, executive producer of *Hawaii Five-0* Reboot, in an interview with Tim Ryan published in *Hawaii Film and Video Magazine* (Issue one /2012), talked about advancements in technology in production since the original *Hawaii Five-0* and *Magnum P.I.*: "Now we can upload what we shoot and it gets sent directly to

LUIS REYES ARCHIVES

Series-star Jack Lord directed a number of episodes of *Hawaii Five-0*. The long-running series functioned as an on-the-job training program for local cast and crew members.

Left to right: Hawaii Five-0 excutive producer Peter Lenkov, *Magnum P.I.* producer and co-creator Glen Larson, and event promoter Tom Moffatt.

Al Burns joined the local in 1968 as a permit electrician on the film *Tora! Tora! Tora!*

Donovan Ahuna worked in craft services on several productions in Hollywood and is credited with starting Aloha Shirt Fridays, where the cast and crew would come to work on the set wearing Aloha shirts. If they didn't have Aloha shirts, Ahuna would bring them over from Hawai'i. This new practice carried over into the national work place as "Casual Fridays."

Emmy®-winning *(Lost)* special effects supervisor Archie Ahuna, the only Native Hawaiian to be so honored, learned his craft on *Hawaii Five-0* starting as an electrician. His career has come full circle as Ahuna is now working on the new *Hawaii Five-0* Reboot.

Lost second-unit key rigging grip Brian Vollert started working in the industry as a seventeen year old on *Hawaii Five-0*. John Rodriguez, a second-unit transportation coordinator, also began his career on *Hawaii Five-0*.

STEPHANIE SPANGLER

Development of the Modern Hawai'i Film Industry

Doug Mossman as Detective Frank Kamana reports to James MacArthur (left) as Danny and Jack Lord (right) as McGarrett, in his Iolani Palace office.

Right: Curt Lofstedt of Island Helicopters.

Far right: Pictured are (left to right) Producer Howard W. Koch, Frank Sinatra and Jack Harter. Harter provided helicopter location service on Kaua'i for the only film Sinatra directed *None But The Brave* (1965).

the editors over the internet. Back then you're shooting on film, the logistics were insane. We put our digital video on DAT to upload. The cameras today also are so small. We've shot some things on the fly with a (DSLR) Canon D5 that ended up in the show. Technology makes it easier. I can look at a cut scene on my iPhone and make notes on my iPhone and get it right back to the editors in LA and then get immediate answers within five minutes."

To filmmakers, the Hawaiian islands offer access to a tropical look without the currency, security and language obstacles of other far-off locations. There is a wealth of locations in one place, with production industry support. Hawai'i is a union state and has the same labor and insurance codes.

IATSE Hawai'i Local 665 is a mixed local chapter with 300 members representing a wide variety of stage and film-related crafts. Local 665 was started by a handful of projectionists in 1937. These projectionists were responsible for screening all of the films that were to be seen in the movie houses of the day as well as at schools, libraries and military bases. Two events changed the course of the 665 union, *Hawaii Five-0* and the Neal Blaisdell Center (then called the Honolulu International Center, built on the Ward Estate).

In the early 1960s after years of showing plays at McKinley High School, the Neal Blaisdell Center opened,

John Nordlum worked on *Hawaii Five-O* as Jack Lord's stunt double and stand in as well as Tom Selleck's on *Magnum P.I.* and founded the Hawaii Stunt Association. Colin Fong is a local stunt man whose credits include *Jurassic Park*, *Pearl Harbor*, and *Windtalkers* and for television *Lost* and the *Hawaii Five-O* Reboot.

Curt Lofstedt has been flying helicopters in Hawai'i since 1973, and *Hawaii Five-O* was his first film production credit followed by *Magnum P.I.* Along with his wife, Bonnie, they are the owners of Island Helicopters, Kaua'i. Curt's expertise in finding just the right location or piloting the camera helicopter or crew transportation has been utilized on such productions as *King Kong*, *Raiders of the Lost Ark*, *Jurassic Park*, *Tropic Thunder* and *Soul Surfer*. Prior to moving to Hawai'i in 1973, Curt received his helicopter training in the U.S. Army where he flew helicopters in Vietnam and received a Silver Star. During the filming of *Six Days Seven Nights*, he taught actor Harrison Ford to fly a helicopter while on location in Kaua'i. So enthused was Ford that he later received his helicopter license and purchased his own helicopter on the mainland. Jack Harter Helicopters, also of Kaua'i, has been servicing the film and photography industry for more than fifty years since 1962 from Frank Sinatra's *None But The Brave* to *Jurassic Park*.

Development of the Modern Hawai'i Film Industry

and stage hands were organized and added to the Union. The Blaisdell Center put Honolulu on the map as a destination for symphony orchestras, opera and legitimate theater and dance companies. The Center shifted most of the work away from projection and towards stagecraft, especially with the closing of single-screen movie theaters and the trend toward automated multi-plexes.

Up until recently, Hollywood film and series producers never hired department heads from Hawai'i, but now more and more people are being hired in these positions.

"*Lost*, ABC Television's mega-global series—more than any other show filmed on O'ahu—took a look at what visual assets the island has to offer and used them so nimbly and creatively that it opened people's eyes to Honolulu and the island of O'ahu as a production center," remarked Walea Constantinau, Film Commissioner for the Honolulu Film Office.

Notable theatrical feature films that have been made and produced locally on modest budgets with local industry support include *Goodbye Paradise* in 1992, Kayo Hatta's *Picture Bride* in 1995, Nathan Kurosawa's *The Ride* in 2003, and Rob Hedden's *You May Not Kiss The Bride*, which was produced by Hawai'i Film Partners in 2009. Hawai'i Film Partners also produced *Flight 29 Down*, the first network series produced by a Hawai'i-based production company.

TalkStory productions, a Hawai'i-based independent production company, teamed up with Chartoff Productions and Artemis films to produce *The Tempest*, a theatrical feature starring Helen Mirren and directed by Julie Taymor that filmed on Lāna'i and the Big Island. TalkStory's projects included *Beyond the Break*, a cable TV series filmed on the West side of O'ahu, the Sci Fi Channel Movies: *Aztec Rex, Heatstroke* and *Cook and The Goldsteins*.

Beginning in 1968, *Hawaii Five-O* alone constituted a four-million-dollars-a-year industry for the state. In 1977, the film and television industry contributed a total of some forty-five million dollars to the state's economy. In 1978, the Hawai'i State Film Office opened to become the one-stop central coordinator for film and photographic use of state-administered parks, beaches, highways and facilities. The office worked with some agencies to assist filmmakers acquiring film permits and to provide location, tax incentive and production resource information to filmmakers.

In 2012 the total estimated production expenditures totaled $245.6 million, and the total estimated economic impact is $398 million.

"*Hawaii Five-O* has made a big impact on Hawai'i, not just in production, but what they do to help promote the destination. Both the original *Five-O* and the new show have become part of our community's vernacular," says Donne Dawson, Hawai'i State Film Commissioner

---

Brian Keaulana is one of the most experienced watermen in the world. His credits include *Soul Surfer, Blue Crush, Waterworld, Point Break, North Shore, War and Remembrance, Baywatch Hawaii* and *Johnny Tsunami*. Brian is a professional surfer, stuntman and stunt coordinator, lifeguard, actor and rescue and risk management specialist. He was the first one to use jet rescue crafts with an attached rescue sled, which he invented. Keaulana was joined by Greg Barnett on *Soul Surfer* and *Blue Crush* in which they mounted cameras on surfboards and jet skis as well as on land in order to capture the aquatic surf action.

Paul Atkins, who runs Moana Productions with his wife Gracie, lists among his credits nature and water filming for National Geographic Channel, PBS, BBC and The Discovery Channel. Because of his experience, director Peter Weir hired him as Director of Photography to shoot an actual storm off of Cape Horn in South America that would be used in the film *Master and Commander: Far Side of the World* (2003). Atkins was part of the team that helped earn the film's Cinematographer Russell Boyd, an Academy Award® for Best Cinematography in which he captured visually stunning 50 ft. seas, up to 85 mph winds and snow from the deck of a replica of an eighteenth century sailing vessel.

Island Film Group, run by Ricardo Galindez and Roy Tjoe, is a Hawai'i-based entertainment and Financing Company. The enterprise financed the theatrical feature film *Princess Ka'iulani* and co-financed and co-produced Sony Pictures' *Soul Surfer*.

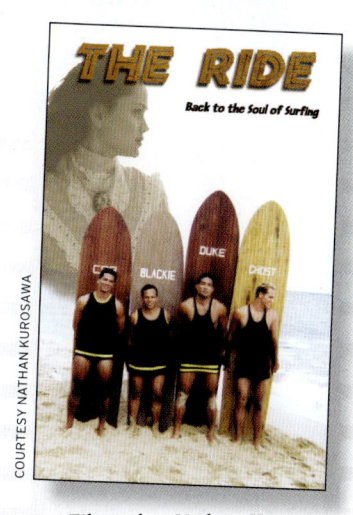

Filmmaker Nathan Kurosawa's *The Ride* is contemporary story about a surfer who travels back in time to 1911 Hawai'i after a surfing accident. He meets Duke Kahanamoku and learns life lessons in and out of the water. Filmed on location with a local cast and crew. The local cast featured Scott Davis, Mary Pa'alani, and Sean Ka'awa as young Duke Kahanamoku. Local crew member department heads were production designer Rick Romer, costume designer Cathie Valbovino, prop master Alvin Cabrinha, and vintage surfboard collector Jay Behrens who crafted period surfboards for the film. The director of photography was Ron Condon who was aided by Brian Keaulana in the surf sequences. Wesley Nakamoto of Waipahu is the Executive Producer. Prior to this 90-minute feature, Kurosawa received awards for his short film *Kamehameha*. *The Ride* premiered at the Hawai'i International Film Festival.

Development of the Modern Hawai'i Film Industry

Left to right: Adam Sandler, director Peter Segal, and Drew Barrymore on the set of Columbia Pictures' romantic comedy *50 First Dates*.

Left to right: Behind the camera photo of Daniel Dae Kim, Scott Caan, Grace Park and crew filming a scene from an episode of *Hawaii Five-0* Reboot on location in Waikīkī.

who took over the office in 2001.

"On average, a television series of 22 episodes brings in an estimated $60 million in economic activity per year." Dawson says, "This doesn't include the value of on air promotions, brand awareness and the ancillary market benefits which in *Hawaii Five-O's* case is significant. And the series creates around 400 full time jobs for local residents," she added, "The Film Industry is such a good fit; it's an environmentally friendly industry. It is also a perfect partner for tourism in that films productions such as *Hawaii Five-0* provide primetime exposure for the state in a way that we now really gravitate toward destinations where popular film and television shows are made."

Through cooperative efforts between the state of Hawai'i, the television and film production studios, labor unions and other interested parties, a lucrative production tax incentive was passed in the state legislature in July of 2006 in order to make Hawai'i more competitive with other film friendly states with similar incentives for location filming.

The diverse number of blockbuster films ranging from *Raiders of The Lost Ark*, *Jurassic Park*, *Waterworld*, *Pearl Harbor* and *Pirates of The Caribbean: On Stranger Tides*, to the more modest budget *50 First Dates*, *Forgetting Sarah Marshall* and *Soul Surfer*, to the award-winning and critically acclaimed television series *Lost* and the Oscar®-winning worldwide theatrical hit feature *The Descendants*, have proven the islands of Hawai'i is the perfect venue not only because of its versatility and beautiful scenery but also the experienced local crews,

Hawaii Five-O employed local Hawaiian, Asian-American and Polynesian actors and entertainers as regulars in the supporting cast. This included the late Glenn Cannon (district attorney Anthony Manicote), Herman Wedemeyer (Duke Lekela), Harry Endo (as forensic scientist Che Fong) and Doug Mossman (George Kealoha, Frank Kamana). Local nightclub entertainer Al Harrington went from bit parts to assuming a major regular role as Ben Kokua, part of the *Five-O* team in the fifth through seventh season when Zulu left the series after a personal disagreement with Jack Lord.

Also contributing to the authentic atmosphere of the show were the bit and walk-on parts filled out by Island residents, the majority of them non-professionals who received on-the-job training. Everyone, from the doorman of a well-known hotel (cast as a legislator) to real legislators, lawyers and housewives, auditioned. Kwan Hi Lim, a practicing attorney, acted on the series in 31 different episodes in which he portrayed different characters. Lim went on to have a recurring role as Lt. Tanaka on *Magnum P.I.* Moe Keale, a pure Hawaiian from the island of Ni'ihau, was a laborer pulling cable on the set when he was asked by Lord to take on a small acting role. For ten years, Keale played all sorts of bad guys on the series, and in the final season, when the original *Hawaii Five-O* team changed, Moe was cast as Truck Kealoha. Legendary Hawai'i-based newspaper columnist Eddie Sherman played a recurring *Five-O* character named Detective Parker as well as other assorted characters. Sherman, who died in 2013, was an avid supporter and promoter of *Hawaii Five-O* and the Hawai'i film and television industry.

Development of the Modern Hawai'i Film Industry

union members and governmental support, buttressed by an infrastructure that has proven itself on multiple features and television shows since 1968. It is most appropriate in this centennial celebration year that the new *Hawaii Five-0* Reboot production headquarters are now ensconced at the Hawai'i Film Studio, the site of the old Diamond Head soundstage at Fort Ruger, the home of the original *Hawaii Five-O*.

Film Commissions

The Hawai'i Film Office is the film commission for the State of Hawai'i. The state office can assist productions with permits for state jurisdictions and tax incentive information. The office manages the only state owned film studio facility, the Hawai'i Film Studio, located on the slopes of Diamond Head.

In addition to the Hawai'i Film Office, which serves the entire state, each county has its own film office and commissioner. The county film offices are dedicated to supporting film productions, both local and off shore with location scouting, expediting film permits, and acting as liaisons between government agencies and various support services necessary for filming in the Hawaiian Islands. The goal of each office is to attract film, television, video and internet productions that will result in a positive economic impact throughout the community.

TAMMY HASEGAWA, FILM OFFICE-DBEDT-STATE OF HAWAI'I

The only state-run film studio in the United States, The Hawai'i Film Studio, located in Diamond Head Crater, officially opened in 1994, but the site was the production headquarters for such long-running series as the original *Hawaii Five-O* and *Magnum P.I.*

Aerial helicopter camera crew at the Ilikai Hotel in Waikīkī recreating the classic title visualization of Jack Lord as McGarrett at the penthouse balcony, this time with Alex O'Loughlin as McGarrett for the new *Hawaii Five-O* Reboot. Today the penthouse at the top of the thirty-story Ilikai is a private residence that has no public access.

The film office websites are:
 HAWAI'I FILM OFFICE www.hawaiifilmoffice.com
 HONOLULU FILM OFFICE (O'AHU) www.filmhonolulu.com
 MAUI FILM OFFICE www.filmmaui.com
 BIG ISLAND FILM OFFICE www.filmbigisland.com
 KAUA'I FILM COMMISSION www.filmkauai.com

Hawai'i International Film Festival

Hawai'i serves as the home of two world-class film festivals. Dedicated to advancing cultural exchange and media awareness in the Pacific Rim, the East-West Center, based in Honolulu, established the Hawai'i International Film Festival (HIFF) as a non-profit organization in 1981. Governments, film distributors, filmmakers, scholars, critics and educators laud this premier independent film event. The HIFF now moves across one dozen screen sites on six Hawaiian islands to audiences of more than 80,000 people. The films are gathered from all over the world, and many films screened at the festival have gone on to prominence, critical acclaim and worldwide distribution. HIFF also conducts seminars and workshops with established and emerging filmmakers.

Founded in 1998 by Barry and Stella Rivers, the Maui International Film Festival at Wailea Resort offers outdoor film screenings under the stars in one of the most beautiful island spots in the world. The festival is a favorite of film industry executives and insiders looking to get away from it all while participating in a unique film program.

Development of the Modern Hawai'i Film Industry

ʻŌiwi Film Festival

The ʻŌiwi Film Festival, which began in 2010 at the Honolulu Museum of Art Doris Duke Theatre, highlights film productions directed by Native Hawaiians. Each year the ʻŌiwi Festival chooses the best films by Native Hawaiian filmmakers showcasing Hawaiian storytelling in film about life and culture in Hawaiʻi's past and present.

The South Sea Cinema chapter discussed how island life, either in Hawaiʻi or elsewhere, when used as a backdrop or for story content lead to caricaturing island ways and traditions. Like in all film genres, storytelling conventions or cultural interpretation can lead to misrepresentations by oversimplifying.

Films by Native Hawaiian filmmakers look at the Native Hawaiian experience from the inside out, from and through Native Hawaiian eyes. They show how Native Hawaiians perceive their culture, choose to portray it, and share it through the medium of film. These films shown at the ʻŌiwi Film Festival reveal the strength and artistry of filmmaking by Native Hawaiians. In addition, by encouraging Native Hawaiian talent, the festival contributes to the pool of talent available for Hawaiʻi's film and TV production industry.

Maunalua
1959

DIRECTED BY **Lehman Henry**

One of the first films known to be directed and produced by a Hawaiian, *Maunalua* is a snapshot in time. The film is a vintage look at the area's Kuapa fishpond, the community, and ocean before Henry Kaiser turned it into Hawaiʻi Kai.

Maunalua Fishpond as seen in the 1930s. Keahupua O Maunalua was the largest fishpond in Hawaiʻi encompassing an area of 523 acres.

Happy Birthday, Tūtū Ruth
1996

DIRECTED BY **Ann Marie Kirk**

This is the story of ninety-year-old Ruth Makaila Kaholoaʻa, a force of nature from Waipiʻo Valley on Hawaiʻi island. At ninety years old, she continued to raise taro and pick the island ocean delicacy ʻopihi off the dangerous rocky shoreline of Hawaiʻi island.

Tūtū Ruth at her home in Hilo turning the tables on the film crew by putting them on camera. At 90 years old she continued to raise taro and pick the island ocean delicacy ʻopihi.

Development of the Modern Hawaiʻi Film Industry

Kekohi
2008

DIRECTED BY **Kaniela Joy, Ed Joy, Quddus Ajimine**

A film about the son of a warrior-king selected to be the royal court's message runner during the early- to mid-17th century.

In the eyes of a young man who sees himself as the best warrior in the province, he feels insulted by the appointment. He soon learns the dangers, the prestige, and the accolades of being a royal messenger.

Hawaiian warriors begin their quest to try and capture the royal court's messenger, Kekohi, before he is able to complete his royal task. A journey of awakening to one's responsibility and its importance.

Keao
2008

DIRECTED BY **Emily Kaliko Spenser**

Ancient and modern rituals of Hawaiian culture are challenged when a young woman reflects on their purpose in this piece about the misappropriation of tradition.

Keao contemplates on her plight to find harmony between traditional and modern hula practices. In the forest is where she feels most at home with her culture.

Queenie: The Spirit of a Dancer
2010

DIRECTED BY **Ann Marie Kirk**

Legendary hula dancer Queenie Ventura Dowsett shares her thoughts on the essence of hula. Queenie speaks about how her kumu, which includes ʻIolani Luahine, passed on the knowledge of what a dancer, and a dancer's spirit, possesses.

Queenie Dowsett, a premier hula dancer, wearing the traditional holokū dress of a hula dancer.

Development of the Modern Hawaiʻi Film Industry

Oliver Homealani Kupau became one of the highest ranking U.S. Army officers in Hawai'i in the 1930s and 40s. He successfully navigated between traditional Hawaiian ways and introduced Western culture to serve as an example of how to find balance in a changing Hawaiian world.

This sign along the road in East Maui reflects the Native Hawaiian communities desire to cease having the water from their streams diverted to other parts of Maui.

Homealani
2010

DIRECTED BY **Ann Marie Kirk**

Homealani is the story of Oliver Homealani Kupau, the grandfather of the filmmaker Ann Marie Kirk. Born the year her grandfather died, the filmmaker takes us on a journey of discovering who he was as an indigenous Hawaiian, everyone whose life he has touched, and the legacy he left for them.

Release Our Water
2010

DIRECTED BY **Kelly Pauole**

For the last 100 years, billions of gallons of water have been diverted from East Maui Stream to Upcountry and Central Maui.

More than half the population of East Maui is indigenous Hawaiian. *Release Our Water* interviews people from the community about the water issue. The film reveals that the displacement of East Maui's native peoples, the loss of their culture, and an overall decline in the health of the land and its people can be directly related to the water diversion.

KELLY PAUOLE

The Sweepstakes
2011

DIRECTED BY **Jamie Poliahu**

Kaimana enters a cereal-box sweepstakes to win a surfboard prize and the friendship of his next-door neighbor, David.

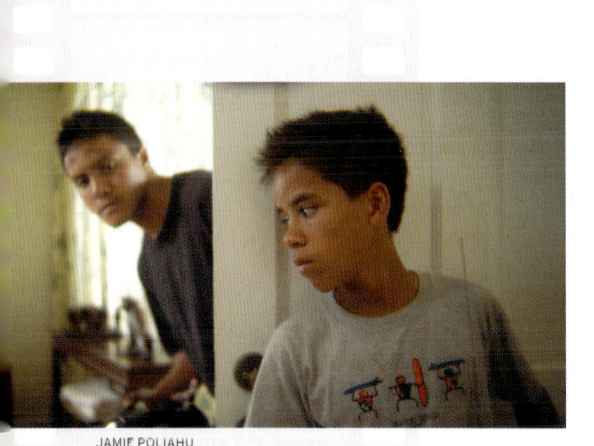

JAMIE POLIAHU

Local boy Kaimana hiding from David, a young man Kaimana is trying to befriend.

Pa'ahana
2012

DIRECTED BY **Lana Dang**

Kekoa is stuck between jobs and struggling to make ends meet but finds solace in his ability to teach his daughter to speak Hawaiian.

Development of the Modern Hawai'i Film Industry

The Hawaiian Room
2012

DIRECTED BY **Ann Marie Kirk**

In 1937 the legendary Hawaiian Room opened in the Hotel Lexington in New York City. The Hawaiian Room showcased hula dancers, singers, and musicians from Hawai'i and transported the beautiful sights and sounds of Hawai'i to the bustling city of Manhattan. The entertainers who brought the Hawaiian Room to life carried with them the true aloha spirit from one island, Hawai'i, to another island, Manhattan. *The Hawaiian Room* explores the experiences of the people who worked in the Hawaiian Room and the legacy they and the Hawaiian Room created.

One of the earliest pictures of the dancers and musicians in the Hawaiian Room taken in the late 1930s. Included in this picture is famed dancer and entrepreneur Tutasi Wilson Steinhilber.

Kai Wahine
2012

DIRECTED BY **Ann Marie Kirk**

Follow the women of the Waimanalo Canoe Club as they prepare for and then race in the 2011 Na Wahine O Ke Kai, forty-one mile outrigger canoe race from Moloka'i to O'ahu across the Ka Iwi Channel.

South Seas Cinema Society

In 1989, the South Seas Cinema Society was established in Hawai'i by four motion picture buffs: the late Robert C. Schmitt, longtime State statistician and author of the pioneering book *Hawaii in the Movies, 1898-1959*; DeSoto Brown, Bishop Museum historian and author of books such as *Hawaii Recalls: Selling Romance to America—Nostalgic Images of the Hawaiian Islands, 1910-1945*; Matt Locey, a veteran Hawaiian assistant director and second unit director, producer and assistant producer, who has worked on many prominent TV series, features, commercials and music videos; and this book's co-author, film historian/critic Ed Rampell.

The women of the Waimanalo Canoe Club pictured in the famed Ka Iwi Channel as they participate in the 41 Na Wahine O Ke Kai race.

The purpose of the South Seas Cinema Society is to study, document, promote and enjoy the genre and the Native and local talents and filmmakers who work in and create Pacific Pictures. The Honolulu-based film society has a pro-indigenous outlook, although it is open to all who love features, documentaries, shorts, cartoons, etc., about Hawaiians and other Polynesians, Melanesians, Micronesians and their Isles. In 1996 the Society presented the South Seas Cinema Fest at what was then the Honolulu Academy of Arts. These moving images are screened at semi-regular meetings/lū'au, more often than not hosted by Dan Long of Long's Audio Visual and his wife Tura.

Matt Locey is the indefatigable "Ali'i Nui" and president of this fan club. This veteran first assistant director began his career as a trainee on *Magnum P.I.* His credits include the theatrical features *Race the Sun, Snakes on a Plane, Charlie's Angels: Full Throttle,* and *Pearl Harbor,* television series such as *Marker, Jake and The Fatman, Baywatch: Hawaii,* the locally produced *Flight 29 Down,* and the new *Hawaii Five-O* reboot. Locey is also one of the first Hawaiian members of the prestigious Directors Guild of America.

The Society's website is chock full of photos and info at: www.southseascinema.org.

Development of the Modern Hawai'i Film Industry

Hollywood Goes

This page, left to right: (Top row) Robert M. Luck, Hilo Hattie, Joan Blackman, and Elvis Presley; Montgomery Clift; Jack Lord. (Middle row) Connie Stevens and Troy Donahue; Deborah Kerr; Maria Montez; Robert Wagner. (Bottom row) Dolores Del Rio and U.S. Army personnel; Dorothy Lamour; Halle Berry; James Garner; Adam Sandler.

Opposite page, left to right: (Top row) Paul Rudd; Boris Karloff and Beverly Tyler; Poncie Ponce and Robert Conrad. (Middle row) Debra Paget, David Hasselhoff, Tom Selleck, Haunani Minn, Liam Neeson. (Bottom row) John Wayne, Jane Russell, Henry Fonda, Harrison Ford.

Hawai'i!

Bibliography

Barclay, Barry. *Our Own Image*. Auckland, New Zealand: Longman Paul Limited, 1990.

Bennett, Tara, and Paul Terry. *Lost Encyclopedia*. New York: DK Publishing, 2010.

Bergan, Ronald. *The United Artists Story*. New York: Crown Publishing, 1988.

Berlin, Howard M. *Charlie Chan Film Encyclopedia*. Jefferson, NC: McFarland and Company, 2000.

Charlie Chan's Words of Wisdom. Rockville, MD: Wildside Press, 2001.

Berry, Paul, and Edgy Lee. *Waikiki in the Wake of Dreams*. Honolulu: Filmworks Press, 1998.

Cook, Chris. *The Kaua'i Movie Book*. Honolulu: Mutual Publishing, 1996.

Day, A. Grove, and Carl Stroven. *A Hawaiian Reader*. Honolulu: Mutual Publishing, 1984.

Dennis, Jonathan, and Jan Bieringa. *Film in Aotearoa, New Zealand*. Wellington, New Zealand: Victoria University Press, 1996.

Douglas, Kirk. *The Ragman's Son*. New York: Simon and Schuster, 1988.

Fonda, Henry, and Howard Teichmann. *Fonda: My Life*. New York: New American Library, 1981.

Geiger, Jeffrey. *Facing the Pacific, Polynesia and the U.S. Imperial Imagination*. Honolulu: University of Hawaii Press, 2007.

Giddens, Gary, and Bing Crosby. *A Pocketful of Dreams: The Early Years 1903-1940*. Boston: Little, Brown and Company, 2001.

Graham, Trevor. *Making Hula Girls: A Cocktail for International Co-Production*. Doctorate of Creative Arts UTS, 2009.

Eames, John Douglas. *The MGM Story: The* Complete History of Sixty-Five Roaring Years. New York: Pyramid Books, 1990.

Hanke, Ken. *Charlie Chan at the Movies*. Jefferson, NC: McFarland and Company, 2004.

Hirschhorn, Clive. *The Warner Bros. Story*. New York: Crown Publishing, 1987.

Huang, Yunte. *Charlie Chan: The Untold Story of the Honolulu Detective's Rendezvous with American History*. New York: Norton and Company, 2010.

Lauritzen, Einar, and Gunnar Lundquist. *American Film Index 1908-1915*. Stockholm: Film Index, 1976.

Maltin, Leonard. *Leonard Maltin's 2011 Movie Guide*. New York: Plume Books, 2011.

Marrill, Alvin H. *The Films of Anthony Quinn*. Secaucus, NJ: Citadel Press, 1975.

Maslon, Laurence. *The South Pacific Companion*. New York: Touchstone/Fireside, Simon and Schuster, 2008.

McBride, Joseph. *Searching for John Ford*. New York: St. Martin's Press, 2003.

Mirisch, Walter. *I Thought We Were Making Movies, Not History*. Madison: University Of Wisconsin Press, 2008.

Mitchell, Charles P. *A Guide to Charlie Chan Films*. Westport, CT: Greenwood Press, 1999.

Pukui, Mary Kawena, and Samuel H. Elbert. *Hawaiian Dictionary*. Honolulu: University of Hawaii Press, 1986.

Rampell, Ed. *Progressive Hollywood: A People's Film History of the United States*. New York: The Disinformation Company Ltd., 2005.

Reyes, Luis I., and Ed Rampell. *Made in Paradise: Hollywood's Films of Hawaii and the South Seas*. Honolulu: Mutual Publishing, 1995.

Rhodes, Karen R. *Booking Hawaii Five-O*. Jefferson, NC: MacFarland and Company, 1998.

Riordan, Ann Fienup. *Freeze Frame: Alaska Eskimos in the Movies*. Seattle: University of Washington Press, 1995.

Robb, David L. *Operation Hollywood: How the Pentagon Shapes and Censors the Movies*. Amherst, NY: Prometheus Books, 2004.

Schmitt, Robert C. *Hawaii in the Movies*. Honolulu: Hawaiian Historical Society, 1988.

Server, Lee. R*obert Mitchum: "Baby I Don't Care."* New York: St. Martin's Press, 2001.

Simonson, Douglas. *Peppo's Pidgin to the Max*. Honolulu: Bess Press, 1981.

Taylor, Ben. *Apocalypse on the Set: Nine Disastrous Film Productions*. Duckworth, NY: Overlook Press, 2012.

A Tree is a Tree. London: Longman, 1954.

Twain, Mark. *Mark Twain in Hawaii: Roughing it in the Sandwich Islands, Hawaii in the 1860s*. Honolulu: Mutual Publishing, 1990.

The Universal Story. New York: Crown Publishing, 1987.

Vaz, Cotta Mark. *The Lost Chronicles: The Official Companion Book*. New York: Hyperion, 2005.

Vidor, King. *Monarch Film Studies*. New York: Monarch Press, Simon and Schuster, 1976.

Zolotov, Maurice. *Shooting Star: A Biography of John Wayne*. New York: Simon and Schuster, 1974.

Index

50 First Dates, 104-105, 142, 156, 186

A

Academy Award, 5, 31, 36-38, 41, 43-44, 53-54, 61, 71, 73, 82, 87-88, 92, 111, 116, 120-122, 126, 130, 163, 185
Adler, Buddy, 39, 45, 47
Ala Moana Park, 50
Allerton Gardens, 46, 169
Aloha Stadium, 98, 100
Aloha Tower, 15, 19, 60
Andrews, Julie, 53-55
Apana, Chang, 12, 14-15
Asner, Edward, 27
Avatar, 116-117, 126

B

Baa Baa Black Sheep, 48
Baker, Brandon, 85
Barrymore, Drew, 100, 104-105, 156, 186
Battleship, 59, 144, 164, 166
Bay, Michael, 88-89, 129
Baywatch Hawaii, 86, 161, 185
Bellisario, Donald, 24
Berry, Halle, 69, 97
Beyond Paradise, 75-76, 91-92
Big Eyes, 151-152
Big Island of Hawaiʻi, 57, 90, 114, 123, 175
Big Jim McLain, 10, 16-17, 28, 158, 160, 181
Bird of Paradise (1932), 3-4, 6-7, 34, 38
Bird of Paradise (1951), 3-4, 6, 8, 37-38
Birkmyre Estate, 46
Black Camel, The, 13-15, 160
Black Sheep Squadron, The, 19, 48
Black, Jack, 66, 111
Blake, Cricket, 8, 18, 48, 161
"Blue Hawaii", 36, 49-50, 138, 158, 161, 172, 181-182
Blue Hawaii, 36, 49-50, 138, 158, 161, 172, 181-182
Blue Lagoon, The, 3, 8, 74, 148
Bonham Carter, Helena, 90
Brady Bunch Movie, The, 70
Brazzi, Rossano, 45
Bridges, Beau, 131-132, 134, 177
Bridges, Jeff, 61
Brissac, Virginia, 32-33
Bruckheimer, Jerry, 88-89, 110, 138
Bunker, Archie, 54
Burns, Gov. John A., 28

C

Caan, Scott, 8-10, 26-27, 124, 126-127, 186
Cadiente, David, 124, 182
Cadiente, Jeff, 124
Calvin, T.C., 24
Cameron, James, 66, 116-117
Carpenter, Pete, 24
Carrere, Tia, 92-93, 141
Castaway Cowboy, The, 168
Central America, 64, 77, 123
Chamberlain, Richard, 83-84, 168
Chan, Charlie, 5, 10, 12-15, 28, 160
Chandler, Jeff, 37-38
Chapman, Duane "Dog", 25
Charlie Chan and the Curse of the Dragon Queen, 13
Charlie Chan At The Racetrack, 13, 28
Charlie Chan Carries On, 12-13
Charlie Chan in Reno, 13
Charlie Chan's Murder Cruise, 13
Charlie Chan's Secret, 13
Chinaman's Hat, 60, 84, 103-104
Chun, Dennis, 27, 57
Clift, Montgomery, 39-40, 163
Clooney, George, 31, 131, 133-135, 168, 178-179
Coco Palms Hotel, 172
Coco Palms Resort, 37, 46, 50, 138, 172
Conrad, Robert, 8, 10, 18-19, 29, 48, 161
Costner, Kevin, 66-67, 97
Cox, Paul, 82-83
Crichton, Michael, 64, 91
Crosby, Bing, 6, 31, 35-36, 50
Cunningham, David, 75-76, 91

D

Da Kine Bail Bonds, 25
Dacascos, Mark, 26-27, 124, 128
Dae Kim, Daniel, 9-10, 26-27, 106-107, 124, 126, 186
de Veuster, Father Damien, 83
DeBlois, Dean, 92-93
Del Rio, Dolores, 4, 34, 38
Denning, Richard, 8, 20, 56, 58, 124
Depp, Johnny, 110, 138
Derek, Bo, 80
Derr Biggers, Earl, 12, 14-15
Descendants, The, 1, 9, 30-31, 87, 131-133, 135-136, 168, 173-174, 176, 178-179, 186
Dhiegh, Khigh, 20, 56, 58
Diamond Head, 19-20, 49-50, 57, 68, 84-85, 105, 163, 176, 187
Dog the Bounty Hunter, 25, 30
Dole Food Company, 105
Donovan's Reef, 17, 51-52, 124, 169, 171
Downey Jr., Robert, 13, 31, 111-112
Dreyfuss, Richard, 78
Duff, Hilary, 171
Duncan, Michael Clarke, 90

E

Eastwood, Clint, 1, 31, 57-58, 121
Elvis: Aloha From Hawaiʻi, 50
Emmy, 9, 24, 27, 58, 62, 87, 100, 107, 124, 126-128, 183

F

Fantasy Island, 81, 164, 173
Fleischer, Richard, 59-60
Flight 29 Down, 108, 141, 185
Flirting With Forty, 115
Fonda, Henry, 31, 43, 156
Fong, Kam, 8, 20, 27-28, 56-57
Forbush, Nellie, 45-47, 168
Ford Island, 60, 89, 166
Ford, Harrison, 63, 74-75, 114, 184
Ford, John, 7, 17, 31, 43-44, 51-52, 73, 171
Fort Shafter, 60
Freeman, Leonard, 10-11, 20-23, 26, 28, 56-58, 124, 182-183
Freeman, Morgan, 68, 103
Freeman, Rose, 58
From Here to Eternity, 8, 30, 39-42, 53, 159, 163, 181
Frye, Dwight, 15
Fuqua, Antoine, 102

G

Gajdusek, Karl, 147
Gaynor, Mitzi, 45-47
George of the Jungle, 72
Giamatti, Paul, 90
Girls, Girls Girls, 4, 49-50, 131, 138, 140, 150, 182
Godfather, The, 79, 126
Godzilla (1998), 77, 155-156
Godzilla (2014), 150, 180-181
Gooding Jr., Cuba, 68, 89
Grand Waimea Hotel, 108
Grove Farm Property, 112
Guzman, Luis, 99, 145

H

Hāʻena Beach, 45-46
Hackman, Gene, 53-54
Haleʻiwa, 102-103, 113, 167
Haleʻiwa Bridge, 103
Hālona Cove, 8, 40-42, 105, 139, 159
Hāmākua Coast, 68, 117
Hamilton, Bethany, 139
Hamilton, Laird, 66, 97, 131, 133
Hanalei, 37, 45-47, 91, 93, 110, 134-135, 140, 158, 168, 177-179, 182
Hanalei Bay, 37, 45-47, 134, 168, 178-179
Hanalei Pier, 140, 168
Hanalei Plantation Resort, 110
Hanalei Town, 177
Hanamāʻulu Beach, 52
Hanapēpē, 92-93, 172
Hanauma Bay, 50, 158
Hang ʻEm High, 57-58
Happy Birthday, Tūtū Ruth, 188
Harris, Richard, 53-54
Hasselhoff, David, 86, 141
Hatta, Lori "Kayo", 68
Hawaiʻi Film Partners, 108, 141, 185
Hawaiʻi Film Studio, 68, 90, 102, 105, 107, 181, 187
Hawaiʻi Volcanoes National Park, 122
Hawaii, 53, 55, 57
Hawaiʻi Film Office, 187
Hawaii Five-0 (reboot), 8-11, 18, 20-22, 24-29, 56-58, 107, 124-128, 155-156, 161-162, 164, 166, 174, 181-184, 186-187
Hawaii Five-O (original), 8, 11, 18, 20-23, 27-29, 56-58, 124, 129, 162-164, 181-187
Hawaiʻi International Film Festival, 185
Hawaiian Eye, 8, 10, 18-19, 28-29,

48, 161, 182
Hawaiian Love, 4, 6, 31-33
Hawaiian Room, The, 191
Hawaiian Village Hotel, 18
Hawaiians, The, 26, 36, 53-56, 58, 87, 90, 120, 130, 162, 172
Heʻeia Kea Harbor, 105
Heʻeia State Park, 150
Heatstroke, 116, 185
Hereafter, 121, 173
Heroes, 22, 83, 128
Heston, Charlton, 55-56, 90, 130
Hickam, 60, 150
Higgins, Jonathan Q., 23-24, 62
Hillerman, John, 23-24, 62
Hilton Hawaiian Village, 18, 151, 161, 180
Homealani, 190
Honokaʻa, 121
Honokaa Boy, 121
Honolulu Advertiser, 29, 54, 60, 84, 103
Honolulu Police Department, 13-14, 28-29, 124, 167
Honolulu Police Department Law Enforcement Museum, 29
Honopū Valley, 61, 170
Honopū Beach, 138
Horsely, Lee, 80
Hudgens, Vanessa, 145
Huleʻia River, 63
Hunger Games, The, 150
Hunger Games, The: Catching Fire, 150
Hurricane Iniki, 65, 172

I

Ilikai Hotel, 26, 107, 187
In God's Hands, 74, 80
In Harm's Way, 17, 156, 180-181
Indiana Jones, 63, 114
Isaac Hale Beach Park, 122
Island Son, 84

J

Jackson, Janet, 100
Jackson, Samuel L., 64, 109, 126
Johnson, Dwayne, 101, 145, 156
Jurassic Park, 1, 64-65, 71, 91, 155-156, 169, 173, 184, 186
Jurassic World, 152

K

Kaʻaʻawa Valley, 73, 77, 95-96, 102, 105, 156
Kahanamoku, Duke, 5, 12, 17, 44, 47, 83-85, 185
Kai Wahine, 191
Kaimū, 37
Kainoa's Sports Bar and Restaurant, 103
Kalalau Trail, 118, 140, 168, 170

Kalapana, 37, 175
Kalihi District, 60
Kalihiwai Bay, 52
Kāneʻohe, 3, 34, 44, 105, 138, 157, 164, 180
Kāneʻohe Bay, 44, 84, 105
Kāohikaipu Island, 104
Kasdan, Lawrence, 63
Kauaʻi, 9, 30, 37, 44-47, 49-50, 52, 58, 61, 63-65, 67-68, 70-71, 74-75, 81, 86, 91-93, 97, 110, 112, 117-118, 132-135, 138-143, 152, 168, 172-173, 176-179, 184, 187
Kauhi, Gilbert Francis Lani Damian, 21, 57
Kawaihae, 66-67
Kawela Bay, 150, 165
Keao, 189
Keʻe Beach, 93, 168
Keʻehi Lagoon Beach Park, 150
Keahua Arboretum, 117
Kekaha Kai State Park, 122
Kekohi, 189
Kelly, Chin Ho, 20, 26-28, 56-57, 124, 126
Kerr, Deborah, 8, 39-41, 159
Kīlauea Falls, 143, 173
Kilcher, Qʻorianka, 119-120
Kimo, 35-36, 98, 113
King Kong, 6, 31, 61, 64, 73, 170, 184
King Vidor, 34
Kipu Kai Bay, 177
Koko Head, 60
Kolekole Pass, 40, 60
Kona, 34, 37, 66, 69, 76, 143
Kona Pali High School, 69
Kono, 20-21, 26-27, 56-57, 124, 127
Krippendorf's Tribe, 78
Kristofferson, Kris, 8, 66, 82
Kurtzman, Alex, 26, 124, 129

L

LaGarde, Jocelyn, 53-54
Lahti, Christine, 27
Lamour, Dorothy, 5-7, 51, 58, 75
Lānaʻi, 122, 151, 174, 185
Lancaster, Burt, 8, 39-41, 159, 163
Lange, Jessica, 31, 61, 73
Larson, Glen, 23-24, 62, 183
Last Resort, 147
Lee, Edgy, 87
Lee, Jason Scott, 92-93
Lemmon, Jack, 30, 43-44
Lenkov, Peter M., 129, 183
Leonard, Elmore, 103
Lilo & Stitch, 92-93
Liu, Dan, 16, 28

Locey, Matt, 32, 69, 148, 183
Logan, Joshua, 43-45, 181
Logue, Elizabeth, 53-54
Lord, Jack, 8, 10, 20-23, 26-28, 56-57, 164, 174, 182-184, 186-187
Lost, 9, 106-108, 113, 124, 126, 155-156, 164-165, 167, 183-186
Lucas, George, 63, 114, 128
Lugosi, Bela, 14-15, 160
Lumahai Beach, 46, 168
Lydgate Park, 50

M

MacArthur, James, 8, 20, 27, 56-57, 126, 184
Maccabee, Danny, 142
Mackenzie State Park, 122
Magnum P.I., 1, 8, 10, 23-24, 62, 163-164, 182-184, 186-187
Magnum, Thomas, 23-24, 62
Makahūʻena Point, 52
Makapuʻu, 105
Mākua Beach, 54-55
Malloy, Turk, 127
Mānoa Falls, 102, 150
Marshall, Robb, 138
Martin, Ross, 13
Marvin, Lee, 51-52
Master, The, 148
Maui, 19, 54, 58, 66, 74, 81, 86, 97, 110, 121, 142-143, 148, 149, 173-174, 187, 190
Maui International Film Festival, 185
Mauna Loa, 37-38
Maunawili Valley, 102
McCrea, Joel, 3, 34, 38
McDowell, Malcolm, 81
McGarrett, Steve, 8, 10, 20-22, 26-28, 56, 58, 124-125, 127, 162, 164
McKern, Leo, 82
Meet the Deedles, 78
Michener, James A., 53, 55
Midler, Bette, 54
Mifune, Toshiro, 67
Mighty Joe Young, 31, 73, 102
Miller, Dorrie, 89
Miss Sadie Thompson, 30, 168, 172
Mister Roberts, 30, 43-44, 155-156
Mokoliʻi, 84, 103-104
Mokuleʻia Beach, 106, 167
Molokaʻi, 17, 82-83, 91, 110, 174, 191
Molokaʻi: The Story of Father Damien: 82-83
Montalban, Ricardo, 22, 81

Mossman, Douglas Kinilau, 18
Mount Kīlauea, 90
Mount Tantalus, 50

N

Nā Pali, 61, 63, 81, 118
Naish, J. Carol, 13
National Botanical Gardens, 138
Navajos, 95
Nāwiliwili Harbor, 52
Neal S. Blaisdell Center, 50
Nobriga, Ted, 28, 53-54
North Shore, 108, 165, 185
North Shore (Oʻahu), 68-69, 80, 86, 94, 98, 100, 103, 106, 108-109, 113, 115, 129, 138-140, 150, 165, 167
North Shore (Kauaʻi), 168, 177, 179
Nuyen, France, 5-6, 45-47

O

Oʻahu, 4-6, 8, 21, 23, 28, 31, 33, 37, 39, 41-42, 44, 49-50, 55, 62, 65, 68-70, 72-73, 77-78, 80-81, 84-87, 89, 91, 94-96, 98, 100-110, 113-116, 120, 124, 130-131, 133-135, 138-142, 144, 146-147, 150-152, 155-159, 163-165, 167, 176, 180-182, 185, 187, 191
O'Connor, Carroll, 53-54
O'Loughlin, Alex, 8-10, 26-27, 124-125, 126, 187
O'Quinn, Terry, 106-107, 124
O'Toole, Peter, 82-83
Ocean's 11, 127
ʻŌiwi Film Festival, 188
Oka, Masi, 26, 124, 128
Oland, Warner, 10, 12, 14-15, 28, 160
ʻŌpana Point, 60
Orci, Roberto, 26, 124, 129
Oscar, 8, 24, 30-31, 36, 38-39, 43-45, 54, 59, 61, 63, 66, 69, 73, 82, 110-111, 121-122, 131, 138, 150, 156, 181, 186
Owens, Harry, 35-36

P

Paʻahana, 190
Paget, Debra, 8, 37-38
Paniolo O Hawaiʻi—Cowboys of the Far West, 87
Paradise Hawaiian Style, 50
Park, Grace, 9-10, 26-27, 124, 127, 186
Payne, Alexander, 30-31, 91, 131
Peahi Beach, 97
Pearl Harbor, 7, 15, 88-89, 124, 155-156, 160, 163-164, 166, 184, 186

Pearl Harbor, 7, 17, 39, 50, 59-60, 88-89, 144, 166
Perfect Getaway, A, 118
Picture Bride, 67-68, 185
Pirates of the Caribbean, The, 110, 138, 159, 165, 169-170, 172, 186
Police Beach, 106, 167
Ponce, Poncie, 8, 18-19, 48, 182
Post, Mike, 24
Predator, 123
Presley, Elvis, 36, 49-50, 138, 158, 172, 182
Prestidge, Mel, 18, 28-29, 48
Princess Ka'iulani, 79, 119-120, 162, 185
Pulver, Ensign, 43-44
Puna District, 37, 114
Punchbowl, 13-14, 50, 144, 162, 164, 176

Q

Queenie: The Spirit of a Dancer, 189
Quinn, Anthony, 35-36

R

Race the Sun, 69
Raiders of the Lost Ark, 63, 71, 114, 184, 186
Rampage, 57, 124, 175
Rebel Without a Cause, 32
Release Our Water, 190
Return of Charlie Chan, The, 13
Rise of the Planet of the Apes, 130
Robb, AnnaSophia, 139-140
Roth, Tim, 90
Royal Hawaiian Hotel, The, 14-15, 17, 40, 99, 151, 160
Ryan, Shawn, 147

S

Saldana, Zoe, 116-117
Sanders, Chris, 92-93
Sandler, Adam, 1, 99, 104-105, 142-143, 156, 186
Schneider, Rob, 104-105, 141
Schofield Barracks, 39-41, 60, 163
Schwarzenegger, Arnold, 123
Sea Chase, The, 17
Selleck, Tom, 8, 10, 23-24, 62, 184
Selznick, David O., 34
Shark God, The, 4, 6, 9, 31-33
Sheen, Charlie, 103
Shipman Estate, 37
Shipman Ranch, 114, 123, 175
Sinatra, Frank, 24, 30-31, 39-41, 58, 163, 173, 184
Six Days Seven Nights, 1, 74-75, 137, 170, 184
Sizemore, Tom, 124
Slater, Christian, 94, 96

Snakes on a Plane, 109-110
South Kohala, 66-67
South Seas Cinema, 1-9, 32, 64, 76, 131
South Seas Cinema Society, 191
Spangler, Randy, 154
Spangler, Stephanie G., 154
Special Delivery, 115
Speedman, Tugg, 111
Spielberg, Steven, 31, 63-64, 71, 114, 121, 124
St. Regis Princeville Resort, 46-47, 179
Star Wars, 114, 128
Stevens, Connie, 8, 18, 48, 161
Stiller, Ben, 104, 111-112
Sutherland, Kiefer, 91-92
Sweepstakes, The, 190
"Sweet Leilani", 35-36

T

Tagawa, Cary-Hiroyuki, 15, 67, 85, 88, 90
Tahiti Nui Restaurant, 134, 177
Taradash, Daniel, 39, 53
Tears of the Sun, 102, 156, 162
Ten, 80
Theron, Charlize, 31, 73
Thorn Birds, The, 168, 172
To End All Wars, 91-92
Toler, Sidney, 13
Too Rich: The Secret Life of Doris Duke, 47, 83-85
Tora! Tora! Tora!, 59-60, 183
Tropic Thunder, 111-112, 170, 184
Trumbo, Dalton, 53
Tupou, Manu, 53-54
Turtle Bay Resort, 100, 106, 108, 113, 139-140, 150, 165
Tyrannosaurus Azteca, 115

U

Umezu, Art, 67
Uncommon Valor, 111
USS *Arizona*, 7, 17, 50, 59, 89, 166
USS *Missouri*, 144, 150, 166
Ustinov, Peter, 13

V

Ventura, Mary Ann, 38
Very Brady Sequel, A, 70
Von Sydow, Max, 53-55

W

Wackiest Ship In The Army, The, 44
Wahlberg, Mark, 90
Wai'alae Golf Course, 40
Waialua, 68-69, 103, 105, 167
Waikīkī, 176
Waikīkī Beach, 176
Waikiki Wedding, 31, 35-36, 50

Wailua Falls, 81
Wailua River, 50, 52, 68, 91, 117, 171-172
Waimānalo, 23, 62, 105, 163
Waimea Canyon, 52, 171
Waipio Valley, 66
Walston, Ray, 45-46
Warner, David, 90
Waterworld, 66-67, 77, 185-186
Wayne, John, 7, 10, 16-17, 28, 51-52, 156, 158, 160, 171, 180
Wenham, David, 82
Wheeler Fields, 60
Wild Wild West, 19, 48, 58
Williams, Danny, 20, 26-27, 56-57, 124, 126-127
Williams, Elmo, 59
Willis, Bruce, 102, 156
Wilson, Owen, 103, 109
Wily, Taylor, 113, 128
Wind On Water, 80
Windtalkers, 30, 52, 94-96, 156, 184
Winters, Roland, 13, 49
Woo, John, 94, 156
Wray, John Griffith, 32-33
Wright, Rick, 23-24, 62

Z

Fred Zinnemann, 39-40, 55, 163, 181
Zulu, 8, 20-21, 56-57, 75-76, 186

About the Authors

Ed Rampell spent much of his life writing about film and the Pacific. After college, in Tahiti, Samoa, Hawai'i, and Micronesia, Rampell reported on culture and the nuclear-free and independent Pacific movement for ABC News's "20/20," Reuters, Associated Press, Radio Australia, Radio New Zealand, *NewsWeek*, etc. In 1989, Rampell co-founded the South Seas Cinema Society. During the 1990s, when he lived on O'ahu's Waianae Coast, Rampell wrote more *Honolulu Weekly* cover stories than any other freelancer living in Hawai'i.

Rampell co-authored with Luis Reyes the film history books *Made In Paradise, Hollywood's Films of Hawaii and the South Seas* and *Pearl Harbor in the Movies*. He is the author of *Progressive Hollywood, A People's Film History of the United States* (2005) and appears in the 2005 Australian documentary *Hula Girls, Imagining Paradise*.

In 1999, Rampell relocated to Los Angeles and went on to contribute to "The Finger" column for *New Times L.A., Variety, Written By, The Nation, L.A. Times, L.A. CityBeat, AlterNet, L.A. Daily News, Financial Times, New York Press, Guardian, The Forward,* and the *San Diego Reader.* He currently covers the L.A. culture and arts scene for *The Progressive Magazine, Hollywood Progressive.com* (which he co-founded), *Jesther Entertainment, LAProgressive.com, Rock Cellar Magazine, The Daily Dissident, L.A. Stage Times*, etc. In December 2007, Rampell created The Progie Awards to highlight the year's best progressive films and filmmakers. This award led to the creation of the James Agee Cinema Circle, an international group of film critics, historians and scholars, which votes on The Progies annually. In 2007, Rampell initiated a 60th anniversary commemoration of the Hollywood Ten at L.A.'s Skirball Cultural Center.

Rampell wrote the screenplay for the upcoming feature film *First Landing* about the initial occupation of Kaho'olawe to stop the bombing of the "target island."

Named after legendary CBS broadcaster Edward R. Murrow, Rampell graduated from Manhattan's Hunter College, where he majored in cinema. His Polynesian daughter, Marina Davis, is a singer who lives in Auckland, New Zealand.

Top left: Ed Rampell, aboard the *Aranui*, somewhere between Tahiti and the Marquesas. DONNA WENDT

Top right: Luis I. Reyes and daughter Arlinda Marie Makamae Reyes on Kaua'i. LUIS REYES ARCHIVES

Luis I. Reyes is a nationally renowned scholar, author, archivist and lecturer who specializes in the film history of ethnic minorities in Hollywood and is one of the leading scholars on the history of Latinos in the Hollywood film industry.

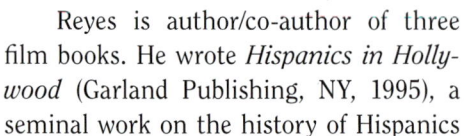

Reyes is author/co-author of three film books. He wrote *Hispanics in Hollywood* (Garland Publishing, NY, 1995), a seminal work on the history of Hispanics in the Hollywood and television industry, with Peter Rubie as co-author. In 2000, Lone Eagle Press republished and updated this book. Reyes wrote his second book, *Made in Paradise* (Mutual Publishing, Honolulu, 1996), and third book, *Pearl Harbor in the Movies* (Mutual Publishing, Honolulu, 2001), with Ed Rampell. As a seminal work, *Made in Paradise* led to the recognition of the South Seas movie as a distinct film genre.

Reyes's film articles have appeared in many publications including *The Los Angeles Times, The Oakland Tribune, Hawaii Magazine,* and *Hemispheres,* United Airlines's in-flight magazine.

Reyes has lectured on film at California State University, Northridge, and University of California, Los Angeles, and delivered a speech as a guest speaker along with co-author Ed Rampell at the 2001 60th anniversary Pearl Harbor Conference in Honolulu, Hawai'i. Reyes served as one of the organizers of Mahalo Con—the historic *Hawaii Five-0* reunion convention—which took place in 1996 in Burbank, California, and Honolulu, Hawai'i. Reyes also delivered a speech as a guest speaker at the worldwide executive IBM convention in Kaua'i, Hawai'i. In December 1994, Reyes was invited as part of a special Hollywood contingent to attend the Summit of The Americas in Miami, Florida. U.S. President Bill Clinton presided over the summit, which hosted the leaders of over thirty of the Western Hemisphere countries.

As a veteran Hollywood publicist, Reyes has worked on such films as *Hoosiers* with Gene Hackman, *American Me* with Edward James Olmos, *Man On Fire* with Denzel Washington, and *Bandidas* with Salma Hayek and Penelope Cruz. His television credits include *Dr. Quinn: Medicine Woman* with Jane Seymour, Showtime's *Resurrection Blvd,* and HBO's *The Josephine Baker Story*.

Reyes holds a bachelor's degree in Education and Inter-American Studies from Elbert Covell College, University of the Pacific, in Stockton, California. He serves as a member of the Directors Guild of America and the Publicist Guild.